Unearthing the Stories of Eleven Murdered
Jewish Footballing Greats

DIGGING DEEP

DAVID BOLCHOVER

Biteback Publishing

First published in Great Britain in 2026 by
Biteback Publishing Ltd, London

ISBN 978-1-83736-032-1

10 9 8 7 6 5 4 3 2 1

A CIP catalogue record for this book is available from the British Library.

Set in Adobe Garamond Pro

Printed and bound in Great Britain by
CPI Group (UK) Ltd, Croydon CR0 4YY

FSC www.fsc.org MIX Paper | Supporting responsible forestry FSC® C013604

To Janie, Yael, Joe and Tali

'Earth, do not conceal their blood; let there be no resting place for their cries.'

From a Hebrew memorial prayer for the victims of the Holocaust

CONTENTS

INTRODUCTION

Zygmunt Steuermann was one of football's big-game players. He rose to the occasion when his team needed him most, sending his many fans into raptures. Although he scored goals galore as a striker over a long period for the Polish Jewish club Hasmonea Lwów, two especially big performances catch the eye. Neither were in the colours of Hasmonea and only one happened for certain. About the other, we can't be 100 per cent sure.

The first game, the historically documented one, took place in 1926. Steuermann was making his debut for the Poland national team in the picturesque city of Lviv, now situated in Western Ukraine, but then in Poland and known as Lwów. In a devastating twenty-minute spell against Turkey, Steuermann announced his arrival on the international stage by smashing a hat-trick – the first ever scored by a Poland player – to help his team to a 6–1 victory.

The Polish Jewish community would have been proud of his achievement on that September day. We can assume that Steuermann's name was still on many lips just a few days after the game, as millions of soon-to-be murdered Jews crammed into thousands of soon-to-be-ransacked synagogues for the Day of Atonement, Yom Kippur.

The second of Steuermann's stand-out games was also said to have taken place in Lviv, but on the other side of the city, more than fifteen years later. And not this time in a packed stadium, but in a slave labour camp known as Janowska, somewhat ironically built right next to the stadium formerly occupied by Steuermann's now erased former club.

Between 1941 and 1943, approximately 200,000 Jews were sent from elsewhere in the region to Janowska. Many were immediately sent elsewhere to be gassed or shot, while the remainder were retained as slave labourers. Steuermann was in the lucky latter category – a daily witness to brutality and murder, but not yet dead himself.

Kazimierz Górski, who later became a distinguished coach of the Poland national team in which Steuermann had once starred, was a young man in Lviv during the war. In his memoirs published many years later, he wrote that a match between prisoners and guards took place in Janowska. Steuermann was in his early forties by the time he found himself in Janowska, but he had nevertheless continued to play football at a reasonably high level up to that point. Despite his advancing years, it seems that he still knew where the back of the net was. According to Górski, Steuermann scored twice in a 3–1 victory for the prisoners. The other goalscorer was apparently named 'Berger', a man even more lost to history than Steuermann.

We can suppose that most if not all of the players in the prisoner team were Jews, as they made up the overwhelming majority of the camp population. For that reason, we can reposition this game in our imagination closer towards something resembling the grim truth, and away from the match famously depicted in the film *Escape to Victory* between camp guards and comparatively gilded Allied prisoners of war.

The Janowska contest would have been fought between representatives of a people in the process of being exterminated on the one side and their exterminators on the other. One last desperate display of defiance in the face of certain death. Górski reveals that the team gave themselves the Latin name *Morituri* – 'those who are about to die'. In the entire history of sport, is there a team name to rival that?

Modern-day football commentators routinely categorise an unusually competitive section of a tournament as the 'group of death'. When local historians refer to this purported match as *match smerti* (the match of death), they are not speaking metaphorically.

What, then, happened to Steuermann himself? We have various stories at our disposal. Some have suggested that he was shot right there in Janowska, perhaps to the sound of the camp orchestra reprising 'The Tango of Death', the special tune which Yakov Mund, the Jewish former director of the Lviv opera and latterly Janowska inmate, was forced to compose for such occasions. Another eyewitness suggests that Steuermann was shot dead in his native town of Sambir, seventy-five kilometres away, probably after fleeing Janowska. One more claimed that he was shot after trying, quite sensibly, to escape a transport to the Bełżec death camp, in which up to 600,000 Jews were murdered and from which three (that's three, not 3,000) emerged alive.

The fact is that we do not know for sure that the *match smerti* took place, and we do not know exactly how Steuermann was murdered. The witnesses to both events were either perpetrators hiding a guilty secret or were themselves murdered. When you confront extermination on such an all-encompassing scale, memory is smashed into tiny, often incoherent, pieces. Encountering a multitude of frustrations while writing this book over several years, that thought was never far from my mind.

Given their comparatively impeccable survival rate, however, knowledge of what happened to the perpetrators is rather more dependable. We do know, for example, what happened to Fritz Gebauer, the commandant of the camp at the time. Due to his propensity for halting a conversation before it reached its natural conclusion so that he could focus on strangling his interlocutor, Gebauer was known by inmates as 'The Choker'.

Although no doubt miffed at being deprived of his daily dose of Jew-beating, he continued to live life free as a bird for more than two decades after the war. But in 1971, he was unlucky enough to become a constituent part of the estimated 1 per cent of murderers from the European Holocaust who ended up being convicted for their crimes. At the age of sixty-four, Gebauer was judged guilty for such peccadillos as strangling a Jewish dentist for warming potatoes on a stove and beating a Jewish musician to the ground and then killing him by standing on his throat.

Despite being awarded a life sentence, Gebauer was deemed too poorly to face even the relative comfort of a prison in the modern state of West Germany. While kicking back to enjoy his country's triumph in the 1974 World Cup on television in the comfort of his home in a sleepy rural town, perhaps his mind wandered back to another football match he had witnessed three decades before. The match when his fellow murderers were roundly beaten by a motley group of foredoomed Jewish inmates – in a very different type of prison.

* * *

This book documents the scarcely believable life stories of Zygmunt Steuermann and ten other Jewish footballing greats – celebrated stars one minute, hunted down and murdered the next. Why have I written it? I would like to start my long answer to that question with a few short questions of my own.

Who was the best Brazilian player of all time? Pelé comes the answer. Argentina? Maradona or Messi. Hungary? Puskás. Holland? Cruyff. Germany? Beckenbauer. Portugal? Eusébio or Ronaldo – take your pick. France? Zidane? England? Perhaps Bobby Charlton?

What about the best Jewish footballer ever? Gotcha! That's one to send even a group of the most historically literate Jewish football nerds into a prolonged silence. Not even a semblance of a suggestion is likely to emanate from their lips. Maybe they will break into a smile to indicate that we Jews are not very good at football, so choosing the best is probably a pointless exercise anyway, because the best would be rather bad in the broader scheme of things.

If you had asked me that question several years ago, I would also have drawn a blank and produced the same sardonic grin. But having now read a considerable number of contemporaneous press descriptions of top Jewish players, I can attempt an educated selection, even though the task is difficult because the standard is in fact extremely high and the competition intense. In the end, it boils down to a choice between two outstanding talents – Kálmán Konrád and József Braun, both right-sided attacking players from Hungary.

My instinct would be to plump narrowly for the latter. Another player featured in this book, Braun was the youngest of twelve siblings from a very religious (or to use the modern parlance, ultra-Orthodox) Jewish family from the small town of Putnok in the north of Hungary, on what is now the border of Slovakia. Such was his immense ability that at the age of just seventeen he was selected for the national team of Hungary, then and for several decades afterwards among the elite footballing nations in Europe. Lightning quick and technically gifted, his displays of footballing genius and glittering international career were cut short in his mid-twenties by a succession of crippling injuries inflicted by vengeful defenders.

By the age of forty-one, Braun too had been murdered, beaten to death as a slave labourer in the snow of a brutal Russian winter by Hungarians who, less than two decades previously, had perhaps spent evenings with their friends talking excitedly about his feats on the football pitch. The last image we have of Braun is of those same

Hungarian guards crouching over his lifeless body, prising open his mouth to extract gold teeth.

Braun was not serenaded by tributes after his death like Eusébio, Johan Cruyff and Diego Maradona were. No public announcement of his death was broadcast. Proud Jews have never lauded his memory, as Hungarians who were born long after Ferenc Puskás retired may wax lyrical about his talents, or as old Brazilians may tell their young grandchildren that nothing will ever quite beat watching Pelé. Most of the people who might have gone all dewy-eyed about Braun left this earth pretty much around the same time that he did, along with their children or grandchildren, and the latter's dreams of having their own children and grandchildren. Thus, the story pretty much stopped in its tracks.

This, as the story about Zygmunt Steuermann's final game intimates, is what genocide does. It eliminates not just the people, but the stories of those people among those who continue to live. The European Holocaust did not only account for the murder of 6 million Jews, but also shattered the chain of Jewish collective memory to such an extent that if you throw up the name of József Braun as a quiz question to those aforementioned Jewish football fanatics, they might well hazard a guess that he was the man behind a famous electronics company, an enemy of five o'clock shadow rather than bewildered full-backs.

* * *

Several years ago, I wrote a book about Béla Guttmann, one of the greatest coaches that football has ever produced. I loved discovering the story of Guttmann, a highly charismatic and influential Jew from

Hungary who recovered from the trauma of the Holocaust to reach the top of his trade.

Guttmann's story was breathtaking enough, but I was even more transfixed by the remarkable wider story that hit me between the eyes as I ploughed through the research. Namely, the huge role European Jews played in football in the years before the catastrophe – the panoply of top players, the innovative coaches who revolutionised training and on-field tactics, the extraordinary personalities, the proud network of Zionist teams, the ubiquitous club presidents and investors, the administrators who played a key role in professionalising and internationalising the sport, the hordes of passionate fans, even the elite referees. I felt like I was on an archaeological expedition, digging deep to reveal a few vestiges of a destroyed society, in particular its fascination for a game in which so many of them excelled.

After the book was finished, I started to think of an entirely separate subject to research and write about. After all, hadn't I already written about the European Holocaust and the Jews devastated by it? But the problem is, when you have entered the subject of the Holocaust in any depth – its bestiality and heroism, the sheer scale of the mass murder right in the middle of supposedly civilised Europe – then little else can compete. I was also mesmerised by the vision, denied to my generation in the real world, of a Europe with millions of highly productive and creative Jews, whose subsequent absence has completely and irrevocably transformed the continent's character.

In my spare time, I started writing and collecting biographical summaries of Jewish footballers and coaches, with often big question marks at the end querying an eventual fate still shrouded in mystery eighty years on. I also read up as much as I could about Jews in other sports, such as the boxer Salamo Arouch from Salonika in Greece, who won 200 bouts in Auschwitz on pain of death just to provide entertainment for the guards and who then lived out his life as a manager of a shipping company in Tel Aviv; or the world-record-holding swimmer Alfred Nakache, a French-Algerian Jew who emerged from the camps at Auschwitz and Buchenwald weighing forty-two kilograms (about six and a half stone) and mourning his murdered wife and two-year-old daughter, only to break another world record the following year.

There are enough similar jaw-dropping stories about Jewish sporting personalities and the Holocaust to fill a good number of bookshelves, many of them barely known. My own attention, however, became especially and increasingly drawn to the many among them who did not live to tell the tale. The against-all-the-odds stories of Guttmann, Arouch and Nakache, and of the other remarkable survivors we see or hear in now rapidly declining numbers on Holocaust memorial days, may offer hope and generate supreme admiration.

But I began to feel that, for all the school courses, films, books and television programmes, what many people understood by the Holocaust did not reflect the widespread reality, one often of almost complete obliteration. The Guttmann story represented the exception; I now felt a strong compulsion to write about the rule.

* * *

One reason why people tend to gravitate towards survival stories from the Holocaust is that the alternative is too much for them to stomach. This is particularly true for Europeans. It all took place on their patch and many of their forebears participated in or approved of it or were close to people who did. Obliteration is thus a more exacting narrative, whereas the heroic incidences of extremely courageous non-Jews saving Jews, as was the case with Béla Guttmann, are particularly digestible or even welcomed. This was a point well understood by Steven Spielberg, I am sure, when he centred his Holocaust blockbuster, *Schindler's List*, on just such a non-Jewish hero.

In acknowledging this heroism, however, we surely also have a duty to be brutally honest about its rarity. 'For the record', writes Dara Horn in her book *People Love Dead Jews*, 'the number of actual "righteous Gentiles" officially recognised by Yad Vashem, Israel's national Holocaust museum and research centre, for their efforts in rescuing Jews from the Holocaust is under 30,000 people, out of a European population at the time of nearly 300 million – or 0.001 per cent. Even if we were to assume that the official recognition is an undercount by a factor of *ten thousand*, such people remain essentially a rounding error.'

Pan-European surveys suggest that remembering the millions of *un*saved Jews is often more likely to generate irritation than honest reflection. According to the latest data from the Anti-Defamation League's antisemitism survey, the following percentages are happy to agree with the statement that 'Jews still talk too much about what happened to them in the Holocaust' – 70 per cent in Greece, 65 per cent in Lithuania, 62 per cent in Poland, 53 per cent in Latvia, 44 per cent in Austria, 43 per cent in Ukraine, 43 per cent in Hungary, 38 per cent in Italy, 38 per cent in Russia, 33 per cent in Germany and 29 per cent in France. Given that most people will be well aware, particularly in more woke-conscious Western Europe, that this statement does not rank in the 'politically correct' category, I would suggest that some of these percentages are under-reported to a significant degree.

Nor is it only people from countries in which the Holocaust was perpetrated who roll their eyes in boredom at the mere mention of what Winston Churchill referred to as 'probably the greatest and most horrible crime ever committed in the whole history of the world' – a crime, one may add, that people who are still alive remember seeing with their own eyes. At the age of seventy, Matthew Parris, the esteemed British commentator and former Member of Parliament, offhandedly and without any apparent negative reaction admitted in the centre pages of *The Times* that he had been 'on occasions heard to grumble to Jewish friends (sic) for "going on" about something the world knows all too well'.

But surely the overriding reason we hear more about the survivors is that the obliterated cannot speak, while their near-obliterated network of family, friends and community cannot speak much for them either. The murdered Jews often need a more distant third party to find out about them and then cry out on their behalf.

As you will see in these pages, that in itself is no easy task. Shortly before his death, Raul Hilberg, one of the great historians of the Final Solution, admitted that 'we know perhaps 20 per cent about the Holocaust'. With all due respect to the late Professor Hilberg, I suspect that even that figure was the product of more than a little sugar-coating.

And we know almost as little about the society the obliterated left behind.

* * *

Many have heard of Auschwitz-Birkenau, the camp that came to symbolise the Holocaust, perhaps even picturing in their mind's eye the iconic entrance arch they have seen so often on their television screens. The main reason why Auschwitz has become so notorious is that despite the mind-boggling scale of the mass murder that took place there, the liquidation was not total. Whilst 960,000 Jews were murdered (865,000 of whom were gassed on arrival), at least 50,000 survived by the skin of their teeth after being forced on so-called death marches back to Germany, and were able then to inform the world about what had happened. They survived because Auschwitz-Birkenau, as well as functioning as a death factory, also hosted a network of slave labour camps (not to mention a prisoner-of-war camp for British and Commonwealth soldiers which was strictly separated in terms of both geography and in the way it treated its inmates). As a result of starvation, disease and persistent beating, the average life span of a slave labourer in the camp was a matter of a few months. However, survival was nevertheless a remote possibility, particularly if the victim was dispatched there late on in the war.

Many British people have also heard of Bergen-Belsen, a concentration camp that British forces stumbled across in April 1945. Around 50,000 people were murdered there. Of the skeletal inmates the soldiers saw on their arrival, around 15,000 eventually survived, and it is their stories we usually hear. Dachau occupies a similar place in the American imagination, after the US army entered the camp two weeks after the discovery of Bergen-Belsen and found 30,000 prisoners hanging on to life by a thread.

Other camps, however, operated purely as instruments of death, and the statistics put even the respective hells of Auschwitz and Belsen in the shade. At the death camps of Sobibór, Bełżec, Treblinka and Chełmno, for example, approximately 1.9 million Jews were murdered, primarily through gassing, while a maximum of 140 in total survived, and only through the most incredible escapes. That equates to a survival rate of one in 13,570. Apply that rate to a packed Wembley stadium with a capacity of 90,000, and you would get six people staggering out at the end, with the remaining 89,994 sprawled dead on their seats or lying heaped on the concrete stairwells and concourses.

Even the lucky six survivors would spend the rest of their days in a state of mental torment. Then repeat that process twenty-one times over to make the 1.9 million.

Some might think it strange that I make this Wembley analogy. But I make calculations of this nature all the time. I would wager, too, that quite a few other Jews of my generation, born in the dark shadow of the Holocaust, sometimes think along similar lines without necessarily saying so out loud for fear of seeming obsessed or even unhinged. For example, tourists visiting Central Europe might talk enthusiastically about a wonderful evening in a beautiful concert hall, with their thoughts firmly fixed on the present and their enjoyment of it. My mind would be on other matters, thinking to myself that if I had visited the same concert hall in, say, 1930, a significant proportion of the audience and even the orchestra would have been Jews, and now there are no Jews, save for me and a couple of Israeli and American tourists.

'Beginning in the breathtaking Bohemian capital of the Czech Republic, Prague, this hugely popular holiday takes you through the heart of Bohemia', read one cruise holiday advert that I saw in a British newspaper. 'Visit magnificent Vienna, home to stunning palaces, vibrant culture and the very best coffee and cake. See the cosmopolitan Slovakian capital, Bratislava, and the majestic "twin city" of Budapest, which sits astride the mighty River Danube'.

Please forgive me if palaces don't immediately come into my head when I think of these places. Nor cake.

The footnotes that you will see throughout this book reflect my wandering Jewish mind. It is difficult for me to move on from mentioning a Jewish footballing personality from the 1920s, or one of the many European towns or villages with a Jewish population, without at least trying to find out what happened to them during the years of the inferno. After the Holocaust, as the writer Michael Elkins put it, 'there was no step (in Europe) a Jew could take that would not leave him standing on his brother Jew, dead and buried and shoved underground'.

I digress. Let's return to the comparison between the camps lodged in the popular consciousness and the other, barely known death camps utilised in the frenzied war against the Jews, and listen to someone who could compare them at first hand.

Hershl Sperling,* whose job as a teenager was not to wait tables but to drag the asphyxiated bodies of fellow Jews out of the gas chambers at Treblinka and then incinerate them, managed in remarkable fashion to escape that hyper-efficient death factory, before being apprehended and sent to Auschwitz instead. He frequently used to describe the latter, in which tens of thousands of Jewish babies and toddlers were gassed to death, as a 'walk in the park'. He settled in the leafy suburbs of Glasgow after the war, before throwing himself into the River Clyde in 1989.

Or to illustrate my point about this downplayed obliteration a little further, we can turn to a summary of the relevant series of events that took place in Sambir, the birthplace of death match hero Zygmunt Steuermann. The historian Aharon Weiss recorded what happened to the town's Jews when the Germans and their Ukrainian helpers arrived and set about their work with the zeal of Rentokil technicians incentivised by life-changing bonuses. It is hardly the sort of material you hear on Holocaust Memorial Day in Europe:

> The first mass Aktion took place on August 4, 1942, when 4,000 Jews were 'selected' and sent to Bełżec death camp. On September 4,

* To the best of my knowledge, Hershl Sperling was no relation of Leon Sperling, the great Jewish footballer whose story follows later in the book.

> about 100 aged persons were executed and 2,000 Jews were sent to Bełżec, followed by 3,000 on October 17, and more on October 22. On December 1, 1942, the ghetto was closed down. A small number of remaining Jews were sent to the (slave) labor camp of Janowska, in Lvov.*
>
> On March 14, 1943, the remnants of the Jewish community were brought to the Jewish cemetery. Mothers were ordered to put their children in a central open space, where they were forced to watch them being shot. Nine hundred persons were killed on this day. Two months later 1,200 Jews were murdered. An attempt by some Jews to leave the ghetto through sewage canals was thwarted. By July 1943 the Jewish community of Sambir ceased to exist, and the city was declared '*judenrein*' (free of Jews). The last remaining Jews were executed in a forest near Radlowicz. In the summer of 1944, 165 Jews in hiding were found and executed. When the Russians occupied the city in August 1944, a handful of Jews were still alive. No Jewish community was re-established.

And that, in case you were wondering, is what real genocide looks like.

* * *

My growing sense of the under-discussed reality of obliteration and the resulting destruction of Jewish collective memory ultimately led to an article I wrote for *The Guardian* newspaper, documenting the names of international Jewish footballers I had managed to identify, including Steuermann and Braun, who were murdered in the

* The Russian spelling of Lviv.

Holocaust. I wanted to see their names all together on the internet, recorded for posterity if anyone wanted to search for them.

I noted in the article that the absence of a goalkeeper meant that I did not have a full and proper team. However, one highly knowledgeable reader informed me shortly afterwards that Paul Goldberger, who was murdered in 1942, had played one game in goal for Hungary, way back in 1908.

I therefore had the makings of a complete football team, and the idea of this book – detailing the lives and careers of each of the team's players – started to take shape in my mind. I even had a top candidate for player-coach. Árpád Weisz was murdered in January 1944, probably picturing in his dying moments his wife and two young children who had suffered a similar fate fifteen months before. He had not only won seven international caps for Hungary, but was also the most celebrated coach in the great Italian league of the 1930s, winning the Championship once with Inter Milan and twice with Bologna.

I also had an on-field captain. Austria international Max Scheuer led the great Hakoah Vienna, the avowedly Zionist team which – quite remarkably – won the domestic league championship amid often vicious hostility and just a few short years before that country spiralled into an unbridled mania of Jew hatred.

But I still had choices to make. For the sake of the book's structure and symmetry, I decided to limit my purview to eleven players, a traditional football team. I also resolved to include only those players who graduated to full international honours. These were men who had once stood tall and proud as they walked out on to the pitch to represent what each no doubt thought was their country. Several of the eleven also risked life and limb in the First World War. But not so long later, in a vicious repudiation of what turned out to be extreme naivety, they were to be gassed, worked to death, beaten to a pulp or shot into pits, very often with the enthusiastic assistance of their fellow national citizens.

Most historically literate Jews, in my experience, do not need to be told that our existence in any country in the diaspora is fragile and has been untenable over time, but such reminders never do any harm. As we will see in these pages, to say that the destructive assault on European Jewry was some sort of historical blip or carried out and supported only by an elite cadre of committed German Nazis, constitutes a highly underestimated and sophisticated form of Holocaust denial.

Unfortunately, my focus on internationals meant losing some players who might have vied for inclusion on merit, such as Eddy Hamel, the flying Ajax winger of the 1920s who never got to represent the Netherlands, and was later murdered along with his wife, four-year-old twin sons, both parents, three sisters and all their young children, as well as around 75 per cent of Dutch Jewry (about 100,000 murdered, or the traditional capacity of Barcelona's Camp Nou – for those who haven't been there, I can tell you that the stands look like they reach the sky).

After much deliberation, my chosen team for this book is therefore as follows:

- Paul Goldberger – Goalkeeper, Hungary (1881–1942)
- Max Scheuer (captain) – Defender, Austria (1895–1942)
- Józef Klotz – Defender, Poland (1900–41)
- Henrik Nádler – Midfield, Hungary (1901–45)
- Antal Vágó – Midfield, Hungary (1891–1944)
- Otto Fischer – Forward, Austria (1901–41)
- József Braun – Forward, Hungary (1901–43)
- Leon Sperling – Forward, Poland (1900–41)

- Árpád Weisz (player/coach) – Forward, Hungary (1896–1944)
- Julius Hirsch – Forward, Germany (1892–1943)
- Zygmunt Steuermann – Forward, Poland (1899–1943)

You may notice several things in this line-up. First, you will see the preponderance of attack-minded players in the team and the lack of defenders. That is because tactical formations of the era included fewer defenders than they do today. My team will exude the intent to create and move forward, accurately reflecting the extraordinary enterprise and energy of the Jewish Europe that once was. You may also note the generational bias of the team. Most of these players were at their peak in the early inter-war years as international football was really taking off, and before the idea of Jews representing these countries became highly improbable or even impossible as a result of burgeoning antisemitic.

Finally, although their life stories take us the length and breadth of Europe – from Norway to Italy, from France to Latvia – you will see that all the players hail originally from the middle of the continent. This Central European dominance reflects the geographical reality of the Holocaust. These four countries (Poland, Hungary, Germany and Austria, stated in the order of the overall number of victims) contributed between them around 3.75 million (more than 60 per cent) of the murdered Jews. But the territorial concentration also reveals something important about the Jewish contribution to football before the catastrophe. Hungary and Austria, in particular, were at the vanguard of continental football between the wars. And where there is a vanguard, you will often find Jews.

Despite my research for *The Guardian* article, my understanding of these players' lives (and deaths) was at that stage still very sketchy and even, it later turned out, sometimes inaccurate. I set myself the task of excavating much more from this buried civilisation, to do my bit for truth and memory, the two concepts that lie at the very root of my motivation for writing this book and instilled in me the strength to combat the many obstacles I confronted along the way.

Which cities, towns and villages were these players from, and what were they like to grow up in? Who were their parents and siblings and what happened to them? How did they get started in football? What were the ups and downs of their footballing careers? Which clubs did they play for, and what did these clubs represent? What type of player were they? What was football like when they played, and how did Jews fit in? What were they like as people? Who were their wives and children, and what happened to them? What was it like for them to live and play football in a continent which – after centuries of recurrent persecution, torture, murder and expulsion – was about to embark on a project to eradicate the Jews once and for all? Why didn't they leave when the writing was on the wall? How were they captured? What was life like for them in captivity? How were they murdered, and who was responsible? What are they imploring us to say about them from their non-existent graves?

What I managed to discover from rummaging around the broken pieces of European Jewry is set out in this book. Some of the chapters deal with individual players, while others combine the stories of two players whose life stories intersect to a significant degree. The chapters vary a little in detail, for several reasons: the inevitable limits of the available evidence on some of the players' lives and deaths due to the scale of the obliteration; my own wish to avoid unnecessary repetition; and, to some extent, the respective footballing greatness of these largely forgotten players, and any resulting obligation I felt to record more information.

Through telling the stories of these eleven footballers, I have several aims in mind: to convey some semblance of the savage reality of the European Holocaust through the prism of the magnificent game of football; to establish definitively, for posterity, the crucial Jewish contribution to the development of the world's most popular sport, a remarkable tale that was lost amid the ruins of Jewish collective memory; and, more than anything, to award these eleven men their rightful place in history, thereby restoring just a few fragments of the vast, intricate European Jewish tapestry that was ultimately ripped to shreds.

'We could not prevent their deaths the first time,' said the writer and survivor Elie Wiesel on receiving his Nobel Peace Prize in 1986. 'But if we forget them, they will be killed a second time. And this time, it will be our responsibility.'

CHAPTER 1

THE HEBREW RONALDO

On 6 April 1924, Benito Mussolini consolidated his grip on power in Italy, winning a landslide victory at the polls. It was to be the last multi-party election to take place in that country for more than two decades. The descent into dictatorship and barbarism in Europe had begun in earnest, a process which was to culminate, among other things, in the annihilation of the continent's Jewish population.

Italian football fans could perhaps point to the tribulations of their national team on that very same spring Sunday as a harbinger of dark times ahead. In the Hungarian capital, Budapest, Italy were hammered 7–1, blown apart in front of 40,000 delirious fans. Even today, it remains the heaviest defeat ever suffered by that proud footballing nation. Italy's only goal was the last of the game, as a rampant home side belatedly and mercifully took their boots off their opponents' throats.

If you look up the details of the game on the Internet, you can see the facts for yourself. If you want, you can reflect for a few seconds on what a great team Hungary must have been in those days, ask yourself momentarily why they have fallen from that pedestal and then move on to something else. You might notice too that the pulverised Italian team were coached that day by a young Vittorio Pozzo, one of the titans of football history, and later known as *Il Vecchio Maestro* (The Old Master) after he gifted Mussolini two World Cups in the 1930s.

A closer examination of the game, however, reveals what to me is a far bigger story, offering a precious insight into a lost society. What the bare statistics will not tell you is that the scorers of Hungary's first six goals were Jews. Italy 0, Jews 6.

György Molnár, the Jewish inside right whose speed and mobility earned him the nickname *hangya* (the ant), smashed a second-half hat-trick within the space of ten minutes. József Eisenhoffer, a left-winger who converted to Judaism to marry his Jewish bride, scored another. Even the Czech-born referee Max Seemann was a Jew, as indeed were many top European referees in that era. Three minutes before half-time, with Hungary then only one up, he entered the spotlight after the Juventus defender Virginio Rosetta bundled into Eisenhoffer in the penalty area. Seemann, reported the newspaper *Nemzeti Sport*, 'deliberated for several seconds', before pointing to the penalty spot, demonstrating the unhurried assurance of an official in total control of his work.

Molnár and the rugged and powerful defender Károly Fogl had a quick on-field conflab, but both declined the responsibility to take the vital kick for Hungary. Only one player could rival Seemann for coolness under pressure. With barely any run-up, as if he was showing off to his friends in the park, the team's right-winger stroked the ball 'confidently' into the left-hand corner of the net. József Braun, the son of a *yeshiva bochur*,* whose footballing skills are unmatched by any Jew before or since, had just scored his second goal of the game.

* * *

In 2012, fifty-seven graves in the Jewish cemetery in the town of Putnok in north-eastern Hungary were daubed with antisemitic slogans. The

* A student at a *yeshiva*, an Orthodox Jewish seminary.

living Jews had long since disappeared, but the dead Jews were clearly still troubling some of the local populace. It is very possible, given the small size of the town, that one or two of the graves of József Braun's ancestors were daubed with familiar themes, perhaps similar to that scrawled on the Holocaust memorial in Budapest that very same year – 'This is not your country, you filthy Jews' – a modern-day reverberation of the message which the vast majority of Hungarian Jews had heard loud and clear on their way to the gas chambers back in 1944.

When we think of history's great footballers and their early childhoods, we may visualise the beaches and favelas of South America or the urban streets of working-class Europe. We wouldn't necessarily imagine them spending their first years wearing *tzitzit* or their days reading Hebrew and studying Torah.* But that is exactly how we should picture the young József Braun, a gifted son of Putnok.

From the beginning of the nineteenth century, major tensions had developed within Hungarian Jewry, resulting in a fundamental schism around thirty years before Braun's birth. The progressive camp, mostly comprising urban and rapidly assimilating Jews, emphasised the need for more secular education and favoured a more relaxed adherence to religious ritual. They embraced Hungarian patriotism and the country's language and culture. The Orthodox Jews, on the other hand, clung zealously to age-old traditions, believing that divine law is immutable and that any loosening of religious obligations would open the floodgates to a wholesale abandonment of the Judaism that had been their lifeblood for countless generations.

The simmering conflict inevitably came to a head at a stormy national Jewish congress in 1869, followed by an acrimonious split between the rival camps. Communities throughout the country

---

* A *tzitzit* is an undervest with tassles or fringes worn by Orthodox Jews. The *torah* comprises the Five Books of Moses.

discussed their choice of allegiance. The result in Putnok, however, was never in doubt. The town came down firmly against assimilation into Hungarian society, and for maintaining the minutiae of Jewish religious precepts.

The highly religious Rozália and Lipót Braun therefore fitted in very well to the local community. Indeed, the football world should perhaps be grateful that they were such eager advocates of the biblical commandment to 'go forth and multiply', and its interpretation expounded by the great medieval Jewish theologian, Maimonides. A person should 'not refrain from being fruitful and multiplying as long as he has the strength to do so,' explained Maimonides, 'for anyone who adds a soul to the Jewish people is considered as if he built an entire world'.

Rozália (née Binét) and Lipót built twelve entire worlds between them, seven girls and five boys. Rozália started giving birth when she was twenty and was still going strong almost two decades later, when the couple's youngest child József entered the world, on 26 February 1901. The name József will not just have been chosen because his parents liked the sound of it. The twelfth child of Jacob, the biblical patriarch of Israel, was similarly named. It was perhaps at this point, too, that little József was awarded the moniker Csibi, derived from the Hungarian for little chick. It was a nickname that stuck with him throughout his truncated life.

Putnok is situated on the left bank of the River Sajó, around forty kilometres from the major city of Miskolc, and now just a few minutes' drive from the border with Slovakia. The Jewish community grew to more than 700 in the 1930s, around one in four of the total population. Although farming was the town's largest industry, the majority of Jewish men were engaged in commerce, particularly in the wine or grain trade. Lipót himself managed to scratch out a living through grain trading, although he spent much of his time teaching in the community cheder.* As a young man, he had studied for a period at the Pressburg (Bratislava) Yeshiva, the largest and most influential such institution in Central Europe at that time.**

Shortly before the First World War, when they were in their fifties, Rozália and Lipót left behind their close-knit community and large, ornate white stone synagogue in Putnok to join the huge exodus of Jews from the provinces to the capital, Budapest. Some of their children were grown up and had already moved there, and they doubtless wanted to secure proximity to family as they got older.

The move bore two major and welcome, albeit unintended, consequences. For the young Csibi, Budapest provided the perfect conditions for his talent to flourish and be swiftly identified during his teenage years. Abandoning the provinces in favour of the capital also substantially increased family members' chances of survival three decades later. A mere half of Budapest's Jews were murdered, while the slaughter in the provinces was almost total. Indeed, the community the Brauns left behind was liquidated in 1944. Eva Brown, daughter of Putnok's community rabbi at that time, Solomon Rosenfeld, provides us with invaluable testimony of what happened in the days, months and years preceding the deportation and extermination of the town's Jews.

Before the Nazi occupation of March 1944, the antisemitic

* A school for young Jewish children where Hebrew and the basics of the Jewish religion are taught.

** The charismatic founder of the Pressburg Yeshiva, Moshe Sofer (better known as Chatam Sofer), was one of the leading rabbinic scholars of the nineteenth century and provided much of the intellectual weight in the fierce argument with the progressives. His motto, *He-chadash asur min ha-Torah* (the new is prohibited by the Torah) became the slogan of Orthodox resistance. The Pressburg *yeshiva* was closed down in 1941, shortly before the deportation of Slovakia's Jews to the death camps. It was re-established in Israel in the late 1950s, a few years before its historic building in Bratislava was razed by the Communist authorities.

Hungarian government had independently ordered the rounding up of many younger Jewish men for deportation to slave labour camps. Rabbi Rosenfeld had somehow been spared this torment until the Nazis efficiently snuffed out the anomaly soon after their arrival. His daughter escorted him to the station to say her heart-rending farewell.

'I started noticing the crowds of people,' she wrote. 'Hundreds of gentiles were lined up at the station, applauding and cheering, jubilant at the event: the last able-bodied Jewish man was leaving their town'.

A week later, it was the turn of the remaining Jews in József Braun's birthplace to experience a scene replicated in countless locations across the length and breadth of Hungary. This time, the destination, after several days crammed together in sealed cattle cars, was to be the death camp, Auschwitz-Birkenau.

'It was June 9, 1944 … Again, hundreds of our gentile neighbours showed up at the train station,' recalled Brown. 'They were applauding and cheering. The town would be free of Jews. They would have it to themselves. The sights and sounds cut into my heart like a knife. The expressions on their faces as they jumped up and down were terrifying. Parents, children, young and old – celebrating our departure as if it were a soccer championship.'

A trickle of surviving Jews returned in 1945 and lovingly restored the synagogue. No matter. By the early 1970s, the last trace of Jewish life in Putnok had vanished. The synagogue is now a shop.

* * *

Ármin Beregi was a man who defied the overwhelming trend: he was a Budapest-based Zionist at a time when the vast majority of the capital's Jews considered the idea of a renewed nation-state in the ancestral Jewish homeland to be ridiculous or even hateful. 'When we started our task at the turn of the century,' one Hungarian Zionist historian wrote in 1934, 'the word "Jew" was considered a disgrace, even among Jews'.

Playing down the ethnic or national connotations of Jewishness (in favour of a strictly limited religious self-definition) in a bid to ward off antisemitism and gain acceptance in Hungarian society was the pervasive and driving goal. Zionism also took some time to flourish in small provincial towns such as Putnok, where Orthodox Judaism still held sway.

Having emigrated to Palestine in 1935 and avoiding the fate of close to 600,000 fellow Hungarian Jews, we can imagine that Beregi spent a large portion of his twilight years staring at the sea in the warmth of Tel Aviv, contemplating how seemingly ridiculous and hateful ideas can prove so eminently sensible and desirable.

Back in the early years of the century, one of the first tasks embraced by Beregi and his small band of fellow Budapest Zionists was to set up a sports club open exclusively to Jews and defined by an assertive Jewish nationalism. This was a model followed later by their peers in many other cities in Central Europe, with the forceful Hebrew names of new clubs devoted to heroic feats or individuals in biblical Jewish history – such as Hasmonea Lwów, Maccabi Brno or Bar Kokhba Berlin – or denoting Jewish strength, such as Hagibor (The Mighty) Prague and the most famous of them all, Hakoah (The Power) Vienna.

The Budapest Zionists applied to register with the simple name 'Jewish Gymnastics Club', but the idea was rejected by the authorities on the basis that it was too sectarian. In 1906, the Zionists circumvented this bureaucratic obstacle by opting for the neutral Vívó és Atlétikai Club (Fencing and Athletic Club), but with the initials VAC shaped on the club's crest to resemble the Star of David.

'Through VAC, the idea that a Jewish sports club should be belittled or ridiculed came to an end,' remarked a defiant Beregi in 1920, a period in which up to 3,000 Jews were being slaughtered throughout the country during the so-called White Terror, orchestrated by the then Hungarian government. 'The Fencing and Athletics Club not only wanted to take a Jewish name but has cried out to Hungarian society with all its might: "Anyone who wants to see Jewish strength and a Jewish team should look at us; we have created something meaningful from nothing but a heart and a symbol."'

It was in this highly charged environment at VAC that József Braun honed his football skills during his early teenage years, having first become acquainted with the sport by kicking a stuffed rag around Almássy Square with other underprivileged children from his local neighbourhood. It seems likely that this formative period at VAC, together with his unambiguously Jewish upbringing, bore a long-lasting imprint on his soul. In 1929, travelling on a ship to the United States to play professional football, Braun crossed out 'Hungarian' as his 'race or nationality' on the ship's manifest, and replaced it with 'Hebrew'.

* * *

Braun's performances in the VAC youth teams reverberated among the footballing cognoscenti of Budapest, a city that had become transfixed by this British-imported sport since the turn of the century. One of those with his ear close to the ground was himself a British import, a Lancastrian innovator and disciplinarian by the name of Jimmy Hogan, who had recently become coach of MTK Budapest.

Hogan's appointment by the club's Jewish chairman Alfréd Brüll – whose own incredible life story appears later in the book – followed a defined strategic pattern. He was given the task of building on the solid foundations put in place by previous British coaching exiles, John Tait Robertson and William Holmes. Legend has it that Hogan spotted Braun's talent while on a leisurely stroll in Angol Park (English Park), a popular haunt of the city's heavily Jewish-dominated middle classes, with its open green space, amusement arcade and its restaurant and pub open until the small hours. The park was situated a thirty-minute walk away from the Braun family apartment on Wesselényi Street in the Erzsébetváros district, where Jews made up almost half the population.

According to Hogan, Braun was having an informal kickabout with his (non-Jewish) friend, György Orth, and the three struck up a conversation. Braun and Orth, both fifteen at the time, had been enthusiastic students of English at high school, and Hogan offered them an appealing blend of top-class football coaching and language practice if they chose to work under him at MTK. 'I pounced on them and said "they are mine, my very own",' Hogan recalled.

The story is surely too simple, with perhaps a touch of self-aggrandisement on Hogan's part, seeking to convey the impression that only he possessed the footballing intuition to identify something special about two boys playing three-and-in with their jumpers as goalposts. More likely, he opportunistically seized on a chance meeting with two prodigious talents who were already becoming known. While Braun had been making sparks fly with VAC's youth team, Orth had by this stage already broken into the first team at Vasas, one of the many football clubs to have sprung up in the city over recent years.

Hogan need not have bragged about his coaching insight; there were plenty of others who would do that for him. In later decades, two Manchester United managers of the modern era were just as bowled over by Hogan's coaching as Braun was to be. Tommy Docherty, who worked under Hogan at Glasgow Celtic in the late 1940s, referred to Hogan as 'the greatest coach the world has ever known'. Some praise from a man who lived and breathed football until he died at the age of ninety-two.

A young Ron Atkinson was similarly rapt by Hogan's coaching sessions as a young player at Aston Villa. In an interview in 2020, more than a century after the Burnley-bred Hogan had fallen for Braun at first sight in Angol Park, Atkinson said, 'There was no one like him at the time (in England in the early 1950s) ... He laid the foundations for many coaches that followed.' Bear in mind, too, that by the time he tutored Atkinson, Hogan was already in his early seventies, his most fruitful and energetic years long behind him.

In November 1953, Hogan took Atkinson and several of his young Aston Villa charges to Wembley for what he hoped would be a footballing education. He was not to be disappointed. Hungary, a country that had been hugely influenced by Hogan's ideas, set about crushing England, a country that had rejected his methods for decades and forced him to spend his peak coaching years as a footballing migrant, plying his wares not just in Budapest, but also in Holland, Germany, Austria, Switzerland and France.

The scoreline, 6–3 to Hungary, flattered England. The return match in Budapest six months later finished with a scoreline which more accurately reflected the gulf in class – 7–1 to Hungary. The results and performances shocked a complacent footballing establishment in the country which had founded the sport. They triggered a painfully slow, decades-long process which culminated in English football eventually relaxing its obsession with physical strength and stamina, and finally embracing an emphasis on technique, ball control, passing, possession and perpetual movement for which an English coach, Hogan, had been the most persuasive and pioneering advocate.

The young Atkinson had no idea of Hogan's past until he started reading in the newspapers that the visiting Hungarian players, such as the great Ferenc Puskás, were waxing lyrical about *Jimmybacsi* (Uncle Jimmy), a veritable legend in their home country. 'Jimmy Hogan taught us everything we know about football,' confirmed the president of the Hungarian football association, Sándor Barcs.

It was at the feet of this coaching revolutionary that Csibi Braun learned his trade, lapping up every single word. For Hogan, meanwhile, it was to be the start of a love affair that ended with a broken heart. After Braun's untimely death, Hogan's eyes would well up at the mere mention of his name.

* * *

Braun and Orth developed quickly under Hogan's watchful gaze. 'They were both intelligent lads attending High School in Budapest,' recalled Hogan. 'Every day after school I had them on the field, instructing them in the art of the game.'

Hogan had to determine how to shoehorn Braun's talent into his multi-talented team. Braun had played in the inside-right position for the VAC youth team, but that position was occupied at MTK by Kálmán Konrád, a player with flawless technique, impeccable balance and the rare ability to play a penetrating pass. Instead, Hogan earmarked Braun as a potential upgraded replacement for the right-winger Imre Taussig, who had played alongside Konrád in the Hungarian national team. Both Konrád and Taussig were Jews.*

'It was hard to compete with the inside forward at the time,'

---

* Imre Taussig qualifies for my team. Born in Martonoš in what is now Serbia, he played five times for Hungary during the First World War, all against Austria. In November 1944, he was murdered in a slave labour camp in Budapest, aged fifty-four. After a distinguished playing career, Kálmán Konrád became coach of several top clubs in Europe, including Bayern Munich. He sensibly found a job in neutral Sweden in 1939 and stayed there for the rest of his life.

recalled Braun a few years later in an interview with *Nemzeti Sport*. 'Jimmy also saw that, so we started to work on my game on the far right, where there was still some grass growing.' Hogan focused on developing two areas of Braun's game in particular – dribbling at pace and crossing the ball into the penalty area with pinpoint accuracy.

'I only wish that the British player who argued with me a few months ago that swerving and feinting were natural gifts which could not be taught had the opportunity to play against these two wonders [Braun and Orth],' Hogan later said. 'Their body control was learned by simple exercises, such as dribbling the ball round sticks and controlling it first with the inside and then the outside of the foot, coupled with gymnastic exercises to make the body loose at the hips.' In Braun's case, Hogan was only perfecting high-quality raw material. With a slim and muscular build, and about five foot eight inches tall, young Csibi had also excelled in sprinting and long jump.

It was not long before his eye-catching performances on the training pitch earned their due reward. Powered by the prolific goalscorers Imre Schlosser and Alfréd Schaffer, MTK had waltzed to the wartime championship title in 1917, before embarking on a summer tour to Vienna. It was here that Braun made his bow in a 2–0 victory against Wiener Athletiksport Club. He was sixteen years and three months old, an age at which breaking through to the big time was still a distant dream for even some of the most talented stars of football history.*

---

* Braun's niece Veronika Mermelstein left me confused when she told me that her uncle had first impressed for MTK in a game in Vienna, a story which has stayed in the family for more than a century. I only understood what she meant when I saw the relevant match report.

In October 1917, Braun and Orth were both drafted into the team for the league game against Újpest. Braun immediately made his mark, scoring twice in a 6–1 thrashing. 'The youth players performed excellently,' enthused the *Népszava* newspaper. 'If all the forward line had worked with the same sharpness as the two young strikers, Újpest would have suffered an even more severe defeat.'

Hogan used Braun sparingly during that 1917/18 season, carefully allowing him time to learn his trade among great players in a high-achieving environment and to gain gradual exposure to the rigours of top-level sport. Raw talent, however, is difficult to constrain indefinitely. It was in the autumn of 1918, as Europe finally emerged from the horrors of war, that Braun bashed down the door of opportunity and demanded that football sit up and take notice.

A game against the touring DFC Prag cemented Braun's reputation as a rising star. DFC were at that point a major force in Central European football. Founded by German Jews in Prague at the end of the nineteenth century, DFC had been several-time winners of the Bohemian championship and had already beaten MTK at home 6–2 earlier in 1918, no mean feat considering the latter's total supremacy in their own country.*

Few of the 12,000 MTK supporters eagerly anticipating the return match could have foreseen the complete turnaround in fortunes, as their heroes hammered the visitors 8–0. The *Az Újság* newspaper praised Braun's 'ruthless and brutal' play as he punished

* The players and administrators of DFC Prag were comprised mostly of Jews right up to 1939. Max Seemann, the referee who featured at the start of this chapter, was one such administrator. The club was dissolved in 1939, having been banned as a 'Jewish club'. Several of their Jewish former players were murdered in the Holocaust, including long-time goalkeeper Fritz Taussig, murdered at Gleiwitz, a sub-camp of Auschwitz, in December 1944.

DFC's tiring defenders, 'amazing his supporters' with the two final goals of the rout. *Sporthirlap* even advocated that Braun should be catapulted straight into the national team, given the evident magnitude of his talent. 'Braun on the right wing,' gushed the newspaper's correspondent, 'with his extraordinary speed, lovely passes and several shots on goal, showed form truly worthy of representative honours.'

* * *

The national selectors moved quickly to assuage the growing public clamour, selecting Braun for the trip to play arch-rivals Austria in October 1918. 'He is an outstanding player, who has earned the velvet cap even though he is only seventeen,' declared an approving *Sporthirlap*, praising his 'incomparable agility' and 'explosive shooting'.*

Braun's debut game on the international stage could be billed in retrospect as the closing ceremony for the Austro-Hungarian empire, which crumbled just three weeks later in the wake of military defeat. The home team was coached by Hugo Meisl, a Jew who had previously worked closely with Hogan in Vienna to develop the country's top players, laying the foundations for Meisl's infamous *Wunderteam* of the early 1930s. Alexander Popovich, a muscular, quick and wily defender, was given the task of subduing the threat from Hungary's debutant express train on the right wing. By the end of an ill-tempered game, Popovich could be forgiven for wondering whether he was in Vienna or Vladivostok. Braun

* Although several players to have already made their debut for the national team had been even younger than Braun (including Antal Vágó – see Chapter 8), no player has played for Hungary at a younger age in the more than one hundred years since Braun's appearance against Austria (seventeen years and 222 days).

ran his dizzy opponent ragged and put the icing on the cake of a dream first performance with a goal late in the second half of a 3–0 victory. 'Braun gave the best performance we have witnessed for a long time from a right-winger wearing the national colours,' reported *Sporthirlap*. 'His speed and great technique are combined with an amazing calmness, and he deserves special respect for not respecting even Popovich, whom he left for dead several times.'

A common misconception is that aggression and tribalism among football crowds are a relatively modern phenomenon, that the audience of yesteryear must somehow have been more sportsmanlike, an impression consolidated by the available newsreels of smiling fans throwing their hats in the air. Closer examination of József Braun's debut may dispel any such naivety. After the German referee Otto Kehm awarded two penalties for the away team, venom poured from the terraces. At the final whistle, only the police saved Kehm from a severe beating on the pitch at the hands of marauding fans. Braun and his Hungary teammates were also pelted with punches before they managed to escape to the sanctuary of the dressing room.

The region's passion for football had become all-consuming. In front of up to 40,000 fans at the eagerly anticipated return fixture the following April, the only international game played during the short-lived Hungarian Soviet Republic of 1919, Braun smashed in a late winner from outside the penalty area to give his team a 2–1 victory.

At club level, too, Braun was soaring to the heights. He was an almost ever-present fixture in a MTK team that once again lifted the championship in the 1918/19 season with a remarkable 116 goals in twenty-two games. To gain some perspective on this achievement, the second-placed team, arch-rivals Ferencváros, managed only forty-three goals. And Braun's ability to run like the wind with the ball seemingly stuck to his feet, as well as his powerful long-range shooting and imperious heading ability, had already become crucial components of one of the greatest club sides in football history.

Thirty years later, Gábor Kompóti-Kléber, who played alongside Braun with MTK and Hungary before becoming a football journalist, succinctly summarised the storm the teenage sensation had generated when he burst on to the scene. His description was one of several which brought to my mind a close likeness in style to the modern-day great, Cristiano Ronaldo:

> We had never seen an outside right blessed with the same skills as he was. He controlled the ball in an amazing way, with every single part of his body … Even while he was running at maximum pace, he would keep his head up and see which team-mates had kept pace with him. When he got the ball, he headed off towards goal immediately as if he was being pulled by a magnet. He could shoot from the tightest of angles.

If Braun had needed to endear himself yet further to his adoring fans, he also scored that season in each of the fixtures against Ferencváros in the always hotly contested Budapest derby, known locally as the *Örökrangadó* (the eternal rivalry).

Braun's performance in the latter of these games, played at MTK's stadium towards the end of the season, sparked another riot. With five minutes left on the clock and MTK already winning 1–0, Alfréd Schaffer played a through ball for Braun to run on to. The defence had a metre head start but Braun outpaced them with ease, sprinting through to score. The Ferencváros team protested bitterly, simply unable to grasp that Braun could have won the race to the ball so decisively if he had started from an onside position.* The Jewish captain of Ferencváros, Zoltán Blum, led his players off the pitch in protest and the referee was forced to end the game early. Once again, Braun was assaulted by opposition fans as he left the pitch, saved this time by the Communist militia, the Red Guard.

On one occasion that season, Braun's protection came from an unlikely source. The Terézvárosi left-back Ármin Fried was no different to many of his peers. The only way these mere mortals could hope to stop Braun was through violence, and Fried's preferred method in one particular game was to kick him in the stomach. He did not go unpunished. According to the newspaper *Népszava*, 'Braun's elder sister slapped Fried in the face.'

'That would have been Etel,' laughed Braun's niece Veronika Mermelstein when I asked her about this incident. Etel was apparently the most devoted and feisty member of a very substantial family fan club, which also included Braun's proud parents who overcame any initial misgivings about their son's chosen career to stand among the crowds waiting to applaud him as he left the stadium after matches.

Hogan's protégé was inspiring worship and enmity in equal measure, a teenage celebrity in a football-mad city.**

---

* Until a rule change in 1925, a player was considered offside unless three players of the opposing side were in front of him (including the goalkeeper), rather than the two players stipulated by modern rules. Braun therefore had to outpace two defenders, despite their head start.

** In 1919, Béla Szenes wrote a very popular children's story in Hungarian, entitled *Csibi* and inspired by Braun, about a boy who becomes a football star. The book was translated into Hebrew in the 1950s, possibly due to the then iconic status in Israel of the author's daughter. Hannah Szenes, a Zionist who had emigrated from Hungary to British-controlled Palestine in 1939, was parachuted behind enemy lines by the British army in 1944 to assist both Allied forces and the persecuted Jews in occupied Europe. She was captured by Hungarian forces, tortured for several days, and executed in her birthplace, Budapest. She was twenty-three.

* * *

The Communist regime soon collapsed in the summer of 1919. The new nationalist government of Miklós Horthy rounded on the Jews for the next couple of years during the White Terror, trading on the widespread bitterness about their success in Hungarian society, as well as the popular myths that they were somehow responsible for Hungary's defeat in the war and/or had played a leading role in the subsequent revolution.

In October of that year, Hogan also departed Budapest to return to England. But despite the loss of his inspirational mentor, and the fanatical and murderous antisemitism all around him, the Jewish boy from Putnok remained unstoppable for the next two years. Hogan had got to him at the perfect age, implanting invaluable habits and techniques that would stand him in great stead for the rest of his career. Meanwhile, the pervasive antisemitism did not yet possess the fully genocidal quality that Europe would witness a quarter of a century later. Hungarian football was a source of great patriotic pride, and it needed its Jews.

MTK walked the league in 1919/20 and 1920/21, scoring an average of almost four goals a game and losing only two games in total during those seasons. Csibi continued to shine in Hungary's colours as well. 'Braun was the focal point of all Hungarian attacks on the right side and was the most dangerous striker,' *Nemzeti Sport* reported after a typically bravura performance by the young winger against Austria in October 1920. 'His ferocious shot, with which he scored the only Hungarian goal, was especially impressive.'

He was a popular fixture in the dressing room too, and not just because he helped his team to so many victories. 'His eyes and face were always smiling, and he was always up to some mischief,' recalled

Gábor Kompóti-Kléber. 'He was the best kind of friend. If he had enough money in his pocket, nobody could have asked anything of him that he would not have done.'

It was only a matter of time, however, before brutal treatment by defenders had their intended impact, and deprived Braun's meteoric rise of its previous momentum. Proper protection of highly skilled attacking players through refereeing has been a relatively recent phenomenon in football, only emerging after a veritable 'who's who' of talent had their careers cut short by injuries inflicted by vicious defenders. After all, even Diego Maradona, a world star of the 1980s and 1990s, suffered notoriously at the hands of his markers. We have to imagine that the game in the 1920s, only a few decades after association football and rugby football diverged from similar origins, was even more tolerant of savage tackling. If Braun was going to humiliate defenders with his pace and trickery, they were content to resort to brute force without too much fear of heavy punishment.

Moreover, while some of the victims responded in kind to deter their assailants, perhaps even revelling in the conflict, it seems that Braun was a good-natured and even-tempered man who just wanted to excel at football. 'He never played dirty,' wrote Kompóti-Kléber. 'He loathed violence. He couldn't stand it if the opposition was playing rough.' A crosshairs symbol, it seems, was painted in bright red on his forehead.

In November 1921, in a home international against Sweden, Braun received the first of several devastating injury blows. Justus Gustafsson, the uncompromising Swedish left-back, clattered into Braun, who 'got up and limped off the field' in what might be termed a display of foolhardy machismo. His tibia was broken, and he soon went under the surgeon's knife for the first time.

In love with the game and desperate to get his stellar career back on track, Braun rushed back too quickly. He was again badly injured in a match against 33 FC in the spring of 1922, necessitating another operation. The cycle had been set in motion from which Braun, at that point still only twenty-one, would never fully escape – repeated wounds to progressively weakened limbs meted out by calculating defenders well aware of his growing vulnerability; the comparatively primitive orthopaedic treatment of that era; and the failures of both club and the player himself to give his body sufficient time to recover. According to one legend, when Braun walked into a crowded train carriage during these years, old men would vacate their seats so that their idol could rest his precious legs.

* * *

Such was Braun's huge talent (not to mention courage) that for the next two years at least, he still managed to overcome these serious injuries to register outstanding performances on a consistent basis. After missing much of the 1921/22 season, he recovered to become an almost ever-present in MTK's following two title-winning seasons.

One particular game, in the first of those seasons, was an intensely dramatic encounter, a footballing reflection of the bitter division in Jewish society between a greatly outnumbered and youthful minority who saw no future for European Jews on the one side, and those who turned out to be wrong on the other. It was a gulf which had become more pronounced in the wake of the White Terror and the widespread lynching of Jews throughout the country.

Braun's former club VAC had been promoted for the first time to the Hungarian first division in 1921 and looked forward with relish to their encounters against the mighty MTK, a club that the Zionists scorned. Despite being founded by Jewish businessmen in 1888, being predominantly supported by Jews and boasting a playing staff that was more than 50 per cent Jewish in the first three decades of the twentieth century, MTK very much swam with the trend by battling hard to play down its roots. Its name Magyar Testgyakorlók Köre (Circle of Hungarian Fitness Activists) attested to the club's enthusiastic belief in assimilation. In 1926, the club even temporarily changed its name to Hungária in a desperate, yet vain, attempt to be accepted as part of the local furniture.

In their debut season in the top flight, VAC were responsible for MTK's one and only defeat of the league campaign, winning 1–0. They even held on for a goalless draw in a very physical return game when the referee struggled to keep the peace.

Revenge was therefore still in the air for the two teams' first meeting of the following season at MTK's home Hungária Körúti Stadium, on Sunday 1 October 1922, the eve of Yom Kippur.* Halfway through the second half in another highly charged atmosphere, VAC were ahead again, by two goals to one. At that point, the normally placid György Molnár was ordered off the pitch by referee Frigyes Klug for vehement dissent after the official had denied MTK what looked like a clear penalty and instead awarded a free kick just outside the area. When the resulting free kick was crossed into the box, Klug, perhaps realising that he had made an error in the first incident, this time blew his whistle for a penalty, claiming that Gyula Weisz had elbowed MTK's Antal Siklóssy in the stomach. The VAC players erupted with fury and vitriol, pushing Klug and screaming at him to consult with his

* Yom Kippur, or the Day of Atonement, is widely considered the holiest day of the year in the Jewish calendar. It involves a 25-hour fast which even many non-Orthodox Jews still observe today.

linesman, who insisted that he had seen no offence take place. Klug was unmoved, and as rival fans poured on to the pitch to join with the players in a riot that the police found impossible to control, he calmly strolled off to the dressing room.

On the Monday morning, when most of the offending players were in synagogue atoning for their sins of the previous day, the Hungarian Football Federation met to discuss the affair. The committee decided that the remaining minutes of the game should be played a few days later, this time behind closed doors and at a neutral ground. The game was to restart with the awarded penalty to MTK. In what turned out to be a critical error, the committee ordered Klug to play a further twenty-eight minutes, rather than the twenty-two minutes actually left on the clock.

Among his many strengths as a footballer, Braun was known for his ability to strike a dead ball cleanly. He fizzed his corner kicks into the penalty area with spin and swerve, making them extremely difficult to defend. He had a high scoring rate from direct free kicks from outside the area. And he had the ice-cool temperament common to many of football's great penalty takers, consistently and nonchalantly dispatching the ball into the corner of the goal with hardly any run-up. Notwithstanding his near-unblemished record, he spent all week before the resumption practising his penalties against MTK's own goalkeeper, Ferenc Plattkó, himself a Hungarian international who was to be transferred to Barcelona at the end of the season. Paying scant regard to Plattkó's substantial presence, every single one of Braun's countless practice kicks ended up as one would have expected: in the back of the net.

When the big moment came, it was not VAC goalkeeper Lajos Fischer whom Braun saw standing opposite him. It turned out that

Klug had sent Fischer off in the midst of the previous Sunday's pandemonium for appearing to be intent on maiming the MTK star Zoltán Opata. Instead, the forward István Kovës had donned the keeper's jersey. However, when Klug blew his whistle for the restart, Braun's penalty against the makeshift keeper hit the outside of the post. The great winger stood with his head bowed in shame as the VAC players danced around him in mocking celebration.

Could Braun and MTK recover mentally from this unexpected setback in the short time available? They continued to attack relentlessly, only to be repelled by VAC's stubborn rearguard. But then, twenty-three minutes after the restart and one minute after the game should by rights have ended, MTK were awarded a free kick twenty metres from goal. Braun walked up to the ball slowly, as if about to lay it sideways to either Opata or Siklóssy. However, after glimpsing a slight gap in the defensive wall, he suddenly unleashed an unstoppable thunderbolt which screamed into the net behind Kovës, earning his team a 2–2 draw.

Here was a true champion, a sportsman blessed not only with outlandish talent but also with supreme self-confidence and the spirit of a lion.

* * *

Braun was in fine form in the season leading up to the Olympic Games, to be held in Paris in the summer of 1924. Until the World Cup was founded a few years later, the Olympics was the most prestigious football tournament on the planet.

As well as his prominent role in the 7–1 demolition of Italy in April of that year, Braun had made aficionados purr with his exemplary performance in a 3–1 victory against Finland in Budapest. *Sporthirlap*'s report of the game captures the essence of a great footballer in his pomp, less than two decades before his emaciated body was left lying to rot in the depths of the Russian snow:

> In the line of forwards, it was mainly Braun who stood out with a classic display – his swiftness, his inventiveness, his centres and headers, his whole game … Spectators were delighted with his splendid play, which he made even more memorable with his goal as well as a cleverly placed penalty. From the first minute Braun was in complete control of the situation and he handled his opponents with such elegance and ease as if he was playing against a junior team … He kept the Finnish goalkeeper busy with several excellent shots while his corner kicks were also good.

Hungary demolished Poland 5–0 in their first knockout game at the Olympics, raising the expectations of the public back home to fever pitch. But despite having the lion's share of chances in the second round against unfancied Egypt, the team crashed out 3–0, with Braun's own poor performance typified by hitting the bar with a penalty on the stroke of half-time when the team was only one down. After a game dubbed the *Egyiptomi Csapás* (the Egyptian calamity) by an angry Hungarian media, Braun was pilloried for allegedly being intimidated by the huge and imposing figure of the defender, Abdel Salam Hamdy.

Such was the national grief that a formal inquest was held into Hungary's sub-par performance. In the so-called Black Book, players and administrators were asked for their opinions on what went wrong. Braun laid the blame full square on the amateurish preparation and penny-pinching by the Hungarian football establishment:

> In the hotel in Paris we lacked all comforts. There were six of us staying in the same room and we could not keep our own sleeping routine, since everyone went to bed and woke up at different times and always disturbed their mates who were trying to rest. The catering was not good enough, either. It was coffee and butter for breakfast, we got half-raw, bloody meat for lunch; our stomachs just could not take this in. For example, I lost four kilos due to the catering in Paris. It's obvious that because of the accommodation and catering our condition completely deteriorated.

Reading this account, it is difficult not to reflect that Braun would later experience accommodation and food that would make his trip to Paris seem fit for the most gilded royalty. Braun's miserable but brief Olympic appearance would later offer some hope of an escape from that subsequent hell. But as we shall see, even that silver lining was denied to him.

* * *

A matter of months after the Olympics, Braun's career was once again derailed by injury, and this time he would never again soar to the heights of brilliance. In October 1924, MTK and Braun were demolishing Ferencváros in the derby. The score was already 8–1 to the perennial champions when the defender Jenö Jancsár finally ran out of ideas on how to stop the onslaught. He brutally scythed Braun down in the penalty area with a vicious assault on his shins. Before the penalty kick could be taken, Braun had been carried off, a victim of his own genius. Another operation followed. By my calculations, Braun played just twenty-two further league games for MTK in the following four years, although he was also chosen five more times by national team selectors whose romantic memories of a former great trumped any sober realism. Braun's international career finally ended in 1926, at the age of just twenty-five, with twenty-eight caps and eleven goals under his belt.

Yet another operation, in 1927, led to an outbreak of erysipelas on his feet, a type of bacterial skin infection. In the days before antibiotics, erysipelas could be potentially fatal, and critical weeks followed before he eventually pulled through.

Braun eventually left MTK (now also known as Hungária) in 1929. In the seven seasons where he had played a pivotal role in the team, 1918/19 through to 1924/25, MTK had won successive league titles, scoring 547 goals in the process at an average of 3.3 goals per game. In the subsequent three seasons, with Braun pretty much out of the picture, Ferencváros lifted the title instead.

Notwithstanding his outstanding record, the span of his career at the footballing summit was short-lived, and its timing was inopportune. Hungarian football only ceased to be an amateur sport in 1926, that is after Braun's most serious injury, at which point top players could at last be paid legitimately and adequately. Although he tried to supplement his meagre footballing income with jobs as a bank clerk and stockbroker, those careers were never going to last. When I asked his niece Veronika Mermelstein why Braun never married, she replied that he lived only for football, thinking and talking about it the whole time. The last embers of his playing career should be viewed in this rather tragic context.

In late June 1929, he played two games in two days for Hakoah Vienna in a summer tournament. Both Braun and Hakoah had been renowned in the football world for their brilliance in the first half of that decade, and the notion of the flying Jewish winger playing for the pride of the Jewish footballing world would have provoked enormous excitement during that intoxicating period. But now the twin fading giants were subjected to humiliation, with Braun and Hakoah losing 3–1 and 8–0 to MTK and Slavia Prague respectively.

A few weeks later, he rather belatedly followed a significant exodus of well-known Central European Jewish footballers to the United States. He joined his old international teammates György Molnár and József Eisenhoffer at the Jewish club Brooklyn Hakoah. Just like Hakoah Vienna, however, American soccer was already in the midst of decline from its height of popularity a few years before, in its case torn apart by bitter internal strife and a subsequent breakaway league.

Braun soon left Brooklyn Hakoah with Molnár and Eisenhoffer to join another team, Brooklyn Wanderers, that appeared to possess an equivalent propensity to lose football matches. By now, the Wall Street Crash had sent shockwaves through the US economy. Deep recession loomed, and Braun duly returned to Europe, the forthcoming cemetery of the Jews.

His last port of call was at the club where his career had started out with such pulsating promise. He played for VAC in a vital clash against Vasas in June 1930, with both teams vying for promotion to Hungary's top league. Braun was 'a shadow of his former self' (*Nemzeti Sport*) and, lacking confidence and no doubt fearful of further injury, 'was in a hurry to get rid of the ball' (*Az Ujság*). A footballing public which had rejoiced in his wondrous abilities just a few short years before now 'booed him off'. Within a week, VAC had terminated his contract. And that, finally, was that.

* * *

The year 1930 was an *annus horribilis* for Braun. As his football career petered out in a sad anti-climax, his parents Rozália and Lipót passed away within a short time of each other, thankfully spared the horrors of what was to befall their family and people in the coming years. Determined to stay in football, Braun sought a coaching career in which he could apply the many lessons he had picked up from Hogan and from a vibrant and innovative Budapest footballing culture. He was clearly fascinated by the intricacies of the game. 'It is in the stands that a resting player really learns to play football,' he told *Nemzeti Sport*, while recovering from one of his many injuries in 1926.

In becoming a coach, he was among the first of a long list of highly talented Hungarian Jewish contemporaries, such as Béla Guttmann, Izidor Kürschner, Árpad Weisz (whose story appears later), Imre (Emérico) Hirschl, Lajos Czeizler, Ernő Egri Erbstein, Gyula Mándi, Kálmán Konrád, Lipót Hertzka and Gyula Feldmann, who spread their wings and enjoyed success throughout the footballing world, many of them capitalising on their international mobility to evade the European Holocaust.*

Braun's coaching record did not reach the heights achieved by some of his peers and nor could it match the exhilarating achievements of his playing career. But it was highly impressive nonetheless. His first job was as coach of the Norway national team, where he was handed a short-term contract and the specific target of securing the Nordic Football Championship. The regional championship was founded in the 1920s, with Denmark, Sweden, Finland and Norway all playing against each other twice over a four-year period, after which the top team in the mini-league would be crowned as winners. Denmark won the first league, completed in 1928, and Sweden won it nine times

* Having survived the Holocaust, Gyula Mándi coached the Israel national team in two spells from 1959 to 1964.

in succession from 1936 to 1977. But Norway, under Braun, won it for what was to be their one and only time in July 1932, sealing the championship with a 4–1 away victory against closest rivals Sweden in Gothenburg.*

On 30 January 1933, on the same day Adolf Hitler became Chancellor of Germany, a less newsworthy appointment was also announced. József Braun became coach of ČsŠK Bratislava, now known as Slovan Bratislava, in the city where his father had occupied his time in a very different way. He got off to a storming start, with his relative minnows defeating the mighty Ferencváros 3–1 on their tour of Slovakia. He proceeded to build the trust of the players, drumming into them the importance of ball control just as Hogan had done and urging them through his own example to focus on nutrition and fitness and avoid alcohol and cigarettes. That year, Braun also capitalised on his top-level experience and the regional cachet he had built up as a player to write a chapter in a book on the science of football training. His 28-page contribution, translated into Slovak, was entitled *Ako mám futbal hrat* ('How do I play football?').**

For the 1934/35 season, ČsŠK Bratislava competed in the Czechoslovak second division, itself split into five groups along regional or ethnic lines. The five group winners would then play off against each other to qualify for the premier division, the so-called State League. Under Braun's disciplined tutelage, ČsŠK came top of their ten-team

* Eight years later, at the time of the German invasion in 1940, there were approximately 2,100 Jews in Norway, including several hundred refugees from Germany and Austria. In 1942 and 1943, with the help of the Norwegian police, nearly 800 Jews were rounded up and deported, mostly to Auschwitz-Birkenau. Approximately twenty-five survived. As many as 1,000 Jews managed to escape to neutral Sweden with the aid of the underground.

** The book is entitled *Futbalový šport a jeho organizácia na Slovensku* (The sport of football and its organisation in Slovakia). A copy remains in the university library in Bratislava.

regional group and then won the subsequent play-off league for good measure, becoming the first Slovak club ever to reach the heights of the State League. Not only was this a considerable achievement in itself, but Braun's team secured it in the breathlessly exciting style he had imported from MTK. ČsŠK won twenty-one out of twenty-six games during the season as a whole, scoring an average of 3.4 goals in each.

Braun steered his promoted team to a respectable mid-table position in a State League heavily dominated by the big Prague clubs, Slavia and Sparta. However, in February 1936, *Nemzeti Sport* reported that 'he fell out with the management' and his contract was terminated. Rumours also circulated in Slovakia that he had argued with the players and lost the support of the dressing room. Braun clearly knew his own football mind and was not one to be easily thrown off course.

One club's loss was another's gain. Fiľakovo (or Fülek in Hungarian) was a small, predominantly Hungarian-speaking town in south-eastern Slovakia, situated only around sixty kilometres from Braun's birthplace of Putnok and part of the vast swathe of territory that Hungary had lost in the 1920 Treaty of Trianon, signed in the wake of the country's defeat in the First World War. There were only around 4,000 residents in the town in 1936. But among them was Vilmos Hulita, a factory-owning tycoon, the town's mayor and a lover of football, who burned with ambition to get tiny FTC Fiľakovo promoted into the Czechoslovak State League. In the summer of 1936, after the club had already narrowly missed out on fulfilling his dream, Hulita called for the man who had already made waves in Slovak football, József Braun.

Braun was immediately given cash to strengthen the team with high-class players from Hungary and from leading Slovak clubs, such as the talented young defender Viliam Vanák whom he brought with him from ČsŠK. FTC Fiľakovo duly romped home as winners of the regional group to qualify for the mini-league tournament at the end of the season, in which once again the five participating teams would compete for the coveted promotion to the State League.

Intense passions were aroused in the town as the season's denouement approached. Among the club's fans was the young Frank Lowy, born in 1930, one of the few survivors of Fiľakovo's otherwise doomed 200-strong Jewish community. Lowy would not only come through the Holocaust, but later founded the global shopping centre company Westfield, becoming at one point the richest person in Australia and chairman of the country's football federation.

'I think the entire Jewish community supported the club,' Lowy told me.

> My love for football began in Fiľakovo when I went to the games with my late father. I have vivid memories of him and me sitting in the front row and there was just earth in front of us. My father carried a cane, as many men did in those days, and such was his excitement that by the time the game was over, he had dug a very sizeable hole into the earth with it.*

Fiľakovo made solid progress in the play-off league, and promotion to the State League ultimately rested on the final game away at DFC Prag, against whom the young Braun had announced himself to the

---

* Frank Lowy's father, Hugo, was murdered in Auschwitz-Birkenau in 1944. According to a witness, whom Frank Lowy came across through a chance meeting only in 1991, the guards ordered Hugo and the other deportees to put their belongings in a pile on their arrival at the camp. Hugo clutched his small bag and refused to relinquish it. The bag contained his *tallit* (prayer shawl) and *tefillin* (phylacteries) with which he used to pray every morning. The SS guard grabbed it off him and threw it on the pile. When he turned his back, Hugo returned to retrieve his bag. Another guard noticed and beat Hugo Lowy to death with his rifle butt.

footballing world back in 1918. DFC were rooted to the bottom of the mini-league, with no chance of promotion, and had already been beaten 3–0 by Fiľakovo in the corresponding fixture in Slovakia.

Such was the interest in the game that it was switched to the large Letná Stadium, home of Sparta Prague. According to the subsequent memoirs of Viliam Vanák, the change in venue proved to be Fiľakovo's undoing. Due to the comparatively poor quality of the pitches in Slovakia, Braun's team were not used to playing on lush, wet grass and were unable to keep their feet. They lost 5–0 in a shock defeat, and Hulita's dream ended in tears. He withdrew his financial support, Braun and the top players left and Fiľakovo returned to footballing obscurity for good.

* * *

In the spring of 1938, ČsŠK invited Braun to rekindle the spark of his earlier stint at the club. However, the old tensions and disunity soon resurfaced. The returning coach tried to impose order and discipline by dropping the striker and fans' favourite Jozef Luknár to the reserve team for what he perceived to be a poor attitude. However, despite his best efforts, Braun was always fighting a losing battle due to a highly inflammatory cocktail of ethnicity and citizenship. His Jewishness will most certainly have added to his unpopularity at this time in Slovakia, which was on the verge of installing a pro-Nazi regime that participated with a great deal of enthusiasm in the murder of more than 60,000 of its Jews.* To make matters worse, Braun's Hungarian citizenship also provoked a strong reaction in a country which at that point feared the irredentist claims of their neighbour.

* The Slovak government paid Germany 500 Reichsmark (worth around $200 in 1940) for each Jew deported from its territory.

In Fiľakovo, Braun had been accused of seeking only Hungarian company – hardly surprising as there were so many ethnic Hungarians in the town, and he could not speak Slovak. In Bratislava, it was the nationality of the journalists he fraternised with that raised the locals' ire. 'Mr Braun – it must be said openly – perhaps he did not understand his function,' sneered the newspaper *Slovenský Hlas*. 'He liked to give interviews, especially to Hungarian newspapers, to comment on the referees, to criticize their performances and to try to blame them for matches that were lost.' After an 8–0 drubbing at the hands of Slavia Prague, Braun's position quickly became untenable and his brief period in charge came to an end.

Braun's old club MTK, the scene of so many of his previous exploits, came knocking next.* His first task was to take the team on a summer tour of swastika-festooned Germany. Clearly oblivious of MTK's history, and perhaps even the origins of its current coach, the Nazis awarded an honoured welcome to 'the representatives of the Hungarian colours'.** One can only imagine, however, the anger and trepidation Braun must have felt as he stared at the word 'Jew' smeared in thick red paint on the window of every Jewish shop, sometimes with a Star of David added for good measure, as he travelled through Berlin and Leipzig during that summer of 1938.

The team's captain was Gusztáv Sebes, the future coach of Hungary's Wembley conquerors of 1953. In his memoir published in 1981, Sebes recalled Braun's darkening mood on that trip: 'I watched the ever-cheerful Csibi Braun withdraw into himself and stare wordlessly

* The team was now known as Hungária MTK.

** The Hungarian authorities were not so easily duped. In November 1941, Hungária (MTK) refused to comply with new national regulations that excluded Jewish members of sports clubs. The club was officially disbanded in 1942, and its assets confiscated.

into space. His thoughts must have been very far away. I said to him, "Csibi, what's wrong?" He replied melancholically, "Where is humanity sinking to? No one can choose their mother. Can I help it that I was born a Jew?"'

* * *

MTK pushed Újpest close for the title in the 1938/39 season, even beating the eventual champions 6–1 away. Despite both completing impressive seasons at the helm, however, the increasingly antisemitic climate and legal framework in Hungary made it impossible in practice for both Braun and Újpest coach Béla Guttmann to continue in their high-profile positions. Indeed, Sebes describes how tough it became for Braun in the dressing room that season. 'His situation was not easy. He was a Jewish boy. Most of the players loved him, but there were some who simply refused to take his orders, saying they shouldn't be ordered around by a Jew.'

As the Nazis hungrily swallowed up territory, Europe was shrinking fast for Braun. On 15 August 1939, he signed a contract for Nordstern Basel in Switzerland, but the outbreak of full-scale war a couple of weeks later soon put paid to that particular escape route. 'For now, every young man in Switzerland has been called up as a soldier and all football has been terminated,' he told *Nemzeti Sport*. He scrabbled around some more for available opportunities. The same newspaper announced at the end of July 1940 that he had agreed to take over as coach of Gloria Arad in the Transylvanian region of Romania. However, there is no evidence that he ever took up the role, and it is once again likely that inter-ethnic hatred was responsible for foiling his ambitions.

Much of Transylvania had also been taken away from Hungary in the Treaty of Trianon. Seeking to curry further favour with its now close ally, Nazi Germany placed huge pressure on Romania to surrender the territory it had gained two decades before. The eventual 'agreement' of August 1940, known as the Second Vienna Award*, gave the northern part of Transylvania back to Hungary.** As Arad was not included in the ceded territory and remained part of Romania, the atmosphere in the wake of this forced humiliation became increasingly hostile for Hungarian nationals residing in the city. This time, perhaps, it was being a high-profile Hungarian coach in Romania that was not a viable possibility.

Braun had finally run out of options. And then everything went quiet. His name did not appear in the newspapers again until September 1945, almost three years after he was murdered.

* * *

By putting together various pieces of information, we can build a picture of what happened to József Braun in the months and years leading up to his death. It is highly unlikely that Braun found much paid employment between leaving MTK in the summer of 1939 and his deportation to the Nagykáta labour camp in the spring or early summer of 1942. The First and Second Jewish Laws, passed by the Hungarian Parliament in 1938 and 1939, had severely damaged the

---

* The First Vienna Award, signed in November 1938, had given Southern Slovakia, including Fiľakovo, back to Hungary.

** The Jews of Northern Transylvania fared worse than their counterparts in the part of the region that remained in Romania. Between 16 May and 27 June 1944, 131,641 Jews were deported from Northern Transylvania to Auschwitz-Birkenau. According to Veronika Mermelstein, two sisters of József Braun were among those from the region to be murdered. The archives reveal that one of those sisters, Margit Grün, only a year older than Braun, was murdered at Stutthof concentration camp near Danzig (Gdansk), most likely having been sent there from Auschwitz.

ability of Jews to earn a living in a whole host of occupations, throwing tens of thousands of families into poverty.

We know, thanks to his niece Veronika Mermelstein, that he was still living during this time in the same family apartment on Wesselényi Street that had been his base since his arrival from Putnok as a young boy thirty years before. Also in the apartment at that time were his sisters Lídia and her family (including her daughter, Veronika), as well as Etel and Erzsi, who like their younger brother, were both single at the time.* Veronika, then aged ten, remembers waving good-bye to her uncle József and the other Jewish men who had been ordered to report to the Nagykáta camp, around fifty kilometres east of Budapest. Nagykáta served mostly as a staging post, although the draftees were unaware of their eventual destination. After spending some time at the camp, inmates were sent further east to work as slave labourers supporting the Hungarian Second Army on the Eastern Front, which was fighting there alongside Nazi Germany against the Soviet Union.

We know that Braun was in Nagykáta in June 1942 due to the testimony of his brother Béla at the trial of Pál Gidófalvy in the autumn of 1945. From 1941, Gidófalvy's official role had been Ministerial Commissioner of Coaches and Referees of the Hungarian Football Federation. In this government-sponsored position, he had sought with feverish enthusiasm to purge Hungarian football of its Jewish elements and had played a pivotal role in the eventual closure of MTK. Gidófalvy was eventually tried before the people's courts in Hungary, which meted out justice to those accused of war crimes, crimes against the state or crimes against humanity. During the proceedings, Béla Braun, no doubt still raging about the murder of his siblings and whatever unimaginable personal ordeal he himself had been forced

* All three sisters, living with their younger brother at that point, survived the Holocaust.

to endure, stormed to the witness box, making what *Nemzeti Sport* described as 'a dramatic statement'.

Béla had also been a footballer, in his case as a centre-back for the Zionist football team Hagibor Cluj in Northern Transylvania. In 1942, using the network of contacts he had built up as a player, he had managed to persuade István Pluhár, a well-known football journalist and sports administrator, to intervene on his brother's behalf with Gidófalvy. Pluhár was called to give evidence at the trial and confirmed Béla's recollections. He said that he had asked Gidófalvy to release József Braun from Nagykáta, arguing that several other athletes who had represented Hungary at the Olympic Games had received documentation absolving them from labour service. 'Please Pali,' Pluhár had urged his friend, 'regardless of what your opinion is on the Jewish issue, this certificate is due to Csibi Braun'.

Gidófalvy refused to act. By the time Béla had circumvented Gidófalvy to obtain the necessary certificate, it was too late. By September 1942, his brother was already on his way east.* Although it does seem that a few Jewish Olympians may have got special dispensation from labour service at this time (but not from the gas chambers after the Nazi invasion a couple of years later), it could well be that the reverse was true for Braun: his high profile not only failed to save him but actually contributed to his demise. More than 40,000 Jewish men were sent by the Hungarian government to the Eastern Front to work as slave labourers. Most of them were given emergency summonses and were selected on an individual basis, rather than by age – and the

* In October 1945, the People's Court sentenced Pál Gidófalvy to four years in prison for crimes against the people, but in November he was acquitted and released. He later spent a year in police custody, and was convicted again in 1949, but his prison sentence was deemed to have already been served.

more notable and successful they were, the more chance they would be chosen.

'Acting in accord with a secret decree of the Ministry of Defense (22 April 1942),' explains the historian Randolph Braham,

> the recruitment centers saw to it that 10–15 per cent of the field labor service companies were composed of Jews 'well known for their wealth and reputation' ... The recruitment centers called up Jews following lists received from the Ministry of Defense, which in turn often prepared them based on 'complaints' (i.e., denunciations) received from various 'patriotic' individuals and groups.

Gidófalvy's refusal to countenance Braun's release suggests that the Hungarian authorities knew exactly what they were doing when they conscripted this particular prominent Jew.

* * *

At the mercy of the infamous Lipót Murai, the so-called 'executioner of Nagykáta', Braun's initial labour camp experience would have been appalling enough. But it was nothing compared to what lay in store for him later on. As the Jews were deported eastwards, Murai is said to have instructed his company commanders to make sure that none of their charges returned alive. It seems they were listening.

There were 130 labour units on the Eastern Front made up solely of Hungarian Jews, each initially comprising somewhere between 212 and 250 men. Replacements did not normally compensate fully for the subsequent heavy losses in these units, so these numbers were soon greatly depleted. Braun's own labour company was known as 101/3, the number 101 denoting the army unit to which it was formally attached. Among the labourers' tasks, according to Braham, were 'constructing, clearing, and maintaining roads and railroads; loading and unloading munitions, provision, and other materials; building bunkers and gun emplacements; and digging trenches and tank traps'. On many occasions, labourers were also marched through minefields to clear a particular area.

Given the enormity and geographical breadth of the Holocaust, some of its aspects have received relatively scant attention. The fate of the Hungarian Jewish slave labourers on the Eastern Front could be placed in this category. In his book *Conscripted Slaves,* however, Robert Rozett manages to paint a picture of what life must have been like for József Braun, based on survivors' testimony he managed to put together from first-hand accounts and post-war trial records.

Many of the labourers wore clothing that was spectacularly ill-equipped for the conditions. A government decree of March 1942 stipulated that Jewish labour conscripts should not be provided with uniforms but only military caps and, of course, a yellow armband to alert commanders and soldiers that these prisoners were the lowest of the low (Jews who had converted to Christianity wore white armbands). To make matters worse, many servicemen, very possibly including Braun, were called up in early summer and were told to bring only light clothes. Even if they had better protection, there was no way of replacing clothing made threadbare by gruelling work and overuse. Boots were not usually provided, and ill-suited shoes deteriorated to such an extent that some walked around barefoot, even as the temperature plummeted to -40 degrees centigrade by the depths of winter.

István Szlifka, one of the guards attached to unit 101/3, denied murder at his trial in July 1945, claiming instead that 'many in the labour unit did not have any clothing and as a result many of them froze to death'. Due to minimal hygiene, a large number of men were also swarming with lice and caught and died from typhus as a result.

Food rations were utterly inadequate for long days of hard labour in freezing temperatures. The recollections of one slave labourer, Andor Kohn, were typical. Every day, his unit received 200 grams of bread, partly made from straw; warm water, referred to as soup, in the morning; and five or six pieces of potato in the evening. Elemér Saly, who served in the 101/2 platoon, Braun's sister unit, recalled an incident from the eve of Yom Kippur in September 1942 which reveals, in graphic terms, the extent of the labourers' hunger. When an alarm was sounded for a drill, a company commander forced the labourers to dump their food on the ground. As soon as he departed, the starving men licked up the spilt food.

Living quarters were primitive and exposed to the elements. Many men slept in barns which had holes in the roofs and walls. A 1946 report on Braun's unit by the public prosecutor's office reveals that 180 men in the unit – that is, the overwhelming majority – were forced for a period to spend the nights under the open skies in a pit that they had themselves dug. According to the report, three or four men in the unit were dying every day as the weather became considerably colder in November 1942, either through succumbing to weakness, illness, hunger and the freezing temperatures, or as a result of serious physical abuse by the guards.

Indeed, the abuse suffered by the Jewish servicemen took many forms. The guards, possessed by an all-consuming hatred of Jews, 'viciously maltreated them', writes Braham. They 'subjected them to unspeakable cruel tortures, withheld or stole their already low rations … The emaciated and disease-ridden Jews were often also subjected to corporate abuse by the members of the German and Hungarian units for or under which they worked.'

The unit 101/3 had two commanders during its time at the front. József Kreskai was in charge from September until 18 December 1942, at which point one of his assistants, Károly Toronyi, took over. According to the public prosecutor's report, around a hundred men, or half the unit, were already dead by the time this changeover took place. Kreskai habitually referred to the labourers as 'dirty, damn lazy Jews', and his subordinates Toronyi, Szlifka, Gyula Szabó and Ruggiero Tóth inevitably understood from this messaging that they had carte blanche to behave as cruelly as their hearts desired. At Toronyi's trial in July 1945, he admitted to 'tyings', which involved hanging Jews by their hands from a tree or pillar, often with their feet bound to increase the pain. Toronyi advised the court that these punishments were carried out 'according to the rules'. Somewhat unconvincingly, he denied accusations that he poured cold water on the bound prisoners in the freezing temperatures.*

Elemér Saly's story about a fellow conscript's encounter with Szlifka provides a vivid indication of the arbitrary nature of these punishments:

> One afternoon I was carrying water to the horses when I saw a forced labourer hanging near the barn ... When he had entered our quarters, he had bumped into Szlifka and saluted him, according to orders. When he left, Szlifka ran after him and shouted at him, asking why he had not saluted him. Szlifka immediately decided to punish him and decided to hang him by (by his hands).**

---

* Attila Petschauer was another Jewish Olympian conscripted as a slave labourer. The fencer had won two gold medals, in 1928 and 1932. He served in unit 101/4, near to Braun's. He was tied to a tree, naked, at -35 degrees centigrade. One witness said, 'The amused guards ordered him to crow like a rooster, and sprayed him with water. Frozen from the water, he died shortly after.'

** Károly Toronyi, István Szlifka, Gyula Szabó and Ruggiero Tóth were all executed, following the death sentences imposed by the people's courts. József Kreskai was eventually sentenced to ten years' imprisonment, and died in jail in January 1954.

At this point, it is perhaps worthwhile recalling Gábór Kompóti-Kléber's observation that Braun 'loathed violence'. One can only imagine the visceral impact these scenes must have had on him during his last weeks on earth. We can also suspect that Braun's fame would have made him a favoured target of the sadistic guards.

In mid-January 1943, Braun and all his colleagues were finally blessed with an exit from this nightmare. In the so-called Ostrogozhsk–Rossosh offensive, the Soviet forces launched a massive assault near Voronezh in Central Russia, on the banks of the River Don, and managed to encircle and devastate the Hungarian Second Army. Complete anarchy ensued, as the shattered Hungarian forces rushed to retreat under heavy bombardment. 'On encountering groups of labour service men,' writes Rozett, 'some soldiers would fire randomly into the crowd, venting their frustration and hatred'. Companies would fall back thirty to forty kilometres a day, but many starving and frozen labourers could not keep up. Those who fell by the wayside were never seen again.

At Toronyi's trial, it was revealed that just one labourer ultimately survived labour unit 101/3, a piece of information later confirmed by the public prosecutor's report. That one person, Mór Kelemen, had somehow managed to get himself transferred to a military hospital in November 1942.

According to the Budapest city archives, József Braun himself 'disappeared' on 16 January 1943. The records also state that Hungarian authorities took the rather incongruously noble step of notifying his next of kin, presumably his sisters in Budapest, two days later. The location of his disappearance is given in the archives as Krutyec, which perplexed me somewhat until I looked closely at a map of the Voronezh region, which revealed a small town called Korotoyak, sixteen kilometres from Ostrogozhsk. Korotoyak was so heavily bombarded by Soviet forces during the fierce battle that not one of the

800 buildings in the town remained standing. I believe that Braun's remains now lie in the vicinity of this town.

In its two short paragraphs devoted to him, the relevant Hungarian Wikipedia page informed me that József Braun died as a 'labourer' in Kharkiv, Ukraine. That is certainly one way of putting it. Perhaps he fell off some scaffolding on a building site in a tragic accident? In fact, almost every single reference I have seen to Braun's death contains some similar element of evasion or inaccuracy.

The memory of the greatest Jewish footballer of all time does not deserve to be treated in such lackadaisical fashion. For the sake of posterity, the truth needs to be stated with clarity. József Braun, aged forty-one, was brutally murdered by Hungarian guards representing an independent Hungarian government, because he was a Jew, very probably in Korotoyak, Russia, which happens to be around 300 kilometres from Kharkiv.

The writer Ronen Dorfan published a Hebrew-language article about Braun in the newspaper *Israel Hayom* on Yom Hashoah in 2008.* In the article, Dorfan interviews a Hungarian Jewish journalist, Ferenc Molát, whose uncle Tibor Weinberger had been a survivor from a labour unit close to Braun's. According to Molát, who died in 2019, Weinberger had seen Hungarian guards surrounding Braun's body as it lay in the snow and frenziedly using tools to extract his gold teeth.

Other evidence makes such a claim highly plausible. One of the specific charges against unit 101/3 guard Gyula Szabó at his trial in 1945 was that he 'he had smashed the gold teeth out of the mouths of those murdered with the handle of a spade'.

* * *

* Yom Hashoah is Israel's annual day of commemoration for the 6 million Jews murdered in the Holocaust.

'Nothing, completely anonymous,' is Molát's unequivocal reply when asked by Dorfan what Hungarians know about Braun today. Indeed, I found precious few references to him in the post-war Hungarian press. The circumstances of his death at the hands of Hungarians were, no doubt, just too close to the bone. And could a Jew really become an enduring Hungarian legend anyhow? For its part, the Jewish community had, of course, been riven asunder.

But for those still living and lucky enough to have witnessed his talent at first hand, the memory would take some time to fade. In a tribute published in the magazine *Képes Sport* in August 1947, Gábor Kompóti-Kléber indulges in some customary formulaic euphemisms, before speaking for a generation of football fans who understood that they had once been in the presence of a footballing phenomenon: 'Braun died in the Second World War. He perished in tragic circumstances. But everyone who saw him play even just once will cherish his memory with reverence.'

Perhaps the last word should be left to György Molnár, a fellow Jew who so often partnered Braun in that fearsome front line for both MTK and Hungary, and even teamed up with him again in New York at the end of their careers. In October 1976, just six months before his death, Molnár was interviewed by the Hungarian Jewish magazine *Új Élet*. Born two weeks before Braun and by now in his mid-seventies, Molnár should by rights have been spending long and pleasant afternoons with his old friend, reminiscing about their youthful days of heady victory and dressing room banter. But back in the world of cruel reality, Molnár's words soon gave way to darkness, as his mind drifted back to his own close brush with mortality as a slave labourer, and to Braun's own, less fortunate fate.

'The most wonderful winger of all time was tortured to death by the guards … When I think of him today, I still shudder.'

CHAPTER 2

THE WAYWARD PLAYBOY

Politicians have long understood that national sporting success can boost their popularity, particularly when they can get themselves pictured at the triumphant event. Ignacy Mościcki, the sixty-year-old president of Poland, must therefore have thought he was on to a winner as he took his seat in the VIP enclosure for the match against the United States in June 1928.

The fixture had been hastily arranged after the USA's ignominious exit from the Olympic football tournament, battered 11–2 in the first round by Argentina in Amsterdam. Now saddled with a couple of weeks to spare before their optimistically timed boat trip home from Europe, and hoping to salvage just a little of their severely dented pride, the dejected American party had moved on to the Polish capital Warsaw for a friendly game.

With time fast running out, and the unfancied USA leading 3–1, it seemed that President Mościcki had made something of a miscalculation. But then all-Polish hero Wacław Kuchar, veteran of numerous sporting and military feats, got one goal back. Roared on by their fans, the Poles besieged the American penalty area seeking an equalising goal. On eighty-seven minutes, one of the shots raining in on goal struck a defender's hand. The Czech referee pointed to the penalty spot and waved away the furious protests.

Cue pandemonium. 'Some spectators manage to get on to the pitch as the perimeter is badly guarded,' reported the Polish newspaper *Przegląd Sportowy*. 'A black mass of excited people are running along the grass. You can feel the ferment in the air. Whether it will erupt or not will be determined by this penalty kick.'

The police eventually pushed the crowd back beyond the white line of the pitch. Amid the tumult, one man stood focused on the job at hand, bouncing the ball and waiting serenely for everything to settle down. Zygmunt Steuermann, the tall, handsome and flamboyant star striker of the Jewish football club Hasmonea Lwów, known throughout Poland for his penalty-taking prowess, was the only player on the team with the courage to volunteer for the vital kick. Facing him would be the man with the power to start a riot, American goalkeeper Albert Cooper.

'The slim two-metre-high silhouette of Cooper stares at the white penalty spot, with the ball set against the black background of the crowd,' continues the *Przegląd Sportowy* report. 'Everything is as still as death. Is [Steuermann] going to score or will he miss? At last, the referee's whistle pierces the atmosphere. The huge figure of Steuermann is approaching the penalty spot, his leg swishing through the air. Cooper folds like a pocketknife as the ball touches his hand and ends up in the net.'

The referee soon calls full time, allowing the spectators to release their pent-up emotions and flood the pitch, soon to engulf their heroes. The breathless journalist signs off by reporting that 'you can just about make out the red shirts of Kuchar and Steuermann, now in the hands of spectators'.

On the morning of 1 September 1939, a matter of a few hours after the first battles and bombardments of the German invasion of his country, President Mościcki attempted to summon up the same patriotic fervour he had witnessed when Steuermann dispatched his last-gasp penalty eleven years before. Introduced by the stirring tones of the Polish national anthem, Mościcki made his impassioned call to arms:

> At this historic moment, I address all citizens of the country, in a deep conviction that the whole nation will support the commander-in-chief of the Armed Forces in defence of its freedom, independence and honour, and will put up worthy resistance to the attacker, as it has already done throughout the history of German-Polish relations. The Polish nation, united with the army, blessed by God, and in its fight for this holy and righteous cause, will go arm in arm to fight for victory.

Less than a month later, however, Warsaw had succumbed to inevitable defeat. For 3 million Polish Jews, 90 per cent of their total number, the signature on that surrender amounted to a death warrant. Zygmunt Steuermann, the national hero of Poland on that heady summer's day back in 1928, was himself to feature among the never-ending lists of the obliterated.

Albert Cooper, his one-time adversary, went on living in his native New Jersey until 1993, half a century after Steuermann's death. Such were the benefits of not living in Europe – and not being a Jew.

* * *

On the eve of the festival of Passover, 18 April 1943, 1,200 of the still surviving Jews of Sambir were taken to the Jewish cemetery in the town. There they were shot by the German Nazis and their enthusiastic local Ukrainian helpers, before being tossed into a pit next to their buried forebears.

In 1972, the ruling Soviet regime bulldozed the cemetery and used the bulk of the headstones to build the walls of a new sweet factory, while farmers treated the now derelict field as a garbage dump. In 2001, after a Jewish Holocaust survivor and philanthropist living in Canada arranged for a stone Star of David to be placed on the site, locals destroyed it and erected three thirty-foot-tall crucifixes instead.

Given this backdrop, it may come as little surprise that modern-day Sambir, situated in what is now Western Ukraine, is hardly teeming with tributes to the Jew Zygmunt Steuermann, who fell in love with football as a young boy in the open spaces of his home town, nor to his remarkably talented and dynamic Jewish family, and nor to the memory of the town's liquidated Jewish community.*

Indeed, little would alert a visitor to the fact that Jews once comprised up to half the population of Sambir, which they shared with their Ukrainian and Polish fellow citizens. 'When its Jewish residents suddenly disappeared, life in Sambor went on as if they had never existed,' writes Anda Meisels Rosen, one of fewer than a hundred survivors of a pre-Holocaust Jewish population of more than 8,000. 'The locals took over Jewish homes and businesses ... [since that time] strangers have been living in my parents' home, the homes of my grandparents, my aunts and my uncles, and my Jewish neighbours.'

During Zygmunt Steuermann's childhood, Sambir was embedded deep in the heartland of Galicia, a province of the Austrian and then Austro-Hungarian empire for almost 150 years, up to 1918. The Jews of the region, awarded the Yiddish moniker *Galitzianers*, were an integral part of the furniture.** After Ukrainians and Poles, they represented

---

* The town is known as Sambir in Ukrainian, and Sambor in Polish, Russian, Yiddish and German. I refer to it as Sambir when quoting from translations into English, but as Sambor when quoting from the original English text. I will refer to the Polish football club as Korona Sambor.

** The geographical region of Galicia now straddles both south-eastern Poland and Western Ukraine.

the third largest ethnic group in Galicia, numbering 872,000 (11 per cent of the total) by the time of the First World War.

Steuermann's father Josef was what might be termed in Yiddish a *macher*, a big cheese. He was a prominent lawyer in Sambir, chairman of its Chamber of Advocates, and its mayor for fully twenty-five years from 1894 to 1919. The section devoted to the Steuermann family in the Hebrew-language *yizkor* book about the town remarked, 'The length of his tenure would be a rare feat for anyone, let alone a Jew in the Diaspora.'*

Josef and his wife Augusta (née Amster), fifteen years his junior and from a very musical family, had four children. The eldest was Salomea, known as Salka, who became a successful actress on the German-speaking stage in Europe, before establishing herself as a highly prized Hollywood screenwriter after she emigrated to the United States in 1928 with her Viennese Jewish husband and fellow screenwriter, Berthold Viertel. Once ensconced in her new home, Salka soon developed a particularly close friendship with Greta Garbo. Astonishingly, within a few short years after her arrival in the country with only pidgin English, she had co-written the scripts for several of Garbo's blockbuster movies, including *Queen Christina* and *Anna Karenina.*

Salka Viertel also sat at the fulcrum of an uber-creative social circle, many of whom were central European Jews who had fled Nazi terror. In her autobiography *The Kindness of Strangers*, published in 1969, Viertel reels off a list of friends and dinner party guests at the family home in Santa Monica which reads like a 'who's who' of the twentieth century. Just a few of the names I jotted down in my notes include the

---

* *Yizkor* books are memorial books, many of them extremely detailed, commemorating Jewish communities destroyed during the Holocaust. They were written in Hebrew or Yiddish by former residents of the relevant towns. There are more than 1,500 *yizkor* books in existence.

writers Bertolt Brecht, Upton Sinclair, Aldous Huxley, Christopher Isherwood, Lion Feuchtwanger, Irwin Shaw, Heinrich and Thomas Mann, the composers Igor Stravinksy and Arnold Schoenberg, the photographer Robert Capa, the film director Sergei Eisenstein, Albert Einstein and Charlie Chaplin.* It is from Salka Viertel's autobiography and from her personal letter collection that we receive revealing depictions of her younger brother Zygmunt's personality and lifestyle, accounts of some of his movements, and one or two theories about his eventual fate.

Next after Salka in the Steuermann family came Rosa, who married Josef Gielen, a prominent non-Jewish Austrian actor, director and theatre manager. To save her, the couple escaped from Vienna to Argentina in 1939, before returning to Austria after the war. The third child was Eduard, who went on to become a world-renowned pianist and composer. Eduard Steuermann fled Europe in 1938, settling in New York, where he also served as a distinguished teacher at the prestigious Juilliard School.

The first three children were born within as many years, after which came a seven-year gap until Zygmunt arrived on 5 February 1899. 'The youngest, my brother Zygmunt, called Dusko, was born when I was nine, and was not included in our world,' writes Salka Viertel. 'We three ... were an extremely tightly woven entity, sticking together through thick and thin.'

The element of emotional distance from his siblings might go some way to explaining Zygmunt's later misguided reluctance to join them in getting a long distance away from Europe. It certainly influenced his personality, which was free-spirited, independent and irrepressible. Indeed, his nickname 'Dusko', given to him at a young age, is likely to

* Franz Kafka had been a regular visitor when the Viertels lived in Prague prior to their emigration from Europe.

be related to the Slavic words for soul or spirit. In the passage on Zygmunt Steuermann in the Sambir *yizkor* book, his name is presented as *Duszek*, meaning 'little spirit' in Polish.

Zygmunt was a force of nature as a child, in turn infuriating and bewitching his stern, serious and lawyerly father, who was already turning forty-seven by the time his youngest child was born. 'He spent his time outdoors, bullying the peasant boys who were tending the cows, riding his pony like a circus acrobat, swimming and playing games,' continues Viertel. 'He was strong and beautiful … He had our parents completely enslaved. Papa never came home without bringing him a present, and knowing his power, Dusko took unheard of liberties with him. We three older children were amazed that it was Papa, the severe, unapproachable Papa, who spoiled him most.'

While his cerebral and sophisticated elder siblings busied themselves with study, music and literature, Zygmunt craved physical activity and the outdoors. Viertel recalled her impressions upon returning to the family home after a period working away as an actress, at which point Zygmunt was ten years old.

> He was wild, unruly, disobedient, but he played marvelous tennis … and had the habit of vanishing for hours and remaining undetected … Papa reprimanded him with incredible mildness when dirty, smelly, his copper-colored hair disheveled, he would show up for dinner. Dusko sneered at us 'artists'. None of us could ever beat him at tennis and we did not play soccer. But though our parents considered soccer a game for rowdies and had a very limited understanding of sport in general, they were strangely captivated by the physical prowess of their youngest son.

The family lived in an estate called Wychylówka, two kilometres west from the centre of Sambir, on the banks of the Dniester River. The children enjoyed an affluent, wholesome upbringing in an idyllic setting, rigorously homeschooled by various multi-lingual tutors and governesses, rendering them fluent in both German and French in addition to Polish. As was typical of well-heeled Jews in their vicinity, the family spoke German at home and would later send letters to each other in that language.

Summers were especially blissful. 'We bathed in the Dniester, had lunch on the shady veranda, and in the afternoons took long walks to the forest,' Viertel recalled. 'On our way through the wheatfield, we picked bunches of cornflowers and poppies and gathered mushrooms and berries … In the evening, Mama, Rosa and I clustered around Eduard when he sat at the piano and, dividing the parts among us, we performed chorales and oratorios, operas by Mozart, Verdi, Donizetti and the new sensation: Richard Strauss.'

No mention of Zygmunt of course, who, one imagines, was bored senseless by such a pretentious rigmarole and was instead busying himself in the fields to all hours, painstakingly developing the ferocious shooting power that was to define his career.

The family's refined and secular lifestyle was typical of a prominent strand of well-to-do Central European Jewry at that time, clinging on to Jewish traditions only by their fingertips even while continuing to be most comfortable in a particular type of Jewish social milieu.

'I knew that we were Jewish, but we certainly did not belong to those strange people in long black kaftans, with beards and sidelocks, and we did not understand their harsh idiom,' writes Viertel. They put up a Christmas tree and sang Christmas carols, although something inside Josef made him refuse to go the whole hog. He stubbornly visited synagogue every year on Yom Kippur and turned down a lucrative directorship of a major bank in Vienna because an obligatory condition of employment was not to supply adequate references, but to get his entire family baptised.

A classical liberal who believed in a pluralist society, Josef maintained that Jews should not live their lives separately from others. In 1908, when mayor of Sambir, he successfully campaigned against the establishment of a Jewish orphanage, insisting that such institutions should be open to all. One can imagine that he derived deep satisfaction from winning the day, although the ruthless judge of history does now record that his earnest plan to forge a closer understanding between Jewish and non-Jewish children ultimately ended with the former lying dead in ditches and burnt in crematoria little more than three decades later, after which there were no Jews left with whom to forge a closer understanding.

These snippets suggest that the Steuermanns would have fitted in easily with the like-minded assimilated Jewish intelligentsia in Vienna, Berlin or Prague further west, or even with a growing Jewish middle class in nearby Lviv, but much less so among the more traditional, Yiddish-speaking and often impoverished *Galitzianer* artisans and small-time traders inhabiting the streets of Sambir.* The complete ease with which the three elder siblings settled into their new lives elsewhere certainly testifies to their cosmopolitan nature. We can surmise, on the other hand, that Zygmunt's more earthly pursuits and the local hero status he latterly enjoyed tied him more closely, and with tragic consequences, to the land of his birth.

* The city is known as Lviv in Ukrainian, Lvov in Russian, Lwów in Polish, and Lemberg in Yiddish and German. I will refer to the city as Lviv given that it is a constituent part of modern-day Ukraine. I will refer to the football club as Hasmonea Lwów as the city was in Polish territory when Steuermann played for it, and the club competed in the Polish league.

* * *

The outbreak of the First World War in 1914 marked an abrupt end to the untroubled *dolce vita* of the Steuermann family. Terrified by the prospect of an imminent Russian invasion, they temporarily fled their domestic paradise in Wychylówka and hurriedly decamped to the heart of empire in Vienna, joining an exodus of 200,000 Galician Jews during this time. Their fears of Jew-killing rampages by Tsarist forces turned out to be well founded. Plunder and murder of Jews were commonplace; around 50,000 Jews from the region were deported to the Russian Far East; high taxes were imposed on the Jewish population to support Russian troops; and Jews in official positions (such as Josef Steuermann in Sambir, if he had stuck around long enough) were summarily dismissed.

The move to Vienna may have been necessary, but it did Zygmunt's own personal development no favours. The temptations of the big city served only to make him even more feral. 'He neglected his studies, and Papa had visions of him as a soccer-playing hoodlum,' wrote Salka Viertel. He befriended the wrong crowd at school, and began to plough through money as if there were no tomorrow. Salka had her suspicions of what lay behind his profligate behaviour, and they were soon to be confirmed. 'My mother said there was no need to despair about Dusko, that she had had a serious talk with him; he had admitted a gambling debt but promised to reform and avoid bad company. A few days later, I noticed that Grandmother was no longer wearing her diamond brooch.'

What shocked Salka was not so much the gambling itself, which could be put down to adolescent naivety, but 'his complete lack of emotion, his cold disregard for our parents'. When she confronted him, his reply betrayed the short-term hedonism which was later to mar his life and career, while at the same time nourishing his legendary status among football fans.

'His excuse was that in a year or so, he might be in the army – the war would still be on, he might be killed, so at least he intended to have a good time as long as he was alive,' Salka wrote. 'He was only concerned with his pleasures and his dominant position among the young toughs. I looked at him as he sat there, strong, stubborn, handsome and extremely antagonistic. He did not understand what the fuss was about; all he wanted was more spending money.'

As the story about his grandmother's brooch suggests, the family's financial reservoir was running dry. Josef Steuermann, a staunch believer in the Austro-Hungarian empire, had invested all his money in war bonds that were ultimately to be rendered worthless by military defeat. After the Russians had been pushed back from Galicia in 1915, the family (minus Zygmunt, who remained to continue his education in Vienna) returned to a ransacked Wychylówka, but lacked the funds over the years to restore it. It seems that Zygmunt always struggled to adapt psychologically from the well-to-do lifestyle of his youth to these more straitened circumstances. For much of his life, he acted as though someone would soon bail him out. When his sister found wealth in the United States, she became the replacement rainy day fund.

That said, there was scant opportunity for Zygmunt to rack up debts in the three years from 1917. Having turned eighteen, he was summoned for active military duty. His first port of call was training with an artillery regiment in Slovakia to ready him for a war that was swiftly heading for defeat due to the entry into the fray of the United States.

Salka refers to a letter from her mother, seemingly received after the First World War hostilities had ceased, which informed her that

'Dusko had come back from the Italian front'. It seems that Zygmunt was one of around 3,300 Galician soldiers who were sent by the Austro-Hungarian army to Italy in late 1917. In action centred around the Alpine region of Veneto in the north-eastern region of the country, the increasingly demoralised Austro-Hungarian troops were eventually routed by their Italian adversaries at the Battle of Vittorio Veneto in the autumn of 1918. On 3 November 1918, 300,000 of them across the whole front, almost certainly including Zygmunt Steuermann, surrendered and were briefly taken prisoner.

When he came face to face with death on a daily basis in 1941, he would have had a great deal of harrowing experience to draw on. More than 43,000 Austro-Hungarian soldiers were killed on the Italian front in 1918, around one in seven of the total forces that eventually surrendered, and constituting 84 per cent of the army's total losses across all fronts during that calendar year.

Steuermann had not seen the end of bloodshed in his military career either, although his second campaign ended on an altogether more successful note. He volunteered to fight in the Polish war against the newly formed Soviet Union, whose hungry ambitions for Communist expansion threatened various states in east Central Europe, including Poland, which had declared independence after the collapse of the Austro-Hungarian empire following its defeat in 1918.

Immediately after the end of the First World War, conflict had erupted in Galicia – encompassing both Sambir and Lviv – between Polish and Ukrainian ethnic groups competing for control of the disputed area. The Poles ended up winning the day. Symon Petliura, the President of the nascent and short-lived Ukrainian People's Republic, was finally reconciled to this outcome in return for Polish military assistance in the fight against their common enemy, the Soviet Union.

In the Battle of Warsaw, fought in August 1920, Poland avoided what seemed like an inevitable beating, regrouped its forces and then forced back and overpowered the Soviet army in what Vladimir Lenin, the Bolshevik leader, described as an 'enormous defeat'. In the midst of heroic victory, however, Steuermann would have again come face to face with horrific scenes and would have felt fortunate to emerge unscathed. Of around 48,000 Polish soldiers in that battle, 4,500 were killed, 10,000 were declared missing, while 22,000 were wounded.

The victorious Poland sat down to agree what it hoped would be sustainable and stable borders with its defeated adversary and neighbour, the Soviet Union. The Treaty of Riga, signed in March 1921, stipulated that the bulk of Ukraine would constitute a Soviet republic, while substantial areas of Belarus and Western Ukraine, including Sambir and Lviv, would come under Polish rule.

The battle-weary Steuermann returned to his home region to embark on what was to prove to be the most celebrated period of his short life. Having fought for Poland on the battlefield, it was not long before he starred in its fledgling football league and national team, achieving both celebrity and heart-throb status along the way.

* * *

There are various pieces of evidence which suggest strongly that Zygmunt Steuermann was for several years a household name in Poland, and in Lviv in particular. Janina Wiener, a Lviv Jew, escaped from the city to Soviet Central Asia in 1941 at the age of nineteen. She was among 1,200 elderly Jews interviewed after 2000 by Centropa, one of several organisations attempting to salvage a few scraps of memory from an obliterated society. At the age of eighty-three, around seventy years after Zygmunt Steuermann had been the talk of the town, she told Centropa: 'There was a sports club called Hasmonea Lwow, and

Father was an official there … From Hasmonea I remember … Sztejerman (sic) … the name has somehow stuck. Sztejerman. Perhaps I'm mixing something up, I'm not sure.'

Clearer memories of Steuermann surfaced among small pockets of survivors after Salka Viertel's autobiography was published in 1969. 'The publication of *Kindness* brought all kinds of correspondence to Salka,' writes Donna Rifkind, one of her biographers. 'Many warm letters came from Israel, where survivors from Galicia told her how in their youth they admired her brother Dusko, "the football champion".'

Salka Viertel herself recalled a train trip to Sambir (from Germany) during her last summer in Poland before emigrating to the United States. It would therefore have been 1927, when her brother was at the peak of his career.

> I was trapped into a dreary conversation with a fellow passenger. He was a middle-aged, well-fed gentleman, probably a lawyer or a government official, and of insatiable curiosity. After I told him where we were going and why, he asked me what my maiden name was. Collapsing in awe, he repeated: 'Steuermann! Are you by any chance related to the famous Steuermann?' I was sure he meant Eduard who, after the [First World] war, had achieved prominence as a pianist and teacher and had played with great success in Lwow a few months before. The man informed me that he was not speaking of Eduard but of Dusko Steuermann, the famous soccer player.

In his book on the role of Lviv and Vilnius in Polish football, the historian and journalist Andrzej Gowarzewski recounts Steuermann's prominence in the newspaper gossip pages of the time. 'There were dramatic stories that focused on the Hasmonea players, which clearly shows how popular they were in Lviv,' writes Gowarzewski. 'In 1928, for example, the journalists wrote about one eye-catching story that ran for a long time and concerned Steuermann's sister and her husband, both of whom, it was claimed, were striving to become world-famous in Hollywood, where her talent was truly admired.'

Steuermann's cult status can be attributed to several factors. He had a star quality which stemmed not only from his abundant talent as a footballer, but from the way he conducted himself on the pitch. He never seemed to break a sweat. If descriptions of József Braun conjured for me images of Cristiano Ronaldo, then Steuermann brings to mind the effortless brilliance of mavericks such as Dimitar Berbatov, Matt Le Tissier or Zlatan Ibrahimović. He was like the cool boy in the class who never seemed to open a book but still ended up getting the best grades. Gowarzewksi cites a phrase from a football journalist at the time which encapsulates Steuermann's approach to the game: 'Steuermann, lazy as usual, scored three goals again.' There are football fans who have always been drawn to that type of player.

He was also tall, strong and good-looking, popular with women as much as with men. 'It was quite a sight to see him playing, in his white shorts, his golden hair gleaming, and the girls among the spectators chanting "Dusko! Dusko!",' writes Salka Viertel. His antics off the pitch only added to the mystique. He generated endless tittle-tattle, frequenting bars and clubs in the city and by and large parading an image that was the opposite of the clean-cut and committed athlete.

'He had that *je ne sais quoi* that made him the blue-eyed boy of the masses,' says Gowarzewski. 'In short, he had all the features to become a legendary striker but he either couldn't or he didn't want to make the most of them; his popularity was definitely linked to the need [for a sportsman] to abstain from the delights of life, and his inability to resist them.'

His powerful and accurate shooting, especially from free kicks, was the talent for which he was most renowned. The event of a Steuermann free kick became a spectacle in itself, a play within a play, the most dramatic and savoured event in the game as a whole. Gowarzewski writes:

> Everyone at the stadium was waiting for the moment when the referee would blow the whistle to signal a free kick for Hasmonea and the main soloist would enter the stage. He would strike the ball forcefully; he would strike it accurately and goalkeepers would experience profound dread just thinking of Steuermann's shots at goal. In time, a special kind of ceremony developed when a free kick or penalty was awarded; the ceremony was theatrical and the result of the game did not seem to matter at all.

Missing, however, from these few retrospective explanations for the adulation Steuermann received is what to me must have been the most crucial factor – his Jewishness. Wearing the blue and white of Zionism, the national movement to re-establish a Jewish state after an interruption of 2,000 years, Steuermann was the star player of a proudly all-Jewish football team in a city marked by an often extremely hostile environment for its 100,000 Jews, one third of the total population.

It is hardly surprising that Steuermann's specifically Jewish hero status is not dwelt upon. Only a matter of a few hundred of those Jews were still alive after the early 1940s, and the non-Jewish populace was far from blameless in their disappearance. Ashes and bones cannot tell stories, while the living may either harbour guilt and therefore instinctively avoid discussion of a separate Jewish identity and antisemitism, or they may lack empathy with another nation's experience.

The club with which Steuermann was mostly closely associated, Hasmonea Lwów, was founded in 1908. In its short existence, it became the most successful Jewish football club in Poland until it was forcibly dissolved after the Soviet occupation in 1939, never to reopen. To grasp what Hasmonea was all about, and what Steuermann must have meant to the last ever generation of young Jews in Lviv, we must first understand the club's name and ethos, and what those Jews had been going through.

In the second century BCE, the Hasmonean family led a successful revolt against the foreign Seleucid rulers who had attempted to impose Greek customs, destroy the Jewish religion and force Jewish Jerusalem and other areas of Judea to worship pagan idols. The subsequent Hasmonean dynasty, which lasted around eighty years, re-established Jewish independence, expanded Jewish sovereignty into neighbouring territories and created the conditions that allowed Jewish life to flourish unimpeded in the Land of Israel. Steuermann was a striking symbol of a resurgent national self-confidence and a rejection of assimilation, a path which his own family had ironically followed, at least in part.

For Jews in Lviv and surrounding areas, that national self-confidence sorely needed a boost. In the few years leading up to Steuermann joining Hasmonea in 1921, they had been on the receiving end of extreme violence. In his book, *In the Midst of Civilized Europe*, Jeffrey Veidlinger charts the largely unknown history of the murder of more than 100,000 Jews by Ukrainians and Poles between 1918 and 1921, a useful dress rehearsal for the Holocaust.

Some of this mass murder took place in Lviv. After Polish forces had seized control of the city from their Ukrainian enemies in November 1918, they unleashed a ferocious assault on Jewish citizens and their property. 'Polish soldiers doused houses and set them aflame as firefighters stood idly by,' writes Veidlinger.

> Locals could be seen running through the smoke, carrying fur coats and other valuables looted from the burning homes. 'I observed

> that all were watching the Jewish houses burning with pleasure and laughter,' one witness recalled. The soldiers then turned their attention to the synagogues, tearing apart Torah scrolls, destroying antiquities stored in the basements, and setting the buildings on fire, killing several Jews who had barricaded themselves inside.

As many as 150 Jews were murdered and 500 Jewish shops and businesses ransacked. Mass rape was ubiquitous. After the violence ended, sixty twelve-year-old Jewish girls were said to be recovering in the hospital from the 'brutal mishandling of Polish hooligans'.

When Zygmunt Steuermann, proudly sporting the shirt of Hasmonea, blasted the ball into the net past a helpless Polish goalkeeper from twenty metres, I think we can say that this meant more to those watching than a goal on the scoresheet.

* * *

By the time he signed for Hasmonea, Steuermann had already played youth football for various teams while at school in Vienna during the war and at a more senior level for Hakoah Stryj, another Zionist club around sixty kilometres south-east of Sambir.* Throughout his career, according to his sister Salka, the natural athlete also occupied his time 'winning many silver cups in tennis tournaments'.

---

* In 1939, 12,000 Jews lived in Stryj, forming one third of the town's population. In November 1941, 1,200 of them were shot dead in the nearby forest. Most of the remainder were sent to be murdered at Bełżec death camp. On 22 May 1943, the last 1,000 Jews were taken by Germans and local Ukrainians to the Great Synagogue in the town, and kept locked inside for several days. Many died from lack of food and water and the terrible overcrowding. Imprisoned Jews scraped the walls of the synagogue with their nails and were heard screaming for vengeance for their impending murder. Those who did not die inside the synagogue were taken out to be shot at the Jewish cemetery. No Jewish community was re-established.

Prior to 1927, when the first national Premier League (Liga Piłki Nożnej) was formed, the top level of Polish football was divided into various regional A-leagues, including one for the Lviv area, with the best teams in those leagues playing off to be national champions. Steuermann shone in a Hasmonea line-up that consistently finished third in the regional league behind the two frontrunners, Pogoń Lwów and Czarni Lwów, both clubs whose supporters hailed principally from the Polish (and non-Jewish) population of the city.

During that period in the Lviv regional league, Hasmonea made substantial strides as a club, greatly improving its chances of being invited into the eventual Premier League upon its inauguration. First, the club recruited Friedrich (Fritz) Kerr as its coach for a period, a high-profile figure in Central European football who had played for the Austrian national team and the greatest Jewish team of them all, Hakoah Vienna.* Using the pull of his name, the club arranged a series of games against powerful opposition outside of its region, including Legia and Polonia from Warsaw, and Hakoah Vienna themselves.

Top players joined, such as the defenders Izydor Redler, a future Polish international, and Szymon Birnbach, who signed from Pogoń Lwów; the Polish international midfielder Ludwik Schneider, who also defected from Pogoń to play for their Jewish rivals; and the forward Aleksander Mahler, who arrived from Hakoah Vienna.**

In July 1923, the club even moved into new premises in the Krzywczyce

---

* As a Jew, Kerr was later sacked by high-flying Stuttgarter Kickers in 1933 after Hitler's rise to power. In 1939, he fled to Argentina, where he spent the war years as a branch manager in a grain trading company.

** Redler escaped Poland at the onset of war and made his way to Scotland, where he became a doctor for the Polish armed forces, and then emigrated to the United States. Schneider escaped to Russia, and later emigrated to the United States, where he reportedly committed suicide in 1972. Birnbach was murdered in the Lviv ghetto in November 1942. Mahler was murdered in the Stanisławów ghetto (now Ivano-Frankivsk in Ukraine), most likely in 1941.

district of Lviv, unveiled as the swankiest stadium in the city with a capacity of 10,000, including 2,000 seated in an upmarket, covered stand. The occasion of the opening was marked in front of full houses by matches on successive days against fellow Zionist outfit VAC from Budapest and consecrated by a public blessing from a rabbi.

The pristine stadium was to last only nine years. In November 1932, a few months after Steuermann had played his final game for the club, antisemitic riots broke out in Lviv. Polish youths hunted Jews down, beating them up on the streets and on public transport and smashing windows of Jewish homes and shops throughout the city. As rampaging students roamed around campuses seeking Jews to assault, classes at various higher education institutions in Lviv were suspended. Several hundred Jews required hospital treatment. The Polish rioters inevitably gravitated towards one of the most powerful representations of Jewish life and spirit. On the night of 28 November, the Hasmonea stadium was set on fire and burned to the ground.*

A replacement stadium, built on land in the north-western suburbs of the city, was barely ready before the club was disbanded in 1939. By 1941, the new stadium found itself right next to the Janowska concentration camp, to which approximately 200,000 Jews were sent, including the former Hasmonea hero Zygmunt Steuermann.

* * *

As Hasmonea prospered in the 1920s, Steuermann's profile steadily grew. As tends to happen with his type of player, his performances provoked a marked divergence of opinion between those who marvelled

* A few months after the stadium was burned down, Hasmonea Lwów's table tennis team became champions of Poland. Its star player was Alojzy 'Alex' Ehrlich, who survived Auschwitz and later settled in France.

at his ability and those who condemned his apparent indolence. The national team selectors were similarly divided, eventually calling him up but then discarding him despite highly impressive performances.

He scored Hasmonea's solitary goal in both the home defeats against visiting Wisla Kraków and Hakoah Vienna in the summer of 1924. A couple of match reports on the Wisla game exemplified the more negative judgement of certain journalists. 'In the first half, he was far from industrious, while in the second half, he waited for the ball to come to him,' commented *Sport Lwowski*. 'He is a destructive influence on the rest of the attack, depriving it of initiative. The rest of the attackers have limited their role simply to creating opportunities for Steuermann.' *Przegląd Sportowy* bemoaned the lack of energy in the Hasmonea attack, 'primarily caused by the impossibly lazy and conceited Steuermann.' *Tygodnik Sportowy* damned Steuermann with faint praise, expressing hope that he was 'slowly losing his prima donna habits'.

This was a motif consistently applied to Steuermann throughout his career. Commenting on one particular Hasmonea victory in the Premier League a few years later, in September 1928, *Przegląd Sportowy* suggested with some acrimony that the team was more effective in the absence of its supposed talisman, who was suspended for that game. 'The forward line, deprived of their prima donna Steuermann, worked well and diligently and as the situation demanded, rather than just existing to make it possible for the king of shooting to score.' After Steuermann had rescued Poland with that last-minute penalty against the United States a few months earlier, the same newspaper even published a cartoon of Steuermann wearing a Poland football shirt and a ballerina's tutu, with the caption, 'Hasmonea's prima donna as a Poland international.'

His long-awaited international debut had taken place in September

1926. Steuermann's route to the Polish national team had been hampered not just by his seemingly nonchalant attitude but by competition from the likes of Wisla Kraków's Henryk Reyman, possibly the greatest Polish goalscorer before Robert Lewandowski entered the scene in the modern era, as well as Pogoń Lwów's Wacław Kuchar and Cracovia's Józef Kałuża. But the powers that be could not permanently ignore what Gowarzewski describes as Steuermann's 'extraordinary ability to find space and his natural ability for playing football'.

Such was the explosive nature of his debut, played at the stadium of Hasmonea's local rivals Czarni Lwów, that it is still etched in the history books one century later. The opponents were Turkey, whom Poland had narrowly defeated the previous year in Istanbul, thanks to a winning goal from the diminutive Jewish winger, Leon Sperling.

Lining up with Hasmonea teammates Redler and Schneider, Steuermann put the Turkish defence to the sword in the space of twenty-one devastating minutes in the second half. His first goal, reported the sports magazine *Stadjon*, was from a shot hit 'so hard that the Turkish goalkeeper did not even realise what was happening'. His second, wrote the *Przegląd Sportowy* journalist, was 'a beautiful header' from a corner kick. Then came the coup de grâce. 'Steuermann goes on a mazy run down the left,' continued *Przegląd Sportowy*. 'He looks to pass the ball but there is nobody available to pass it to. At the last moment he resolves to shoot. The Turkish goalkeeper raises his hands helplessly just as the ball hits the net.'

Steuermann's debut hat-trick, in a 6–1 rout, has been matched only once in Polish football history.* 'Steuermann,' concluded *Prze-*

* Józef Korbas, the Cracovia striker, scored a hat-trick on his debut for Poland against Bulgaria in 1937.

gląd Sportowy, 'fully justified his selection not only with his hat-trick, but with his effort, commitment and intelligence.' Any temptation to indulge in prima donna preening was seemingly eclipsed by his ambition to impress on the international stage.

No wonder Salka Viertel's interlocutor on the train was so dazzled by meeting the sister of such a player. Perhaps the most unimpressed people in the land were Steuermann's own family. When Salka told the story of that chance conversation to their father, 'he only shrugged', snobbery appearing to get the better of paternal pride.

* * *

Fourteen teams, including Hasmonea, competed in the first Polish Premier League season in 1927, played in the summer months from April to October. Steuermann was very much the lynchpin of a team which comfortably avoided relegation in eleventh place (only one team went down). Steuermann scored twenty-four of the fifty-five goals scored in the team's twenty-six games, despite himself missing several games through suspension for violent play in the derby against Czarni Lwów. Personal highlights included a hat-trick against third-placed Warta Poznań, two before seeing red against Czarni ('Steuermann was perfect: not only shooting well but also working creatively and actively for the team'), and one in a creditable draw against eventual champions Wisla Kraków.

The matches which sparked the most fireworks, however, were the duels against Jutrzenka Kraków, a club that espoused ideals which directly conflicted with Hasmonea's Jewish nationalism. The fans and even players of the club were strongly associated with the Polish Bund, a socialist and Jewish political party which fought discrimination against Jews but remained opposed to Zionism.* As we shall learn in the next chapter, Jutrzenka's derby games against another Zionist opponent, Maccabi Kraków, were particularly known for their bitter rivalry.

Jutrzenka's home game against Hasmonea towards the end of the 1927 season, a match Jutrzenka had to win to avoid relegation as the bottom club, was predictably heated. With the score at 2–2 and with five minutes left on the clock, Jutrzenka's Józef Grünberg kicked out at Hasmonea's goalkeeper, his namesake Adolf Grünberg. When Ludwik Schneider booted a Jutrzenka player in retaliation, rival fans invaded the pitch and mass fighting broke out. The riot police had to intervene in order for the game to be completed.**

In 1928, however, it was Hasmonea's turn to experience relegation, and not only for footballing reasons. Three teams were slated for relegation in an expanded fifteen-team league. With Steuermann again banging in the goals (scoring seventeen out of the team's forty-three),

---

* The Bund attempted to revive its activities after the Holocaust, but the Stalinist rulers soon crushed all competing political parties. The organisation was liquidated in 1948, the same year in which Zionism reached its objective of the establishment of the Jewish state of Israel.

** Hasmonea forgave Józef Grünberg's violence against their player, signing him from relegated Jutrzenka for the start of the 1928 season. He was the eldest of three brothers who all played in the Polish Premier League. Dawid also represented Jutrzenka, while Roman was a top midfielder for Cracovia ('Equally good at defending and with the ball – indeed, some considered him the best in the country just before the war,' writes Andrzej Gowarzewski – although, revealingly, Roman was never selected for the Poland national team, which had increasingly become beyond the reach of Jewish players by this time). According to the Yad Vashem archives, all three brothers were murdered in the Holocaust. After fleeing Kraków in 1939, Roman was last seen in Lviv, where he played for Dinamo. In his encyclopaedia of Polish football between 1918 and 1939, Gowarzewski draws a blank on the fate of their namesake, the Hasmonea goalkeeper Adolf Grünberg. There are no details at Yad Vashem either. In all likelihood, he was murdered too and disappeared into oblivion.

Hasmonea were hopeful they could avoid the drop. But a few games before the end of the season, things started to go awry.

On the afternoon of Sunday 23 September, Hasmonea kicked off their away derby match versus Czarni Lwów, only to be swiftly interrupted. The proximity of the kick-off to the onset of Yom Kippur that evening, with the vast majority of the Jewish community at home getting ready for synagogue, had raised more than a few eyebrows among the religious authorities. 'Two minutes after the start of the game,' reported *Przegląd Sportowy*, 'a representative of the Jewish community of Lwów appeared on the pitch and announced the statement of Lwów rabbis to the Hasmonea players that a ban had been issued for the match. The players, obeying the statement, stopped the game and left the field.'

The Polish Football Association decreed at an emergency meeting that the match was forfeit and awarded it to Czarni. At the same meeting, the authorities imposed a further ban on Hasmonea for not paying 'a required financial contribution' to the league, a clear sign that investment in the club was fast diminishing. The final games of the season were awarded to Hasmonea's opponents, and the team ended up third from bottom and exiting from the Premier League.

According to Henryk Hubel, a striker who played for Hasmonea in their two seasons in the Premier League, the culture at the club was by that stage rotten to the core and the writing had been on the wall for some time. In a letter to Gowarzewski several decades later, he claims that the players began to bemoan the low pay they earned as a result of the tightening purse strings at Hasmonea, while few had other more secure jobs to tide them over. They whiled away aimless hours playing pool and cards at the seedy Teatralna café in the town centre, with

Steuermann no doubt at the centre of things, pursuing his lifelong habit of spending considerably more than he earned.*

* * *

His team may have fallen from the top tier of Polish football, but Steuermann himself was not yet ready to disappear from the limelight. After all, he was still one of the country's foremost strikers and had made that dramatic substitute appearance in the international match against the United States during Hasmonea's relegation season. At the age of thirty, he achieved a notable footballing promotion by joining Legia Warsaw, who had just finished third in the league.

The bright lights of the capital city would certainly have appealed to Steuermann's pleasure-seeking character, but the transfer didn't bear much fruit on the pitch during his one season at Legia in 1929. Everything started well enough, with an uncharacteristically hard-working display and a hat-trick in the Warsaw derby victory against Polonia. 'He was running around in a thoughtful way trying to find space, and was an active element of the forward line, not just a passive component which is usually a problem with him,' reported *Przegląd Sportowy*. In a match against Katowice the following week, it was said that he hit the bar and post with great ferocity no fewer than six times, resulting in a deformed goalframe.

In truth, however, Steuermann was a superfluous signing which disrupted what had been a well-oiled attacking machine. He was also

* Henryk Hubel survived the Holocaust in remarkable fashion. He first hid in the Podolia region of Ukraine and then in Warsaw, and somehow managed to get to neutral Switzerland in December 1943. Hubel, who had previously earned a doctorate in economics at the University of Florence, emigrated to Australia with his wife and infant daughter in 1947.

getting on in age for a player of his generation, particularly one who was said to view fitness training with such disdain. Photographs taken even later on in his career certainly depict the portly figure of a man who had enjoyed life's pleasures to the full.

In the two league seasons before he joined, Legia had scored seventy and seventy-seven goals respectively, largely thanks to their front trio of Marian Łańko, Józef Nawrot and Józef Ciszewski, who together had been responsible for more than 80 per cent of those goals. In 1929, the team's goal tally was cut drastically to forty-four, with that triumvirate only managing to score twelve between them, and Steuermann just eight. It was no wonder that the Legia fans put two and two together and started to protest in vocal terms that Steuermann had stymied the exploits of their heroes. As accusations of laziness proliferated in the press, his swift departure became inevitable.

He never played at the top level again. He first returned to Hasmonea to compete in the Lviv regional league, and then from 1932 and seemingly right up to the Soviet occupation of 1939, he went back to his home town to play for Korona Sambor. His chaotic and troubled life at the time, detailed in the next section, appears to have led to increasingly erratic behaviour at matches. In October 1934, already serving a temporary ban for an unknown misdemeanour, he went completely berserk while watching a Korona game as a spectator. He ran onto the pitch, started a mass brawl, continued fighting as the teams were led off the pitch to the dressing room by a startled referee and then insulted several attending members of the footballing authorities, who promptly handed him a life ban.

Two years later, however, the ban had clearly been overturned, no doubt as a result of a popular outcry. In 1936, thousands of his fans in Lviv, afflicted by nostalgia, reportedly flocked to see their erstwhile hero playing for Korona against Czarni, in the very same stadium where he had blasted a hat-trick in double-quick time on his international debut ten years before.

Despite all his goals for club and country – he ended up with twice as many international goals as international appearances (four in two) – it was one of those sporting careers which cannot be measured in statistics alone. He was both a highly recognisable symbol of Jewish national pride at a time of growing external menace and a man who possessed magnetic personal charisma.

The reason why Salka Viertel received all those letters from Israel fully four decades after his footballing prime is because, to those fans, he was much more than just a football player. Unlike most memories of their home town, recollections of Steuermann would evoke in them past feelings of joy and excitement, rather than of pain, rage and misery.

* * *

Steuermann's departure from top-flight football coincided with economic catastrophe in Poland. During the turbulent era after the Wall Street Crash of 1929, the country suffered one of the most severe and long-lasting depressions in Europe. In the early 1930s, real national income fell by more than 20 per cent, industrial output by almost 40 per cent, while the unemployment rate reached more than 30 per cent.

From the letters and diary entries in the Berthold and Salka Viertel papers held at the *Deutsches Literaturarchiv* (German Literature Archive) in Marbach in Germany, we can gain some revealing insights into Zygmunt Steuermann's considerable financial struggles at this time.

For example, there is this letter to his sister from August 1931, when he was still playing for Hasmonea in the Lviv regional league and Salka had just started to establish herself in Hollywood.

> Dear Salka, I wanted to write to you for a long time, but I never found the courage. Today, however, I have to do it in the hope that you will not hold it against me and that you will listen patiently. I've been out of a job for a few months and my income as a footballer is not enough for me because of the bad situation in Poland. The economic crisis has resulted in total stagnation in everything.

Another letter, in December of that year, repeated a similar message.

> Six weeks ago I asked you to be so good and send me some money to pay off the debt. Although you advised three times that you had done so, I have still not received any money. I am really in a dire position because the people I owe money to have lost confidence in me because I have deceived them a few times … Dear Salka, it is really a serious matter. If you don't send me money right away, it can end very badly for me.

For the first time in his life, Steuermann now had responsibilities as well as debts, surely contributing to the clear anxiety evident in these communications. 'Mama mentioned lightly that a baby had been born to Hania, the pretty housekeeper, and gently indicated that the child was Dusko's son,' writes Salka in her autobiography.

Hania was a Ukrainian non-Jew. The words 'lightly' and 'gently' in this sentence strongly hint at the scandal, even within the context of an assimilated Jewish family, of fathering a child with a non-Jewish maid. There was no civil marriage in the eastern provinces of Poland at this time, so either one party switched religions in order to get married before the baby was born (probably Steuermann, given the comparative ease of conversion to Christianity), or the baby was born to unmarried parents, an even greater scandal. The local authorities have no surviving record of either such a marriage or the birth.

After Josef Steuermann died at the age of eighty-one in 1932, the couple and their son Adam were said to be living with Zygmunt's mother Augusta in Wychylówka, large parts of which had been divided up and rented out to tenants to support the meagre family income and keep the wolf (and the moneylenders) from the door.

In 1933, Zygmunt and his mother took over a small tannery in an attempt to turn their fortunes around. The venture clearly did not take off, because by 1936 he was asking Salka for money yet again, this time for a car repair because he had decided to become a chauffeur.

By the sound of things, that undertaking had an unfortunate ending too. One Friday evening in May 1937, reported the Polish-language Zionist daily newspaper *Chwila,* 'the athlete Zygmunt Steuermann was driving with a few passengers towards Sambor … the chauffeur lost control of the car and drove at maximum speed into a nearby tree. The car was completely wrecked.' Luckily, everyone emerged with only minor injuries.

During these cash-strapped years, in one of those painful anecdotes about Holocaust victims that make the reader want to go back in time and intervene, it appears that Steuermann could have emigrated to British-controlled Palestine, an opportunity that very probably arose through his contacts at Hasmonea. ('He had a chance to go to Palestine, but was not very enthusiastic about the idea,' wrote Salka.) The man who was brought up by his father to believe that Jews very much belonged in Europe, who had fought and played for Poland, whose partner was a non-Jew, opted instead to remain where he was. It was a tragic misjudgement – and not necessarily only with the benefit of hindsight.

After the death in May 1935 of Józef Pilsudski, the de facto leader who enjoyed some degree of popularity among Jews, the ever-present and sporadically violent antisemitism in Polish society became increasingly embedded within the policy of government and institutions.

In December 1935, Lviv Polytechnic, the largest scientific university in the city, introduced the *ghetto ławkowe* (ghetto benches) system, in which Jewish university students were required under threat of expulsion to sit on the left-hand side section of lecture halls, an area exclusively reserved for them. Universities throughout the country introduced an unofficial *numerus clausus* system to limit the number of Jewish students. In 1923–4, 30 per cent of medical students in the country were Jewish; by 1935–6, the proportion had fallen to 12.5 per cent. In 1937, the Ministry of Industry required all businesses to put up signs displaying the full name of their owner, with the aim of facilitating popular boycotts of Jewish shops. That same year, the Polish government even sent an inquiry commission to Madagascar, an island off the south-eastern coast of Africa, to investigate the possibility of resettling the country's Jews there.

At the end of 1937 and the beginning of 1938, Salka Viertel received three letters from her close friend Julia Bonhard, who had been to visit the Steuermanns in Sambir. Bonhard reported that Augusta was being harassed by moneylenders, mostly as a result of Zygmunt's actions, and that she sorely needed help from Salka: 'I can assure you that your dear mother lives an almost ascetic life for herself, but she is heavily burdened with Zygmunt, Viktoria and Adam, whose maintenance she has to take care of.'

Viktoria Holowka was born in 1917, the love child of a Russian army deserter and a maid who both worked at Wychylówka. When the parents went off in their separate directions, Viktoria 'remained a member of our family, spoiled by Papa as he had spoiled Dusko and later his grandchildren'. As we shall see later, this is extremely important background information when it comes to fathoming the denouement of the Zygmunt Steuermann story.

Since her arrival in the country, Salka had coveted United States citizenship, primarily because she believed it would enable her to bring over her mother, Zygmunt (and presumably his wife/girlfriend Hania and son Adam) and Viktoria. In February 1939, she finally achieved her ambition. 'I was hopeful now that I could get my mother and Dusko out of Poland,' she wrote, although her brother's own willingness to emigrate to the United States is far from clear.

Six months later, however, a potential spanner was thrown in the works. The Molotov-Ribbentrop pact, a non-aggression agreement between the totalitarian regimes of Nazi Germany and the Soviet Union, carved up large chunks of Eastern Europe between them. The Eastern provinces of Poland, including Lviv and Sambir, were swallowed up by the Ukrainian Soviet Socialist Republic, complete with a vast repressive bureaucracy which restricted free travel and obstructed the receipt of communications and funds from relatives living abroad, thus further complicating the emigration process.

In the late summer of 1940, Salka received a letter from her mother that had taken nearly six months to arrive. Augusta reported that Wychylówka had been expropriated and nationalised by the Soviets and that she had moved into cramped accommodation nearby with Zygmunt, Hania, Adam and Viktoria, where they all shared one room and a kitchen. She nevertheless took great solace from Zygmunt's apparent flourishing under the Soviet hammer and sickle, having avoided the arrests and deportations to the Gulag suffered by thousands of other Jews in the area.

'Everything has a good side: Dusko has a job,' declared Augusta, almost disbelievingly. 'The Soviets made him chief of the physical culture section and he has an office and a secretary. He works from eight in the morning until three in the afternoon, and for an extra salary he also coaches the soccer team "Spartacus". His Russian superiors appreciate him … I am thankful that he has become a responsible human being.' According to Andrzej Gowarzewski, the forty-year-old Steuermann was also at this time playing for Dinamo Sambor, the Soviet successor club to Korona Sambor.

Augusta discusses other members of the household in her letter too. 'I have no words to describe Hania's selflessness and sacrifice; she has been wonderful. She and Viktoria are employed in a cooperative. Adam goes to school. He is a dear boy and a very good pupil.'

Good news arrived in February 1941, when Augusta's visa for travel to the United States was confirmed. Salka immediately cabled her mother, asking her to request permission from the Soviet authorities to leave Sambir. On 30 May, Zygmunt cabled back to Salka to tell her that Augusta had left for Moscow with the intention of travelling further east to board a ship to the United States. As she waited patiently in a central Moscow hotel, this time for a Soviet exit visa, Augusta expressed the maternal hope in a letter to Salka and Eduard, dated 16 June 1941, that 'Dusko will now work more intensely and not rely upon Salka's checks'. It was a further four months before the 73-year-old Augusta finally arrived in Seattle, after an arduous journey via Vladivostok.

Six days after that letter was written, 22 June, Nazi Germany broke its pact and invaded the Soviet Union. On that day, a Sunday, Salka received a cable from Zygmunt asking for money, perhaps to help him escape eastwards into the Soviet Union. 'But the banks were closed and the telegraph office refused to forward money to the war zone,' explains Salka. 'I tried all day Monday but all connections with West Ukraine were cut. My only hope was that Dusko had fled with the retreating Soviets.'

He hadn't.

* * *

The terror started immediately after the Nazis entered Sambir on 30 June, just one week after Salka had desperately tried to send money to her brother. In the words of Toni Nacht, a Jewish survivor from Sambir, 'as soon as the Germans invaded, the Ukrainian hatred towards the Jews exploded.'

When the Nazis opened the jail in Sambir, they found the bodies of the local leaders of the Ukrainian nationalist movement, executed by the Soviet authorities shortly before they had abandoned the town. Despite the fact that the Soviets had banned Zionist organisations and deported wealthy Jews to Siberia during their two years in power, the local Ukrainian population had somehow believed Communist rule and the Jewish community to be one and the same thing. The Nazis were happy to permit brutal revenge for imagined wrongs.

'The first thirty-two Jews that were caught were dragged to the Jewish cemetery,' documents the Sambir *yizkor* book.

> Placards bearing pictures of Stalin and Lenin were placed into their hands, and a large procession of Ukrainians carrying picks and axes followed them. At the head of the procession was the head priest of the local Orthodox Church and members of the local Ukrainian committee. At the cemetery, the thirty-two Jews were hacked to death by the mob, their heads, legs and hands were torn off and their stomachs ripped open. On the way back, 170 more Jews were caught at random, taken to the jail and murdered in the most savage blood bath. Jewish properties were looted, and there was chaos and much mourning among the Jews of Sambir.

A July report sent back to Berlin by the Nazi occupying forces expressed great satisfaction with the actions of the Ukrainian population in the days after the invasion. 'In the first hours of the Bolshevik withdrawal, the Ukrainian population displayed commendable activity against the Jews,' purred the report writer. 'They set the Dobromil synagogue on fire, and an enraged crowd in Sambir slaughtered fifty Jews. In Lemberg (Lviv), the population rounded up, mistreated, and delivered one thousand Jews to the prison.' Indeed, in Lviv alone, around 4,000 Jews were murdered by Ukrainians in the first days of the occupation.

We know that Zygmunt Steuermann was very close at hand when these events took place in Sambir. But as for exactly when he himself was murdered, and whether he was gassed or shot, we can only sift through the available recollections of events and then apply some reason to determine his most likely fate.

The lack of any certainty derives in part from the bewildering chaos of the period under focus, but mostly from the extremely low Jewish survival rate and hence the shortage of reliable living witnesses. By way of example, Yad Vashem estimates that 110,000 Jews were herded into the Lviv ghetto in November 1941. When a Jewish committee was set up in July 1944 to help survivors in the town, only 820 of those coming forward were from the ghetto itself, less than 1 per cent of their original number.

Before we delve into the specific evidence about Steuermann, we first have to understand some key geographical and historical context. In September 1939, Poland had been divided into three parts: the western third was annexed to the Third Reich; the eastern third, as we have seen, was occupied by the Soviet Union; and the central third was termed the *Generalgouvernement* (the General Government). After the Nazis invaded the Soviet Union in June 1941, Eastern Galicia, including Sambir and Lviv, was added to the *Generalgouvernement*.

The historian Thomas Sandkühler places Galicia 'at the intersection of differing paths to the Final Solution'. He meant by this that Jews in this region were either sent to extermination camps to be gassed – the preferred method of murder in the *Generalgouvernement* and that most commonly associated with the Holocaust – or they were corralled together to be shot, a fate suffered by 1.5 million Jews further east in the so-called 'Holocaust by bullets'. The latter category, in the words of historian Omer Bartov, was no 'distant, neatly organised, bloodless bureaucratic undertaking, but a vast wave of brutal, intimate, and endlessly bloody massacres.'

Janowska, situated on the eponymous street in the northwest outskirts of Lviv and operating as the largest concentration camp in the vicinity, was typical of the hybrid approach followed in Galicia. It operated as a slave labour camp; as a transit camp for deportation to extermination camps (overwhelmingly, Bełżec, just eighty kilometres away on the Lviv to Lublin train line) where Jews were to be immediately gassed; and as a killing site in itself. Around 200,000 Jews are estimated to have passed through the camp, and at least 80,000 to have been murdered within its confines. It is a testament to the enormous scale of the European genocide of the Jews that the camp is little known outside the realm of specialist scholars.

Due to the curiosity of Andrzej Gowarzewski, the Polish football historian, we can make an informed judgement that Zygmunt Steuermann was himself imprisoned in Janowska relatively shortly after its establishment in September 1941, when the camp housed only several hundred slave labourers.

Between 1977 and 1985, Gowarzewski tracked down and corresponded with a number of survivors and non-Jews in an attempt to find out what happened to Steuermann. The varied nature of the replies points to the difficulty of the task he had set himself.

Indeed, some of the testimonies can be quickly discounted. One example is this easily disprovable claim from Wacław Kuchar, his former teammate from the Polish national team: 'Steuermann died in Lviv in his own garden. He was shot by the Germans while trying to defend his father.' A nice story, but we know that Steuermann had been living in Sambir, not Lviv, and that his father had died a decade before the genocide was carried out.

We also have this rather unhelpful statement from Zenon Kruk, a former Lechia Lwów player, who hailed from near Sambir and was in a German prisoner-of-war camp at the relevant time: 'He was murdered in Sambir. I heard it from a lot of people. But maybe it was Lviv? I heard it said too.'

Zygmunt Blumenblatt, who appeared in goal for Hasmonea in the 1928 season, veered towards the Sambir rumour. He wrote from New York to say that he had seen Steuermann play for Dinamo Sambor in 1941 and that 'the Germans shot him in the Sambir ghetto – this is what is alleged anyway, but I heard it said by a number of people.' Izydor Bürgel, whose own identity remains a mystery to me, echoes Blumenblatt's assumption, while adding some detail: '(Steuermann) was shot by a Jewish policeman in the ghetto in Sambir in 1941.'* However, it is worth noting here that the Sambir ghetto, in which almost 7,000 people were crammed, was not established until March 1942.

The most convincing of all the letters came from the multi-talented Marian Wieczysty, a famous non-Jewish dancer and choreographer and friend of the Steuermann family, who had also played football for three Lviv clubs (Pogoń, Lechia and Czarni) when Zygmunt was in his pomp.

---

* A Jewish police force was established in East European ghettos to enforce the orders of the German authorities and the decrees of the Jewish councils (*Judenraete*). Although initially employed to keep order in the ghetto, such as by guarding the ghetto gates and directing traffic, their work later included helping to round up fellow Jews for deportations to killing centres. Jewish police officials, like Jewish council members, were totally subordinate to the German authorities. They were eventually exterminated in the same way as all other Jews.

Unlike the other letters received by Gowarzewski, his included first-hand evidence. '[Steuermann] was arrested in 1941 in Sambir – his mother and siblings had left the town earlier,' Wieczysty wrote. 'He died in the Lviv ghetto at Janowska Street in 1941, or possibly at the beginning of 1942.' He then added a crucial, credibility-boosting line: 'A few days before his death, he sent us a letter with the information that he was staying in Janowska Street.' Wieczysty knew the family history, was aware that Steuermann was in Sambir at the time of the German invasion and had learned of his later whereabouts from the horse's mouth.

We can also speculate that Steuermann mentioned in his letter that he had been arrested in Sambir, and that this information found its way into Wieczysty's statement almost forty years later. Alternatively, given Wieczysty's closeness to the family, he may well already have been aware of the circumstances of this arrest before receiving the letter. The idea that Steuermann would have been arrested so early in the occupation, when the deportations from the region did not start in earnest until the following year, should not surprise us unduly. He was a high-profile Jew who had been working as a senior official for the Bolshevik enemy and was still playing high-level sport at the age of forty-two, all of which made him ideal slave labour material.

Other correspondents support Wieczysty's assertion that Steuermann was in Janowska. For example, former Hasmonea teammate Henryk Hubel wrote that 'there is no doubt that it [Steuermann's death] occurred in the Lviv ghetto in Janowska Street at the end of December 1941.'* We should bear in mind here that given Hubel's own remarkable Holocaust experience documented earlier in the chapter, he himself had probably been some distance away from Lviv at the time in question.

* Janowska was not actually in the ghetto, which was established in November 1941, but nearby. Wieczysty made the same error.

Someone who definitely *was* in Lviv during the war was Kazimierz Górski, a young player at that time who went on to coach the Polish national team that secured third place at the 1974 World Cup in West Germany. As he meandered through his wartime experiences in his 1985 book *Pół wieku z piłką* ('Half a Century With the Ball'), Górski launched into a remarkable story relating to Steuermann and Janowska.

He recounts that he was travelling on a tram in the city when a policeman approached a fellow passenger who was not wearing the requisite armband. 'What are you doing here, Jew? Where's your Star of David?' Górski surmised that the arrested Jew would be taken to 'the concentration camp at Janowska Street'. He continued,

> Many Jews and Poles lost their lives there, sportsmen too, including Steuermann, the famous and popular Lviv football player from Hasmonea. His death occurred in extremely dramatic circumstances – after a match between the prisoners and the perpetrators. The prisoners won 3–1. Steuermann scored two goals, and Berger one. Soon after the competition, a drunken SS man shot the great striker. The name of the team, which was set up for this match and included mainly players from Hasmonea, Kadima Borislav and Korona Sambor, was very telling: 'Morituri' (a Latin word meaning 'those who are about to die').*

* In the Sambir *yizkor* book, a list of names of players in the Korona Sambor team included one man named Berger. The first name was not given. Eighteen people named Berger appeared in the book's list of murdered Sambir Jews. In the Borislav *yizkor* book, one man named Berger (first name not given) is also included in the list of players from the Zionist club, Kadima Borislav. I think it could well be the same person, as Borislav is only forty kilometres south of Sambir. There were more than 13,000 Jews in Borislav in 1939. When Soviet forces took over the town in August 1944, around 200 Jewish survivors were found in the forests and in local hideouts. No one with the surname Berger appears on the list of Borislav victims.

We already know that there was a first-class pitch right next to the Janowska site waiting to be used: the spanking new Hasmonea headquarters which opened in 1939, seven years after the club's previous stadium had been burned down in an antisemitic riot. If Górski's story is true, then this grimmest of football fixtures would have been the only game that Steuermann played on a pitch built specially for Jewish heroes. The detail with which Górski retells this story more than forty years later shows the impact that it must have had on him after he originally heard it on the Lviv wartime grapevine.

Górski does not give any relevant dates, although various Polish and Ukrainian websites citing this story state that the game was in November 1941 and give Steuermann's date of death as December 1941. This tallies more or less with the date of death supplied by Wieczysty and Hubel.

However, Gowarzewski never discusses the death match at all, even though much of his material about Steuermann was written after the publication of Górski's book, an autobiography by a major figure in Polish football history which we can guess he would have read. In his encyclopaedia of Polish football between 1918 and 1939, published in 2017, Gowarzewski's entry for Steuermann gives his date of death as '?.12.1941'. Gowarzewski was seemingly convinced by Wieczysty and Hubel, but not by the story about Steuermann's final game shortly before his murder. I think the websites that claim the death match took place in November 1941 have simply accepted both Górski's story and Gowarzewski's date of death for Steuermann and have then worked backwards.

Gowarzewski himself died in 2020, just before I started researching the life story of Zygmunt Steuermann. His notes on the interviews with former contacts of Steuermann were sent to me by Thomas

Urban, a German journalist and author who has written about Polish football history and who had previously corresponded with Gowarzewski. Importantly, not only did Gowarzweski omit any mention of Górski but his notes also excluded any reference to the evidence provided by Salka Viertel. Unlike with Górski's book, Viertel's writings on the subject were not published in Polish and Gowarzewski may therefore have been unaware of the relevant details. If he had known what Viertel had written, I think he might have hesitated before deciding on 1941 as Steuermann's date of death.

Viertel received two relevant communications in the year or two after the war, when news was still trickling in about what had happened to Jewish relatives in Europe's death factory.

'A woman from Sambor informed me that she had received an unverified report about her own brother, a friend of Dusko,' wrote Viertel about the first of the two letters. 'Apparently both had tried to escape by jumping from a train taking them to a concentration camp and were killed by the SS.' If this story is true, it is very likely to have taken place between March and December 1942, the months that the death camp at Bełżec was operational, gassing around one quarter of a million Jews from the Lviv district alone during this period.*

The second letter came from Viktoria Holowka, the former maid who had been held close to the bosom of the Steuermann family throughout her life. The letter filled Viertel with 'cold horror'. Viktoria

* In just nine months of operation, up to 600,000 Jews were murdered at Bełżec. The killings were stopped in December 1942, because most of the Jews in the *Generalgouvernement* were already dead. There were just three known survivors from Bełżec after the war – Chaim Hirszman, Rudolf Reder and Rabbi Israel Szapiro. Hirszman was murdered in 1946 by the Narodowe Siły Zbrojne (National Armed Forces), a Polish underground military organisation known for its antisemitism. Hirszman, Reder, Szapiro thus represent a survival rate of 0.0005 per cent. No wonder we don't hear much of Bełżec.

was the bearer of 'bad news about Dusko'. She stated, 'In 1943, he came to my house begging me to hide him, but as we are living in a rented place I could not do it, and since the last German *Aktion* I have not heard from him again.' According to Salka, Viktoria had written that she was 'not on speaking terms with Hania', who had left Sambir with Adam. She had concluded the letter by asking if Salka could send a food parcel for her household.

'All her life Viktoria had been a member of our family,' wrote Viertel, 'and the callousness of her report was so shocking that it took me a long time to recover.' She drew up an angry letter back, accusing Viktoria of 'denying shelter to a hunted Jew, whose father and mother had given her love and devoted care since she was born, and that she had allied herself with murderers and torturers'. But then Salka calmed down and persuaded herself that 'this cowardly woman' was only 'one among millions' who 'stood by indifferently when these unspeakable horrors took place'. She tore up her own letter and sent the food package to Viktoria instead.

Salka never told her mother Augusta about the contents of Viktoria's note. 'But Mama must have sensed that I was keeping bad news from her,' she nevertheless wrote. 'She stopped going to the mailbox (and) her trembling got worse.' By this stage, the truth had begun to dawn on Augusta and the rest of the Jewish world. In the central heartland of world Jewry, pretty much every single Jew was dead.

The German term *aktion* which Viktoria uses is a euphemism applied to the particular process that defined the Holocaust by bullets. The principal executioners were the *Einsatzgruppen*, the mobile killing units that followed the German army as it conquered territories in Eastern Europe. In Ukraine, they were ably assisted by the auxiliary police staffed by thousands of volunteers from the local population, who guarded ghettos, rounded Jews up, took convoys to execution sites and then cordoned off those areas. 'All the collaborating Ukrainian policemen were brutal murderers,' writes Anda Meisels, a Sambir survivor. 'In our town, they actively participated in all the raids and the brutal treatment of the victims while they were being held in the fields and the jail, and they participated in the executions.'

The last *aktion* in Sambir took place on 9 June 1943, the first day of the Jewish festival of Shavuot – typical timing by the Nazis, who enjoyed the idea of Jews thinking about what they might have been doing on traditionally joyous days if they weren't watching their children being shot. 'The Nazis did their evil work on the Jewish holidays, in order to intensify the humiliation and the cruel treatment,' reports the Sambir *yizkor* book.

The description of this *aktion* indicates that it was very much in keeping with the later phase of the Holocaust in occupied Poland, known as the *Judenjagd* ('the Jew hunt'). A shared enterprise between the Germans and local populations, the objective was to capture and murder any Jewish remnants, generally escapees from ghettos, camps and transports who had managed to find a place to hide.

'About two o'clock in the morning, men of the Gestapo and Ukrainian police surrounded the ghetto,' the *yizkor* book continues.

> In order to reveal those who had hidden, they destroyed houses, even burning some of them down. They dragged the people out from every hiding place and concentrated them in the prison. At dawn they opened the prison cells and drove the remnants of the Jews of Sambir and the vicinity on their last journey. In the trucks where they were loaded, the Jews were ordered to kneel down and raise their hands over their heads. In the four corners of the trucks

> stood Ukrainian militia with rifles at the ready. Whoever dared to move or raise his head was struck by a rifle butt. The remnant of the Sambir Jewish Community was thus led to the wood near the village of Radlowicz and murdered there. The town was declared *judenrein* (cleansed of Jews).

Was Steuermann indeed among those digging his own grave in the Radlowicz forest in June 1943, before waiting his turn for a bullet in the head?* Or had he, as others testified, already been murdered in Janowska in late 1941, or at some unspecified date after possibly the most poignant match in the history of football? Or had he been shot while escaping from a deportation train from Janowska to Bełżec in 1942?

The testimonies of Marian Wieczysty, and especially Viktoria Holowka, stand out for their credibility. Wieczysty actually received a dated letter from Steuermann and Viktoria says she saw him with her own eyes. I don't see any reason why Viktoria would have lied to Salka Viertel about her alleged meeting with Steuermann. After all, she was asking Salka for material help and the admission that she refused to help Steuermann would hardly motivate his sister to dip into her pocket. I think she felt guilty and needed to get the episode off her chest.

People can get confused with dates, of course, particularly when they relate to incidents a long time in the past. But Viktoria's letter was written just three or four years after 1943. Moreover, her memory of seeing Steuermann in 1943 was juxtaposed with a mention of the final *aktion*, and we know this took place in that same year.

My own conclusion, therefore, is that Steuermann was murdered in 1943. But where? It is possible, even probable, that he was shot near

* The village is now known as Ralivka.

Radlowicz in that final *aktion*. We can recall that some of Gowarzewski's correspondents believed he was murdered 'in the Sambir ghetto', which is near enough saying the same thing.

We can also reason, given that it appears highly likely that he was both in Janowska in late 1941 and Sambir in 1943, that he escaped from the camp before ultimately being recaptured and shot, either near to where he was found or back in Janowska.

Escape from Janowska was extremely difficult and of course dangerous not just for the individual but for their entire family, who were likely to be murdered in reprisal. But it was not a wholly fanciful idea. Waitman Beorn, a rare academic expert on Janowska, writes that slave labourers living at the camp were often outsourced to local enterprises, particularly in its final period before it was dismantled and its inmates all murdered in late 1943.

Beorn writes that 'each morning, work brigades would make the short trip to the city to work for a variety of organizations: the Wehrmacht, the Luftwaffe, the SS housing quarter, multiple clothing manufacturers, the German railways, as well as a cabal of firms tasked with collecting and recycling raw materials. ... In general, external work sites proved safer for laborers.' They were 'away from the sadistic eyes of camp administrators'.

Indeed, there are several recorded instances of prisoners who managed to benefit from the unusually porous modus operandi of the camp. For example, Leon Weliczker Wells, the only survivor of an extended family of seventy-six who later wrote a book about his experiences at Janowska, cleverly exploited this system to escape, before eventually being recaptured and sent back to the camp.* The famous

* Leon Weliczker Wells was brought up as a religious Jew in Lviv. When he died in New Jersey in 2010, he was cremated, despite this being against Orthodox Jewish law. He insisted on cremation because 'my people had gone that way'.

Nazi hunter Simon Wiesenthal was another who managed to flee from Janowska.

A well-known character in the football world and in Lviv's bars and restaurants, and having lived virtually his whole life in and around the area, Steuermann would hardly have been short of non-Jewish contacts whom he could call on after escaping. But despite his former, very evident popularity among Jewish fans, the naked facts speak for themselves. The net result of any help Zygmunt Steuermann received from the non-Jewish world ended in him being shot like a rabid dog at the age of forty-four.

If Gowarzewski had indeed read Górski's description of the death match, I think he was wrong to omit it from possible theories about what happened to Steuermann. Górski was in Lviv during the period and he could have heard stories about the game from friends of friends who were guards at the camp, or indirectly from Janowska inmates who travelled to central Lviv every day to work. The idea that German Nazis would play against Jewish *untermenschen* is too far-fetched, but a game against Ukrainian guards is within the realms of possibility. I desperately want to believe it too. Two goals and a victory against his persecutors would be a fitting final game for this larger-than-life footballing talent.

Augusta Steuermann died in 1953 in the full knowledge that her beloved younger son had been murdered. Her grandson and 'dear little boy', Adam, had vanished into the ether, either put to death by the Nazis for his Jewish blood or successfully camouflaged behind his non-Jewish mother before disappearing behind the iron curtain of post-war Europe. I have made various enquiries in an attempt to discover what happened to him and Hania but have so far come up with nothing.

Perhaps there is now a child somewhere in Eastern Europe who spends all their free time kicking a ball around a field, oblivious to the fact that they are descended from the magnificent Jewish footballer and entertainer Zygmunt Steuermann, memories of whom were all but extinguished in the gas chambers of Bełżec and in the death pits of Ukraine.

CHAPTER 3

THE BOYS FROM KRAKÓW

In 1918, Poland regained the independence that had been lost to the Prussian, Russian and Austrian empires for the previous 123 years. Sporting the country's emblem, the white eagle, its new football team carried with it the hopes of a people galvanised by the spirit of national revival. But before travelling to face Sweden in May 1922, the team had failed to deliver the goods, losing its first two matches without scoring a goal.

There could have been no more awe-inspiring setting in European football for what proved to be a historic chapter in the story of the fledgling Polish state. The venue was the spectacular stadium built to hold the 1912 Olympic Games in Stockholm, with its imposing gothic-style towers on either side of the stand behind one goal. The stadium was packed to the rafters; the heir to the Swedish throne, Gustav Adolf, sat among the excited spectators.

In the twenty-seventh minute of the first half, with the score goalless, the diminutive Poland winger Leon Sperling set off on one of his characteristic mazy runs down the left wing. According to legend, Sperling was such a magician with the ball at his feet that spectators had been known to burst out laughing as they watched him bamboozle defenders. Einar Hemming, the Swedish full-back, was the victim this time. Unable to cope, he resorted to blocking Sperling's attempted cross with his hand.

Hugo Meisl, who also then happened to be the coach of the great Austrian national team of the inter-war period, had few easier decisions to make in his long and distinguished career as an international referee. 'The verdict is a penalty kick. But who should be entrusted with such an important task?' asked *Przegląd Sportowy*.

Cometh the hour, cometh the man. Józef Klotz, a tall and slender central defender whose talent had been identified by the Poland coach Józef Lustgarten, was making his second and what turned out to be his final appearance for the national team. It may not have been the most celebrated of careers, but because of what happened next, Klotz's place in the history books is nevertheless assured.

'The only player who successfully takes penalty kicks in his own club team is Klotz, which is why the team captain asks him to take responsibility,' continued *Przegląd Sportowy*. 'Klotz, composed and unhurried, puts the ball in the top left-hand corner, just below the bar. The goalkeeper does not even move. In this way, the Polish national team scored its first goal in its history of international games.' An eventual 2–1 victory ensured that the newspaper could lead with the headline 'The triumph of Polish football in Sweden', leaving the team members to be feted as heroes who had put their country on the map.

This is a dramatic and momentous sporting story in its own right. And the description of the penalty incident would not look out of place in a report of a major game in a modern-day newspaper. However, upon closer inspection of Poland's first-ever goal, we are again offered a revealing snapshot of how different Europe and European football were before the European Holocaust. All the people who have featured in this story, save the hapless Einar Hemming, were Jews, including the scorer of the first-ever goal for the Poland international team.

Although they were polar opposites as footballers and as Jews, the trajectories of the lives of Józef Klotz and the man who won the penalty, Leon Sperling, followed a very similar path. They were born in the same year in Kraków, a major city in what was then Western Galicia, and the second largest in modern-day Poland. They both played club football in their home city and had the honour of representing the country in which they were both born and raised.

This chapter is devoted to these two boys from Kraków, a city once full of Jews and brimming with Jewish life, and now with almost no Jews apart from those who come from far afield to visit yet one more place in Europe where their people once lived, often thrived, but were ultimately cast out and murdered.

Those visitors are the remnants, the children, grandchildren and great-grandchildren of those who made brave and prescient decisions, or who were the beneficiaries of fortuitous circumstance, who one day turned right rather than left, or left rather than right.

Hugo Meisl himself had the good fortune of dying of a heart attack at the age of fifty-five in 1937 in Vienna, just one year before Jews in that city were on their knees scrubbing streets in front of crowds of guffawing Austrians. Poland's coach, Józef Lustgarten, was a former goalkeeper who, like Meisl, also acted as an international referee. Having somehow managed to flee to the Soviet Union in 1940, Lustgarten was arrested, deported and imprisoned for a decade in a slave labour camp in the taiga of Eastern Siberia, where he toiled as a woodcutter in barely human conditions.

Klotz and Sperling, however, had no such luck. Their deaths were as similar as their lives.

* * *

The two future football heroes arrived in the world within months of each other – Klotz on the second day of the twentieth century and Sperling on 7 August 1900. Their birthplaces, and the apartments in which they were brought up, are all in and around Kraków's medieval Old Town (Stare Miasto). Walking between them all takes less than fifteen minutes.* Standing adjacent to the Old Town was Kazimierz, the traditional Jewish quarter of Kraków.

Both were from large families, with the fathers working in skilled trades. Józef's father Markus was a tailor of women's garments, and Leon's father Salomon Wolf was a watchmaker. Józef was the eldest of five siblings, while Leon was the youngest of seven. But despite the many evident similarities between Klotz and Sperling, the conflicting day-to-day routines and practices of their two families reflected the complexities of a Jewish community that had developed diverse responses to the challenges of modernity and persistent antisemitism.

Their respective attitudes to Jewish religious custom, and their related desire to assimilate into Polish society, were worlds apart. Whereas Salomon Wolf and Ruchel (née Beckman) Sperling clung assiduously to traditional mores, Markus and Szaindel (née Glasner) Klotz would take their family to the progressive Tempel synagogue in Kazimierz, and only on the days of major festivals.** Among other changes that sought to shed the outward habits and mannerisms of Jewishness, the progressives made a special point of introducing local languages and

* The Klotz family lived at Ulica (Street) Bracka 6; the Sperlings at Ulica Dluga 22.

** Szaindel is a Yiddish name meaning 'beautiful'. Szaindel Klotz was also known by the more Polish-sounding name Salomea. From the late nineteenth century onwards, it became more common for Jews in Europe to acquire a native-sounding name alongside a Hebrew or Yiddish name. Which one they used, and in what situations, depended to a large extent on how much they aspired to integrate into the wider society.

church-style organ music into prayer services – innovations, it is safe to say, that would have left the Sperling family cold.

Henryk Vogler, a Jewish writer from Kraków who made the extremely unusual decision to resettle in the city after surviving the Holocaust, recalled the atmosphere in this synagogue in his memoir, published in his old age in the 1990s: 'The typical Eastern rituals were never heard – the throaty cries of voices swelling with passion, as if trying to reach the heavens themselves – nor was the ecstatic swaying of bodies visible. Here, the men observed the rituals almost in silence, trying to show the composure appropriate, it would seem, to Western civilisation.' To fit with the ethos, the Rabbi would give his sermon in Polish, not Yiddish.

Unlike József Braun, Leon Sperling maintained the high level of religious observance inculcated in childhood right throughout his playing career. While Braun could be said to have been the greatest ever Jewish player, Sperling should by rights be a legend among Orthodox Jews who love the game, if only they had the faintest clue who he was.

They would certainly love one particular story about Sperling, as related by Vogler in the same book. The synagogues that Vogler used to visit as a small boy with his Orthodox grandfather were polar opposites of the Tempel:

> The stuffiness and noise, the mass of bodies crowded around the table placed in the centre and the benches arranged against the walls, the liturgical wailing … the fanatically joyful dancing around the table during the [Simchat] Torah festival … all this created an atmosphere of collective folk elation, a sense of community, of almost mystical power, connecting the participants to each other by invisible but inseparable bonds.

Vogler was in one such synagogue on Brzozowa Street in Kazimierz on a Sunday. Those attending synagogue on a Sunday, the day after the Jewish sabbath, would consist only of observant Jews who would commonly aim to be present three times a day for services on every single day of the week, in accordance with the tradition. Sitting that day beside Vogler's uncle, Romek Berwald, was Leon Sperling.*

The service ran over time, and Sperling became concerned that he would be late for the kick-off in the match between his team Cracovia and local rivals Wisla. Together with Berwald and the young Vogler, Sperling took off his *tefillin* (phylacteries) and *tallit* (prayer shawl) and hurried to pick up a horse-drawn cab from the street. Once in the cab, reports Vogler, 'an ordinary little Jew was transformed into a gigantic figure in almost Homeric armour, for who else were the footballers, especially the footballers of Cracovia, but the mythical heroes from the Iliad?'

Such was Vogler's awe of his footballing hero that he recalled the scene in detail some seventy years later.

> Sperling took off the various parts of his civilian clothes – trousers, jacket, underwear, and put on the pieces of his sports kit that my uncle and I had given him in a nervous rush, retrieving them from the suitcase we had prepared: socks, football boots with studs, white shorts and, last but not least, the most sacred thing of all, the red-and-white-striped shirt (of Cracovia). The start time of the match was getting nearer, one had to be ready, and the coachman, urged

* Abraham Roman (Romek) Adolf Berwald became a top league referee in Poland. He was murdered in the Treblinka death camp in 1942, aged forty-six.

on by exhortations and aware of the importance of his mission, dashed off as fast as he could.

The Cracovia team were forced to start with ten men, until a flustered but spiritually refreshed Sperling ran on to the pitch to make up the numbers.

Due to the respective families' conflicting attitudes to religion and assimilation, it is highly probable that Klotz and Sperling also spoke different languages in their home environments, despite being Jews of the same age, being children of parents all born in Poland, spending their childhood in the same streets and making such similar life choices. This might seem strange to those accustomed to a predominantly monolingual environment but would not have raised eyebrows among the Jews of Central and Eastern Europe.

Bernard Wasserstein, in his book *On the Eve: The Jews of Europe before the Second World War*, describes the labyrinthine linguistic intricacies of the Jewish community in Poland, the vast majority of whom were raised in that same country: 'Polish Jewry in the early twentieth century lived in a trilingual environment in which Polish, Yiddish and Hebrew were all known to some degree by most Jews, for whom each language served a specific function.'

For most, Hebrew served as the language of prayer. Meanwhile, Polish clearly had a practical function in allowing trade and social relations with non-Jews and became increasingly popular among Kraków's Jews who, according to the YIVO Institute for Jewish research, spoke 'the Polish language in greater numbers than Jews elsewhere'.

This was particularly true for those families who shunned Orthodoxy, for whom speaking Polish in everyday life was seen as crucial in the battle for integration. As the Polish academic Marcin Wodziński put it, 'choice of language both signified and determined one's particular type of assimilation, or its negation. Far more than an instrument of communication, language labelled its users ideologically.'

According to Danny Dekel, the son of Klotz's younger brother Salomon, the family spoke only Polish at home and his father learned Yiddish almost from scratch when trying to converse with other refugees from Europe while living in Israel in the 1950s.* This indicates strongly that the family made a concerted effort to avoid speaking any Yiddish – which the parents Markus and Szaindel would have known well – in order to appear and become more Polish.

On the other hand, Yiddish would surely have been the preferred language at the family dinner table headed by Leon's father Salomon Wolf Sperling, almost twenty years older than Markus Klotz and seemingly with comparatively little inclination to adopt the foreign ways of the host population.

In the end, of course, any such internal conflict was academic. According to the normal order of things, even at dramatically reduced birth rates, there should now be several dozen descendants of these two large but very different families knocking around modern-day Poland, perhaps still at passionate loggerheads over the same issues. In actual fact, there are precisely zero.

* Salomon's various names throughout his life again demonstrate the fluid and complex identities of Jews from this era and region. The name on his birth certificate was Salomon Stanisław Klotz, but he was known by the Polish-sounding Samek. Having escaped the Holocaust, and presumably seeking to avoid further antisemitism, he applied to the Polish authorities to change his name to the more native-sounding Stanisław Kloc. In 1950, after a spate of antisemitic pogroms and murders inflicted on the few Jewish survivors by the Polish population in the years following the war, he moved to Israel, where he was known as Shlomo.

* * *

The modern-day Kraków authorities have for years been playing a game of catch-up with what seems to be a rather large contingent of passionate local graffiti artists. 'Whore Jews, get the fuck out of Poland' was one message sprayed on the wall of the former Kraków ghetto, in which up to 20,000 Jews were once crammed and from which only a tiny proportion managed to get the fuck out of Poland instead of being murdered.

Another example on the gate of a Jewish cemetery suggests sending 'Jews to the furnace because that's where your place is', which given that the local Jewish population was turned to ashes some time ago, represents another perplexing command to thin air. A Star of David painted with a cross struck through it is the staple graffiti, and seems tame by comparison.

History creates ripples that flow down the ages. The more powerful the history, the more evident the ripples. Much of the graffiti carries messages that have their roots in football, harking back to a time when Kraków's Jews numbered more than 60,000, one in four of the city's total population. One message with particularly large writing hailed 'Cracovia's best tour – Auschwitz, 1940.'* Underneath those words is a Star of David and the hashtag 'Pasyontour', all integrated with drawings of figures wearing red-and-white striped shirts and moving in cattle cars on a rail track towards the infamous death camp.

To understand what this all means, and how Klotz and Sperling

* The graffiti artist did not score full marks for historical accuracy. Jews only started to be deported to Auschwitz for extermination in the spring of 1942.

fit in, we have to go back to the 1920s, when Jews were extremely prominent both in football and in many other areas of Kraków life.

Although a consolidated Polish national Premier League (the Ekstraklasa) was not founded until seven years later, the newly formed Polish Football Association (PZPN) established regional leagues in 1920, with the winners in each region playing off to win the national trophy. Four teams competed in the Kraków regional league in that first season – Wisla Kraków, Cracovia, Maccabi Kraków and Jutrzenka Kraków. These four clubs were sharply differentiated along ethnic and ideological lines.

Maccabi Kraków and Jutrzenka were exclusively Jewish clubs, but their relationship with each other was hostile nevertheless. Indeed, matches between them were known as the *Święta Wojna,* the Holy War. Maccabi Kraków espoused Zionism, while Jutrzenka was latterly attached to the socialist Bund movement, which sought to further the rights of Jewish workers within Poland and saw itself as the guardian of Yiddish (as opposed to Zionist Hebrew) culture.

The two non-Jewish clubs, Wisla and Cracovia, were also riven by an ideological divide. Cracovia's ethos was liberal and democratic, and the club accepted any player into its ranks, regardless of nationality and religion. In 1920s Kraków, what this really meant is that they accepted Jews. Wisla, on the other hand, stipulated in its constitution that no Jew could play for the club. Wisla's followers labelled Cracovia a 'Jewish club' simply for accepting Jews, even though most of their players were not.

Reports from the time reveal the extent of the anti-Jewish abuse that the non-Jewish club Cracovia was forced to endure. 'A number of eyewitnesses came to give evidence at our office,' reported *Tygodnik Sportowy*, a weekly Zionist sports newspaper, after one game between Wisla and Cracovia in October 1924. Among the spectators' accusations were that 'two top-ranking officers, majors, and a certain captain, sitting in and under the boxes in the central stand at the Wisła stadium, shouted "half-breeds, Yids, off with the Jews!"'; that 'after the match people shouted "long live the purely Polish team"'; that the (Wisla) player (Mieczysław) Balcer told one of the linesmen that 'we will deal with the Jews here – away with the Jews! – and I'll deal with you too'; and that spectators shouted 'beat the Jews, go back to Kazimierz!'

One hundred years on, with the Kraków Jewish population destroyed and no Jew having played for Cracovia for decades, rival fans still closely associate the non-Jewish Cracovia with Jews. Cracovia still wear the red-and-white striped shirts of the depicted figures making their way to Auschwitz, and their nickname is still Pasy ('The Stripes'), hence the hashtag 'Pasyontour' on the graffiti. Some of Cracovia's modern-day fans have even responded to the vitriol directed against them by appropriating the club's wrongly attributed Jewish heritage as a badge of honour, calling themselves the 'Jude Gang'.

In the Cracovia team for that match in 1924 was Leon Sperling, by that time an established Polish international. Józef Klotz, meanwhile, was then playing for Jutrzenka, whose intense enmity with Maccabi Kraków was finally terminated in 1939 when both clubs were shut down by the authorities, after which their bitterly divided sets of fans were hunted down and murdered in exactly the same way. In the absence of these two clubs, the contemporary derby between Cracovia and Wisla has assumed sole ownership of 'the holy war' epithet. During these games, vicious anti-Jewish chants emanate from the mouths of people who have never heard of either Jutrzenka or Maccabi Kraków – and have never met a Jew.

Confused? Perhaps the words of Jean-Paul Sartre can help to clarify the matter: 'If the Jew did not exist, the antisemite would invent him.'

* * *

Before they broke through and made their names in football, we again see the very different ways in which Józef Klotz and Leon Sperling viewed their own identity due to their contrasting upbringing.

Prior to the introduction of a more comprehensive conscription system some years later for those aged twenty-one and over, Klotz hurried to volunteer for the army as soon as he turned eighteen. According to research by the historian Jarosław Rokicki, he was first stationed, from March 1918, in a Galician infantry regiment within the imperial Austro-Hungarian army in Tarnów, seventy-five kilometres east of Kraków.* From November 1918, he joined the sixth infantry regiment of the independent army of the nascent Polish state as it sought to consolidate its highly fluid and disputed borders in the Polish–Ukrainian war, and later defend them against a Soviet regime hungry to expand its empire. His regiment saw action first against the Ukrainians and later against Soviet forces, for control of places such as Lida (in what is now Belarus), Vilnius (capital of modern-day Lithuania) and Daugavpils (now in Latvia). In March 1920, he was discharged from fighting duties but still served as a volunteer in the medical unit at the front for several months.

On the other hand, there is no record of Leon Sperling making himself available for military service for empire or nation.

Both had started out in the youth team at Jutrzenka as teenagers during the time of the First World War. In its early years after its

* Klotz would have felt at home in Tarnów. The Jewish population of Tarnów before the Holocaust was 25,000, nearly half the city's population. This increased still further after the German invasion of 1939 due to the influx of Jewish refugees. Almost all were murdered, mostly in the death camps at Bełżec and Auschwitz. Although some 700 Jews returned to the city after liberation, virtually all of them soon fled to escape antisemitism from the local population.

establishment in 1910, before the Bundists began their highly organised takeover around a decade or so later, Jutrzenka was simply considered a club for the Jewish working classes, without the subsequent ideological hostility towards Zionism and religious Orthodoxy. It would therefore still have been a palatable proposition for Sperling and his family as he embarked on his footballing education.

By the time Klotz had returned from his military adventures, however, Sperling had moved to rivals Cracovia. The stage was now set for them both to hit the heights in their own distinctive ways. For they were as different as footballers as they were as Jews.

At a height of 1.85 metres (around six foot one), Klotz was a tall, slender and graceful player, a natural athlete, with descriptions of his prime playing days bringing to mind comparisons with the likes of Alan Hansen or Rio Ferdinand of the modern era. He quickly built a reputation as one of the best defenders in the newly formed regional leagues, with an ability not just to stop opponents but to pass the ball intelligently from the back and build attacks.

He was also a consummate team player, with the instinct of a trained solider to come to the aid of colleagues in need of support. 'He is a footballing philanthropist,' *Tygodnik Sportowy* put it in 1921. 'He runs towards wherever there is danger. He leaves his post and benevolently fights wherever he thinks his team is in trouble.'

In the days when teams lined up with only two at the back, Klotz formed a highly respected defensive partnership for Jutrzenka alongside Ignacy Offen.* His ability as a deadly striker of the ball from both free kicks and penalties served as another string to his bow.

Despite his undoubted ability, Józef Klotz (nicknamed Józek in his

---

* Ignacy Offen was a dentist by profession. He fled to Romania at the start of the war. His wife Selma was still in Kraków in 1941. Their fate is unknown, the latter presumably murdered.

family) faced stiff competition even to be the best player in a family that excelled in sport. The Polish press referred to him as Klotz I to distinguish him from his younger brothers, Jan (Janek, or Klotz II – an extremely pacy left-winger), and Salomon (Samek, or Klotz III), who also both represented Jutrzenka. A surviving team photo from the time shows Józek and Janek posing together in the club's black-and-white striped shirts.

While the primary responsibility for Klotz was to blunt opposition attacks, Sperling performed at the other end of the pitch, probing, weaving and creating. Józef Kałuża, a centre-forward whose outstanding goalscoring record for Cracovia and the Polish national team owed much to Sperling's inventiveness, later remembered him as 'an excellent left winger, top-class technician, a great individualist'. Kałuża compared Sperling to Cracovia's winger on the right side, Stanisław Mielech: 'His style of play was very close to Mielech's; Sperling was not as fast as the latter but was superior to him in the flexibility of his moves and the quality of his shots.'

The writer Henryk Vogler, meanwhile, described him as 'the most outstanding left-winger in the history of Polish football', some statement from a football fanatic who died in 2005, aged ninety-three. 'Leon Sperling ... nicknamed "Muniu" by the spectators,' wrote Vogler, 'was able to manoeuvre his opponents with his skilful dribbling, culminating in an accurate shot or enabling his teammates to score.'*

* There is no Polish word which links directly with Sperling's nickname Muniu. After viewing various online discussions of this particular nickname among Jewish genealogists, I have come to the conclusion that Muniu is short for his Hebrew name, possibly Menachem, Emanuel or Menashe. (Menashe is particularly likely because that was his paternal grandfather's name. I also suspect that he had a second Hebrew name – Leib or Arieh, meaning 'lion' (hence Leon) in Yiddish or Hebrew respectively.) Given Sperling's Orthodox, Yiddish-speaking background, this explanation of his nickname would make sense. The fact that he was so widely known by football fans as Muniu also demonstrates how deeply Jewish culture and language had penetrated into wider Polish society.

Andrzej Gowarzewski, in his encyclopaedia of Polish footballers from between the wars, offers up a similar description: 'A wizard with the ball, with dazzling technique, excellent dribbling, smooth and effortless crossing ability, applauded by even the most discerning of spectators.' He was the ultimate mercurial showman, flaunting his skills to an appreciative crowd, even arguably sometimes to the detriment of his efficiency as a player. 'Sperling had perhaps his best performance in recent years for the national team,' commented *Kurjer Sportowy* later in his career, in 1925. 'This is primarily because he completely abandoned his dancing moves and managed to get his crosses in on time.'

Sperling was the first of the two to achieve prominence, a regular in the 1921 Cracovia side that won the Polish national championship at a canter. The team first came top of the four-team Kraków league and then romped home in the round-robin against the winners of the various regional competitions. In all, Cracovia played fourteen games in the two leagues, winning all but one, scoring sixty-four and conceding ten in the process.

Heavily contributing to Cracovia's total dominance was a new style of passing football that had recently been pioneered elsewhere in Central Europe, not least by the Jewish coach of the Austrian national team Hugo Meisl and the Jewish players of MTK Budapest. Whereas other teams in Poland persisted with their emphasis on physical strength, Cracovia out-foxed them all with intelligence, slick teamwork and skill.

Tygodnik Sportowy hailed brain's victory over brawn after Cracovia hammered Polonia Warsaw 7–1 in May 1921:

> The team from Warsaw consists of tall, strong, athletic and well-trained sportsmen … but as they haven't developed enough football

> and tactical skills, they were bound to lose against the swift and well-organised Cracovia team ... They haven't managed to depart from the old-fashioned style of hitting long, high balls instead of short passing on the floor ... Cracovia's team is a perfect example of the difference between the old and the new style of playing and the match result was the inevitable consequence of this difference.

The return fixture between the two clubs took place in Warsaw at the end of the same month. But being away from home did little to stop the alert and mobile Cracovia attackers running rings round the burly yet flummoxed Polonia defence. In attendance that day was one of Cracovia's most ardent admirers, the Polish Head of State, Marshal Józef Pilsudski, a football enthusiast who later said that 'Cracovia is the club that taught me to be interested in sport'. Writing in 1937, Józef Kałuża recalled that 'we crushed [Polonia] 6–0 thanks to the fantastic work by our attack line of Mielech, [Bolesław] Kotapka, Kałuża, [Adam] Kogut and Sperling. Piłsudski was so excited by our performance that contrary to what had been planned beforehand he remained till the end of the match'.

Sperling, who was also so gifted at playing chess that he represented Kraków at inter-city tournaments, was certainly the antithesis of the muscular but unthinking athlete that had previously been considered the footballing norm. As one might imagine for an impish winger of this type, he was small and thin, standing at 1.64 metres (around five foot four), and known for never heading the ball. Descriptions of him evoke images from footballing folklore of other tricky little wingers hugging the touchline, such as Jimmy Johnstone of Celtic, a breed of player that has gone somewhat out of fashion in the modern era.

Sperling did not have 'physical attributes', confirmed Kałuża, but he made up for that with 'strong legs and a vivid imagination'. There is a picture of the Poland team taken before the game against Sweden in Stockholm in 1922. Klotz and Sperling are sitting cross-legged either side of the Wisla Kraków goalkeeper Mieczysław Wiśniewski. While the rangy Klotz looks uncomfortable, not quite knowing what to do with his long limbs, Sperling takes to the task as if he is sitting in the hall at primary school assembly. Nevertheless, opponents who mistook the slight frame for weakness or vulnerability would do so at their peril. As we shall see, a proud and uncompromising nature lurked within.

The young player was a revelation in Cracovia's victorious 1921 season, earning constant praise from a besotted media. 'Sperling is magnificent – he is definitely the most skilful player in Poland,' reported *Tygodnik Sportowy* after Czarni Lwów were meted out familiar treatment by Cracovia in a 6–1 defeat. 'He never disappoints and always creates danger for the opponents with his mathematically measured crosses of the ball and his beautiful half-volleys.'

His stand-out performances for Cracovia earned him selection for the inter-city Zelenski Cup match between Kraków and Lviv in June 1921. The competition between Kraków and Lviv – named after the first president of the Polish Football Federation, Ludwik Zelenski – had started in 1912 and normally featured two games a year, one held in each city. The rules stated that the first of the two teams to win three games in succession would take the trophy, and the competition would then cease. Before Poland made its international bow in late 1921, the fixture attracted more attention than any other in the footballing calendar.

Since the subsequent Poland team was built mainly around players from the two cities (with players from Kraków dominating), the matches eventually became an ideal platform for players to showcase their talents in front of the national selectors.

Sperling rose to this particular occasion, setting up star strikers Kałuża and Wisla's Henryk Reyman for Kraków's goals in a 2–1 victory. It was certainly an opportune time to display his wares. After being rejected by several nations due to the pervasive ill feeling after recent conflicts, the Polish Football Federation eventually managed to arrange its first-ever game in international football, to be held in Budapest in December 1921 against a powerful Hungary side.

Twenty-two players were initially selected for the squad, whittled down to thirteen after a series of warm-up games in Kraków. Leon Sperling, the 21-year-old Orthodox Jew, was to make the cut for this historic match.

* * *

In actual fact, Sperling was one of seven Jews to take the field that day. In the Hungary team were the captain Vilmos Kertész, Zoltán Blum, Gyula Mándi, György Molnár and Jenö Wiener (the great József Braun was missing, having broken his tibia in the match against Sweden the previous month). Playing for Poland alongside Sperling was another Kraków Jew, his Cracovia teammate Ludwik Gintel, a right-sided defender who stood out for his footballing intelligence, fierce competitiveness and varied passing range.*

The difficult snowy conditions worked in Poland's favour, acting as a leveller against superior opposition, and the team returned home with a respectable 1–0 defeat. Moreover, Sperling acquitted himself

---

* Gintel represented Poland twelve times. Later in his career, he transformed himself into a forward and was the top scorer in the Polish league in the 1928 season with twenty-eight goals, including five hat-tricks. At the outbreak of the Second World War, he escaped to British-controlled Palestine via Romania. In July 1973, after discovering that he was terminally ill, he committed suicide by jumping out of his sister's third-floor apartment in Tel Aviv.

well, taking the eye of the *Przegląd Sportowy* correspondent. 'Sperling was the best in attack,' read the match report. 'He launched several promising forays, but his teammates were not on the same wavelength.' This lack of cohesion was disappointing and surprising, given that club teammates Kałuża and Mielech were playing alongside him up front.

Klotz came into the picture for the return match against Hungary in May 1922. He had impressed the watching Lustgarten by performing well against the likes of Sperling, Kałuża and Wacław Kuchar in two trial fixtures organised by the footballing authorities the previous week, in which a team made up of hopefuls for the national team (also including Klotz's younger brother, Janek (Klotz II)) beat the current first-choice line-up on both occasions.

And so it was that Józef Klotz and Leon Sperling were both selected to play in an event billed by the newspaper *Tygodnik Sportowy* as a 'landmark day ... a breakthrough in the history of Polish football ... the first international match in our own land.' One can only imagine the pride generated in their respective families, whose modest homes were just a matter of a few minutes' walk from the match, to be held in front of a 16,000-capacity crowd at Cracovia's stadium in the Blonia, a vast meadow outside the centre of Kraków.*

Klotz and Sperling were not the only Kraków Jews to inspire such feelings of joy. Also in the Poland set-up were the coach Lustgarten, Gintel and Zygmunt Krumholz, a brilliant finisher and Jutrzenka's

* Jutrzenka and Wisla Kraków also had their stadiums in the area of the Blonia (Maccabi Kraków, on the other hand, played right in the heart of the city, by Kazimierz and the Old Town). The modern-day ground of Wisla Kraków is called the Henryk Reyman stadium, named in memory of the legendary Wisla striker who played together with Klotz and Sperling in that match against Hungary. This stadium, home of a club whose history is blighted by antisemitism, is said to be built on the land once occupied by Jutzrenka, before its players, officials and fans were liquidated.

all-time top scorer, who was making his first and what was to be his only appearance for Poland.* **

Despite the excitement and build-up, the team still lost 3–0 to a depleted, Jewless Hungary side, whose first-choice players were competing the same day in an inter-city match between Berlin and Budapest. The newspaper *Sport Lwowski* bemoaned the defeat ('a pogrom' in its words) to 'a casually assembled team, when a better one was sent by the Hungarians to more worthy opponents. But those who turned up in Kraków were more than enough.'

Various newspapers were critical of Klotz's first-half performance on his debut, noting his poor positioning, indecisiveness and weak

---

* Lustgarten, a First World War veteran, survived seventeen gruelling years in the labour camps of the Soviet Gulag, before returning to Kraków and his beloved Cracovia in 1956, thereafter serving on the club's board. It was Lustgarten who had proposed the name Cracovia (the Latin name for Kraków) upon the club's founding in 1906.

** Krumholz scored seventeen goals for Jutrzenka in the 1927 season, the first in which the league was played on a national basis from the start (the Ekstraklasa), rather than being divided into regional leagues for the preliminary phase. When Jutrzenka were relegated that season, he went to play for Hasmonea Lwów, where he teamed up with Zygmunt Steuermann for one season in the Ekstraklasa. In 1941, he submitted a request to the German authorities in Kraków to receive the compulsory identity card that marked the cardholder as a Jew. He stated his profession as a self-employed maker of leather bags. (An earlier document, from 1939, identified him as a manufacturer of cardboard boxes.) The Polish sports historian Andrzej Gowarzewski writes in his encyclopedia that Krumholz was murdered in Sambir, also in 1941. I don't know where Gowarzewski got this information, and cannot therefore verify its authenticity. There is no information on Krumholz in the Yad Vashem database. If Gowarzewski's information is indeed true, I don't know why Krumholz would have ended up in Sambir. Perhaps he went to hide with Steuermann in the latter's home town? As he was a Jewish international footballer who was murdered in the Holocaust, Krumholz qualifies for my team. Football managers often say that the most difficult job they have is to tell one of their players that he has not been selected for a big game. I would wager that no football manager has ever felt as bad as I do for not being able to select players such as Krumholz. But the competition, particularly in forward positions, was too intense.

tackling. Perhaps this could be put down to nerves on such a big occasion (*Tygodnik Sportowy* remarked that he 'appeared tense'), because the general consensus was that he improved markedly as the game wore on. 'Klotz was very weak until the break, but in the second half he completely fulfilled his task,' reported *Wiadomości Sportowe*. 'Klotz's display constantly improved, and he played more confidently … several times, he brilliantly thwarted very dangerous situations,' agreed *Tygodnik Sportowy*. In its post-match ratings, *Sport Lwowski* concluded that Klotz was 'individually good, but was not a good fit with (his defensive partner) Gintel'.

He had clearly done enough in the eyes of the selectors to be retained for the match in Sweden a couple of weeks later. As indeed had Sperling, whom *Tygodnik Sportowy* praised for being one of the team's two most dangerous forward players against Hungary, along with Józef Kałuża.

* * *

Klotz rose to the occasion in Stockholm, overcoming the nerves that had plagued his debut and registering a superb performance at the back. He perhaps benefited from the absence of Gintel who had to stay behind in Kraków to take a university entrance exam, and from a new-found defensive partnership with Cracovia's Stefan Fryc. 'Klotz turned out to be very good at challenging opponents, he gathered the ball nicely, broke out of defence superbly, always came out victorious in duels, and saved the day several times with his pace,' enthused *Tygodnik Sportowy*.

His conversion of the historic penalty was of course the crowning moment of his display in the team's victory against a Sweden team that had earned a creditable away draw in their previous game against a strong Czechoslovakia side. In an interview in *Przegląd Sportowy* in 1937, fifteen years after the event, Klotz revealed how he was selected to take the penalty in preference to renowned goalscorers such as Kałuża and Kuchar. 'After the referee blew the whistle to award the penalty, the question arose as to who would take the penalty,' he said. 'At first, somebody else was suggested, not me. The captain of our team was (Tadeusz) Synowiec (of Cracovia) who had known me from Kraków, and he knew that I was a good penalty taker. He told me to take it ... There was no time to think too long.'

The domestic Swedish press was particularly taken by his composure at such a suspenseful moment. In his finest hour, Klotz evidently exuded an alluring calm, the personification of cool. 'The right-sided defender, the tall and handsome Klotz, was summoned and shot the ball into the goal just past the Swedish goalkeeper (Frithiof) Rudén,' reported *Svenska Dagbladet*. 'He executed this action with grace and extraordinary elegance; the ball lodged in the top left-hand corner. Rudén had no chance of saving it.'

A couple of weeks later, Klotz seemed to have the world at his feet when he again excelled, this time in Kraków's resounding victory over Lwów in the Zelenski Cup. However, Stockholm was to be the pinnacle of his achievements. Moreover, his demise appears to have been at least partially self-inflicted. He irreparably damaged his relations with the footballing authorities for failing to show up after being selected for the subsequent international match, away in Romania in September 1922.

The Polish Football Federation cited his 'inadequate and disingenuous explanations for his failure to go to Romania' and accused him of 'an unsportsmanlike lifestyle, a desire to have fun at all costs, while keeping company that was not always the best'. Only an intervention by the Jutrzenka club management succeeded in commuting an international ban from the initial three years to a more lenient three weeks.

Nevertheless, the die had been cast and his star quickly began to fade. His form fell noticeably in the 1923 season; he was ignored for the Zelenski Cup matches that year. 'Offen was emphatically better than Klotz I who has not been himself all season,' reported *Przegląd Sportowy* after one particular defeat against Cracovia.

He did recapture some form in 1924, for example starring alongside his 18-year-old brother Salomon (Klotz III) in a much celebrated 1–0 victory against Cracovia. 'The absolutely outstanding display from Klotz I without doubt demonstrates that he is the best defender in Kraków,' reported the magazine *Stadjon*. However, neither the Kraków city nor the national selectors appeared to agree. He left Jutrzenka for good at the end of the season, trying his luck instead with the Zionist club Maccabi Warsaw.

* * *

The change of scene failed to revive a flagging career. A *Przegląd Sportowy* report of a 7–0 thrashing for Maccabi Warsaw by local rivals Varsovia in May 1925 suggests that Klotz's former pace had deserted him. 'It is difficult to assess whether Varsovia's successes should be attributed more to the effective play of their attack, or to tactical errors made by Maccabi's defence, led by Klotz, the former Jutrzenka Kraków star,' reported the paper. 'This player, good on the ball and technically confident, was beset by poor positioning, and could not cope very well with the speed of his opponents.' Meanwhile, a journalist from *Trybuna Polska* lamented that the big-name signing was not all he was cracked up to be: 'It was hoped that he would be a dam on which the attack of any team would flounder. But Klotz today is no longer the Klotz of two years ago.'

Soon after that game, Józef Klotz disappears from view entirely. There are no reports in the available archives of him playing after 1925. So how can we explain his precipitous decline from the giddy heights in the space of just three years? It is not as if age had caught up with him. He was still then only twenty-five.

As Gintel's absence from the Sweden match suggests, football was then very much an amateur sport and many of the players would not have devoted the energy and focus to it that are common nowadays. Indeed, the archives at the Jagiellonian University in Kraków show that Klotz had himself embarked on a course in Law for the final semester of the 1920/21 academic year. He had continued these studies throughout the following year, when he was at the peak of his football career.

According to these documents, the course was extremely demanding (more than sixty hours of study per week were recommended). His failure to prioritise his football, possibly in part due to his studies, appears to have led to his non-appearance at the Romania game and to his subsequent ban. Once the ban was imposed, he lacked the will to put in all the work necessary to fight his way back, when he had other concerns of equal, if not greater, importance to him.*

One of those considerations would have been his marriage in September 1924 to 18-year-old Regina Witkowski, originally from

---

* The *Svenska Dagbladet* report from the Sweden game described Klotz as 'handsome'. In the registration of enrolment for the 1921/22 academic year at the Jagiellonian University, one box asks whether there is anything unusual about the student. The administrator wrote '*przystojny*', meaning handsome – perhaps a clue as to why 'he was keeping company that was not always the best'.

Włocławek.* He moved to Warsaw soon after the wedding, feasibly because Regina had family there, or because he was pursuing a business venture or trade or had been offered a job there. Given Maccabi Warsaw's comparatively low status, the move certainly can't be attributed to any burning footballing ambition. Maccabi were not even good enough to warrant a place in the top regional league of the capital city.

We can also present a rather different theory on Klotz's decline. There is no available evidence that he returned to his studies for the 1922/23 academic year, or indeed that he completed his degree. Perhaps he had failed crucial exams around the time of the Romania game in September 1922, or was retaking them in order to continue with his course? We shall soon see evidence from a few years later indicating that, at some point, he completely lost his way in life. It could be that the rot set in as early as the autumn of 1922 and he found it difficult to regain his equilibrium.

Nor should we completely discount the possible role of antisemitism in his rapid footballing fall from grace. By acquainting ourselves with the country's history and what was going on in other parts of society at that time, we can make an educated guess that not everyone on the disciplinary committee of the Polish Football Federation in 1922 had Jews down as their favourite people. For example, an unofficial *numerus clausus* was being established throughout Poland around that time to limit the number of Jewish students at university. It is safe

* In October 1939, Jews in Włocławek were the first in Europe to be forced by the Nazi authorities to wear stars on their clothing to identify them as Jews. During that year, there were around 13,500 Jews living in Włocławek, around a quarter of the total population. Many were soon sent to the ghettos of other cities, and those left in Włocławek were moved into their own ghetto in October 1940. Between 24 and 27 April 1942, the ghetto was liquidated when the remaining Jews, mostly women, children and the elderly, were sent to be murdered in gas vans at Chełmno death camp. A small number of surviving Jews returned after the war, but the community had completely evaporated by the end of the 1960s.

to stay, at the very least, that Jewish outsiders had to work far harder than the host population to be accepted, or alternatively to return to the fold once ostracised.

Nonetheless, for a few years after the departure of Józef Klotz from the international stage, it was still possible for a Jewish footballer to represent Poland. After all, Leon Sperling managed it, and he was certainly no goody two-shoes.

* * *

Sperling's tenure at the highest reaches of Polish football was as long as Klotz's was brief. He was still a key figure in the Cracovia team that won the Polish national league in 1932, his third such championship. By the time he had hung up his boots, he had made 381 appearances for Cracovia (the third highest for any Cracovia player before the war) and played sixteen times for Poland, scoring two goals for the national team. He had also represented Kraków on twenty-two occasions, including the triumphant game in 1925 when his team beat Lviv for the third successive time to secure the prized Zelenski Cup for good. Sperling's prolonged contribution to Polish football was recognised in March 1931, when the country's president, Ignacy Mościcki, awarded him the Silver Cross of Merit for sporting achievements.

While Klotz may have had his mind on other matters, Sperling's longevity can be attributed to a professionalism that was far from a given in this amateur era. Interviewed after his retirement by *Przegląd Sportowy* in 1935, a year in which Cracovia plummeted from the club's previous heights to be relegated from the Ekstraklasa, Sperling bemoaned the attitude of the players now sporting the red and white stripes, comparing it unfavourably to the dedication and seriousness of the championship-winning teams of yesteryear.

'The football of the past was all about preparing for what was about to happen on the field,' said Sperling.

> A player's preparation used to be more rigorous than today, from winter [off-season] training to how he conducted his private life, always keeping fitness in mind. There was also greater collaboration within the team, which helped to produce harmonious interaction among the eleven on the field. We would sometimes get together and spend long hours drawing up plans on paper for the campaign ahead. There was a thorough mental preparation, which was then transformed into facts on the field.

As his high-level participation in chess might suggest, Sperling thought deeply about football strategy.

His reputation, even far afield, seemingly preceded him. In April 1923, Cracovia embarked on a tour to play matches in Sweden and Denmark. The travelling party, comprising the team, management and journalists, was greeted by a large group of Danish sportspeople at Aarhus railway station. 'From conversations, it turned out that they knew many of our players…,' reported *Przegląd Sportowy.* 'They enquired in particular about Sperling.' The star winger certainly lived up to the billing. 'Sperling is man-marked closely,' wrote the same newspaper about the subsequent game in which Cracovia trounced Aarhus 6–1. 'But he chooses to do whatever he wants with his opponents.'

The Scandinavian tour coincided with the very peak of Sperling's career, when he was both adored by spectators and an indisputable pick for the national team. *Przegląd Sportowy* held a readers' poll in the spring of 1923, asking them to name their preferred players for the Poland squad. Sperling came in top, with 75 per cent of the votes cast. The watching journalists were unanimous in their praise of Sperling a few weeks later in June, despite Poland going down 2–1 to Yugoslavia in Kraków. 'Sperling and Gintel were the best players,' claimed *Przegląd Sportowy.* 'Sperling's solo actions were beautifully performed,' purred *Tygodnik Sportowy.*

The latter newspaper asked the watching Gyula Bíró for his expert comments on the game. Bíró, a Jew from Budapest, was a highly experienced and recently retired playing legend who was now working as coach of Maccabi Kraków. He would certainly have known a thing or two about the game, making his unstinting praise of Sperling all the more powerful. 'I very much regretted that Sperling had to play alone without support, as it was always a pleasure for me when he was in possession of the ball,' said Bíró. 'I wish the Hungary national team had a left-winger like Sperling.' (Hungary's left-winger at that time was another Jew, Árpád Weisz – see Chapter 5 – a top player in his own right).*

But as with all top players, there were certainly bumps in the road for Sperling. Bíró was appointed coach of the Polish national team for the much-anticipated 1924 Olympics, held in Paris. The football tournament included several nations that had recently gained independence from the Russian and Austro-Hungarian empires and were desperate to make a name for themselves on the international sporting stage. Poland was very much among that number.

However, Bíró and his Poland team were unlucky to be drawn in the first round in the knockout tournament against a star-studded Hungary line-up that included József Braun and the future legendary

* Gyula Bíró had represented Hungary on what was then a phenomenal thirty-six occasions, having made his debut at the age of sixteen, still the second youngest player ever to play for that country. He played for MTK Budapest in a number of positions, including goalkeeper. Having coached throughout the continent, he saw the writing on the European wall in 1937. He made the wise move to Mexico, where he died in 1961.

coach Béla Guttmann among others, and were soundly beaten 5–0. This time outmuscled by opponents who could also match his exceptional technical ability, Sperling came in for significant criticism from a traumatised Polish press corps. 'Sperling and (Henryk) Reyman took no more part in the game than the referee,' scoffed *Stadjon* magazine. 'Yes, they ran after the ball, but if by chance they touched it, they immediately gave it away to the Hungarians.'

* * *

Like Klotz, Sperling also experienced some notable clashes with the powers that be. In November 1922, the representative Kraków team took on Bielsko from Southern Poland in an inter-city match at the Cracovia stadium. With his team leading 2–1 at half-time, Sperling unilaterally decided he would not return for the second half, complaining that he felt isolated and redundant on the pitch, receiving few passes. 'I feel too cold as my teammates are not playing with me,' was his reported sarcastic comment. (It is worth at least noting that there were five Wisla players on Sperling's team, and we may speculate that not all will have been entirely enamoured with the self-confident little Jew and his too-clever-by-half party tricks on the left wing.)

The predictably furious press reaction to his refusal to take the pitch took on a schoolmasterly tone. 'The player will be taken care of by the authorities, who will teach him about his responsibilities and about match discipline,' declared *Wiadomości Sportowe*. Nor was that the end of Sperling's dramatic afternoon. 'During the second half, the crowd in the centre stand witnessed a scandalous incident between Mr Sperling, a Cracovia player, and a member of Cracovia who is also a fellow of the Referees' Council, ending with a slap,' continued the newspaper, without elaborating on who dealt the blow. 'This unpleasant incident arouses understandable distaste in every sportsman and is worthy of censure, especially since it is not the first incident of this kind in the Cracovia stands.'

Przegląd Sportowy later reported that the Polish Football Association 'punished Leon Sperling of Cracovia with a disqualification until 1 April 1923 for arbitrarily leaving the pitch as a representative player during the inter-city match between Bielsko and Kraków'. As the Polish season then ran from March to November (the month in which the incident took place), the actual impact of the ban was minimal.*

In August 1924, Sperling was in the thick of it again, this time the victim of an antisemitic referee. Cracovia were playing away at Warta Poznań, in a match refereed by a Mr Wachsmann, also from Poznań, a large city in Western Poland. In the twentieth minute of the first half, Cracovia players surrounded Wachsmann, claiming that a goal scored against them should have been ruled out for offside. Wachsmann took particular exception to Sperling and sent him off, a decision that was not exactly warmly received. 'He [Sperling] refused to leave the field and chaos erupted,' reported *Tygodnik Sportowy.* 'However, he did

* There were up to 6,000 Jews in Bielsko in 1939, around 20 per cent of the population. On 3 September of that year, German troops marched into Bielsko and immediately burned two synagogues. In 1941, a ghetto was created, but it was liquidated on 20 June 1942, when approximately 400 Jews were transported to Auschwitz and murdered. The remaining population was resettled in other ghettos, where the vast majority were murdered. After the war, several hundred surviving Jews moved to the city, now merged with nearby Biala to form Bielsko-Biala. In June 1967, the Polish Communist government launched an antisemitic campaign in response to Israel's victory in the Six-Day War against the neighbouring Soviet-backed Arab nations. Almost all the remaining Jewish residents of Bielsko-Biala managed to leave Poland in the aftermath of the campaign.

finally walk off the pitch, having been asked to do so by the Cracovia captain [Tadeusz Synowiec].'

In an article published a few days later in *Przegląd Sportowy*, Synowiec explained the circumstances behind Sperling's dismissal: 'Sperling, in order to quieten down [his teammate, Zygmunt] Chruściński, who was being exceptionally vociferous [in his complaints], told him in an explicit manner to be quiet. The referee then said, "It doesn't matter if it was said to a team mate or not, the spectators in Poznań are not used to such indecent language."'

The general tumult continued immediately after Sperling eventually left the field. 'The interrupted game is started by the referee with a drop ball, when suddenly [the Cracovia player, Józef] Kubiński strikes the referee's stomach with his leg, quite deliberately,' reported *Sport Ilustrowany*. Unsurprisingly, given his later comments, Wachsmann did not dish out the same punishment to (the non-Jewish) Kubiński as he had to Sperling, despite the much more serious offence.

After having blown for half-time, Wachsmann was reported by several outlets to have turned to the crowd as he was leaving the field, exclaiming that 'they should not bring their Jews [from Kraków] to Poznań'. The comment poured fuel on the flames, and the scenes in the dressing room at the break certainly put Alex Ferguson's teacups in the shade. 'Wachsmann threatened [Józef] Kałuża with a gun in his hand, because Kałuża reacted disapprovingly to Wachsmann's comments about Cracovia's Jewish players,' reported *Tygodnik Sportowy*. According to Synowiec, Wachsmann had been carrying the same gun in his pocket while refereeing the game on the pitch and was heard to say at half-time that 'it will be surprising if someone isn't killed here'.

Although Kałuża refused to return to the pitch, the match was somehow completed, albeit in an atmosphere of uninhibited Jew hatred. 'It has to be mentioned that the antisemitism which is typical for Poznań was evident throughout the stadium,' reported the liberal German-language newspaper *Posener Neueste Nachrichten* (Poznań had a substantial minority ethnic German population).*

Despite these incidents, the latter of which followed soon after his disappointing performance at the Olympics, Sperling's persistently high-quality displays for Cracovia always kept him firmly in the national selectors' thoughts. Indeed, his final appearance for Poland, towards the end of Cracovia's championship-winning season of 1930, came more than four years after his penultimate one.

It turned out to be a fitting denouement. Poland ran out 3–0 winners against Sweden in the same Olympic stadium where Sperling and Klotz, the Jewish boys from Kraków, had combined for the country's first-ever goal back in 1922. All Sperling's teammates from that famous day had long ceased to play international football. He succeeded in outlasting them all – if only, alas, in the footballing sense of the word.

* * *

It would be nice to describe in detail what happened to Józef Klotz, Leon Sperling and to all their families in the years leading up to and including the European Holocaust, as if I were narrating a story in *Who Do You Think You Are?* or another similar television series that

* In 1939, there was a small Jewish population (of up to 3,000) living in Poznań. Soon after the German invasion of 1939, the Jews were deported to Ostrow Lubelski and other towns in Eastern Poland, eventually to be murdered. In April 1940, the Star of David was removed from the opulent and spacious New Synagogue on Stawna Street, a symbolic and triumphant pronouncement that Poznań was now *Judenrein* (cleansed of Jews). On the festival of Rosh Hashana (Jewish New Year) in 1942, the Germans threw a gala party to celebrate the synagogue's conversion into a swimming pool. The building continued to be used for that purpose until 2011, by which time it had fallen into disrepair. The Jewish community in Poznań today is tiny and barely functioning.

offers neat and comprehensive life stories of a celebrity's forebears. But the Holocaust doesn't quite work like that.

In an online presentation from 2020 entitled 'The Search for the Six Million Names', Haim Gertner of Yad Vashem explained the scale of the challenge confronting Holocaust researchers. 'We know most of the names of the Jewish victims murdered on the Western side of Europe,' he says.

> We don't know all their histories, but we know at least the names. But as for the names of the people that were murdered on the Eastern side of Europe, then the further East we go, the less we know … the Einsatzgruppen would come in the morning, take everyone from the village and murder the entire village in a day, or in a few hours. Everything vanished, and we don't have anyone to testify.*

One could also add that there was often nobody left on the planet, whether they were in close vicinity of the eventual murder or not, who had been acquainted in any way with a particular victim.

Indeed, Gertner reveals in this presentation that whereas Yad

* The names held by Yad Vashem come from a variety of sources – mostly from Pages of Testimony, one-page forms with relevant information submitted by surviving family members or friends and acquaintances – and also from any documented records relating to deportations, camps and ghettos. Yad Vashem has said that both early and more recent expert estimates of the total number of Jews murdered in the Holocaust arrive at a figure of somewhere between 5 and 6 million. Such estimates have primarily been reached by comparing pre-war census data with population estimates after the war. The number of six million was first mentioned by Dr Wilhelm Höttl, a senior member of the SS from Vienna, who testified at the trial of Adolf Eichmann in Jerusalem in 1961. Höttl recalled a conversation he had in 1944 with Eichmann, the meticulous spearhead of the complex logistical operations behind the deportation and mass murder of European Jewry. 'Eichmann … told me that, according to his information, some 6,000,000 Jews had perished by then – 4,000,000 in extermination camps and the remaining 2,000,000 through shooting by the Operations Units and through other causes, such as disease, etc,' Höttl said.

Vashem has 90 per cent of the victims' names in Germany, that proportion falls to 40 per cent in Poland and 30 per cent in Ukraine. (That proportion could well be a significant overestimate too. I have encountered a great deal of duplication in the lists, with for example the same victim submitted by multiple people, albeit with a slightly different spelling or biographical detail, such as date of birth.) Moreover, as Gertner himself admits, the circumstances of the murder of even those whose names have been collected may often be largely or entirely unknown.

All we can do is scour all the available archives, assess any available oral histories that are passed down, and build a patchwork narrative. But some very significant gaps often remain. Spending so long studying the career exploits of Klotz and Sperling and the other players in this book, and researching their family backgrounds and upbringing, sometimes even getting to know some of their relatives, left me deeply invested in their life journeys. Not being able to discover fundamental information about the fate of some of their closest family members has been a source of some considerable sadness and frustration for me personally.

Below is what we can know or can reasonably infer.

* * *

Information about the life of Józef Klotz after his move with his new wife Regina to Warsaw in 1925 and the rapid disintegration of his footballing career is scant to say the least.

Much of the capital city was obliterated during the war. There were the massive German air raids of September 1939, the razing of the Warsaw Ghetto after the Jewish uprising of April and May 1943 and then a systematic demolition of the entire city by German forces in

1944 to punish the general population for the later uprising by the Polish resistance.* By the war's end, around 80 per cent of Warsaw's buildings lay in ruins. Not only, therefore, do we have the problem of the lack of surviving murder witnesses, as explained by Yad Vashem's Gertner, but nearly all pre-war documents containing biographical information, such as addresses, occupations or birth and death certificates, were also lost as a consequence of the city's destruction.

An invaluable source of information on Józef Klotz has been his nephew, Danny Dekel, who emigrated from Poland to Israel in 1950, together with his father Salomon and his older sister. Most of this information has come not from family sources but from his own research and collaboration with various interested institutions, such as the Historical Museum of Kraków, which in 2012 hosted an exhibition on the history of Jewish sport in the city.

The information therefore centres mostly on Klotz's football career, rather than his personal life. Dekel spent much of his youth in Israel in a kibbutz orphanage, away from his highly cultured but sick and poverty-stricken father, the former Jutrzenka player Salomon, who eventually died in 1961 when his son was only sixteen. 'Father did not speak much, most of the time he was silent, very pained by the reality he found himself in, one of financial hardship, loneliness, and a cultural gap (with Israeli society),' Dekel told me.

Two more of Józef's siblings, Janek and Genia, had died before Salomon. By the time Dekel had developed a passionate, adult interest in his uncle's life, the final sibling, Maniek (Moshe), had also died and

* The Warsaw Ghetto uprising was the first significant urban revolt against German occupation in Europe. No more than 1,000 young Jewish fighters from Zionist organisations held out against the might of the German army for four weeks, despite few arms and little military training and experience.

there was no one left to ask. His knowledge of Józef Klotz's* life story is therefore sketchy, although still invaluable.**

He does remember being told that Klotz remained in Warsaw after his time at Maccabi until his eventual murder in that city. This seems to be the consensus of post-war Polish footballing historians who have looked into the matter.

Documentary evidence of his existence there is lacking – that is, save for one intriguing exception. Research by the Genealogy Department of the Jewish Historical Institute in Warsaw uncovered one mention of Klotz from the summer of 1930. His name appeared in a *list gończy*, an arrest warrant for individuals suspected of committing a crime who have somehow evaded or escaped trial or detention. The list would have been distributed to police units and border guards and placed in newspapers.

Although the notice erroneously states his father's name as Ignacy, the rest of the relevant biographical information points to our man – born in 1900 in Kraków, mother's name Salomea, Jewish religion, dark hair. It reveals that Klotz had been working as a clerk and his last

* Remarkably, Józef was the only Klotz sibling to be murdered in the Holocaust. Janek died after a heart operation in 1936, at the age of thirty-four. Salomon, Genia and Maniek all escaped to the Soviet Union after the Nazi invasion of Poland in 1939. Salomon served in the Polish People's Army, which fought alongside the Red Army all the way to Berlin. Maniek served in another Polish army formed in the Soviet Union, run by General Władysław Anders, also comprised of Polish exiles and refugees.

** Danny Dekel was born Bogdan Klotz in Warsaw in 1945. He changed his name to Dekel in the early 1970s as the word 'klutz' (which has the same spelling as Klotz in the Hebrew language) means a clumsy, stupid or inept person in both Hebrew and Yiddish. 'I suffered a lot from this as a child, and it was very common to change the family name to a Hebrew name,' he told me. 'We chose the name Dekel, because we lived for many years in the Arava desert together with the palm trees ['dekel' means a palm tree in Hebrew]. I was the only one to change the name. Maniek remained a Klotz. Sometimes I'm sorry, maybe I was wrong. I was the only male child in the family.'

known residences were both in central Warsaw, on Ulica Chmielna and Ulica Widok.*

The notice states that Klotz had been convicted of contravening Article 574 in the criminal code, involving the appropriation of another person's moveable property (in layman's terms, likely to mean theft of cash or other valuable items) and carrying a minimum sentence of three months' imprisonment. We have to assume that Klotz was eventually apprehended for this crime, as he had fully emerged from the shadows in 1937 for an interview by *Przegląd Sportowy* about his famous goal in Stockholm, complete with a photograph of him looking dapper in a suit and rather older than in his playing days.

The crime would fit with a picture of a collapse in Klotz's fortunes following that goal. He dropped out of a prestigious university course, was banned by the international team when seemingly on the crest of a wave and his footballing form had fallen off a cliff within three years of Stockholm. Down on his luck, far away from the stabilising influence of his parents and siblings, unsettled and possibly rather desperate, it seems that he fell into criminality.

Dekel knew that his uncle Józef had a wife and daughter, although not their names. Two photos of them, reportedly taken at some point in the 1930s, were handed down to him. One was of the wife and daughter together and one just of the angelic-looking little girl herself. The girl looks around three years old in the first picture and a couple of years older in the second. I managed to find details of Klotz's marriage to Regina Witkowski in 1924 in a database of Kraków Jewish marriages but could find nothing on the birth of their daughter.

Józef's mother Szaindel (Salomea) died in 1941 in Podgórze, a district of Kraków, around the age of sixty. Podgórze was not where she

---

* The archives in Kraków reveal that he was the only Józef Klotz born in the city around 1900.

and her husband Markus had lived throughout their married lives, but where the ghetto was established in March of that year. Dekel does not believe that his grandmother was murdered, at least not directly through a bullet or gas. Nevertheless, her death was very likely to have been triggered by the malnutrition or disease that were already rampant in the cramped and insanitary ghetto.

At this point, Markus was all alone in Kraków. His eldest son Józef was in Warsaw and his other children had fled to the Soviet Union a couple of years before. It is Dekel's understanding that his grandfather Markus somehow managed to escape Kraków to join Józef in Warsaw. 'The family story has it that Markus hid in Warsaw until very near the end of the war, and the entry of the Red Army into Warsaw (January 1945),' says Dekel. 'The view was that eventually someone had informed on him and revealed his hiding place. From there he was caught and murdered. Whether he was murdered in Warsaw, or sent to a camp, I do not know.'

Dekel's father Salomon, who had fled to the Soviet Union in 1939, marched into Warsaw with the Polish People's Army, alongside the Red Army. 'My father found out the identity of the person who had informed on Markus, equipped himself with a gun and a motorcycle and searched for the informant throughout Warsaw for several days,' says Dekel. 'My sister used to say that he was lucky he didn't find the informant, because there was no telling how it could have ended.'

If Salomon was also looking for Józef's wife and daughter, his search would have been forlorn. There is no information on Regina and the daughter in any Holocaust archive of victims or – however unlikely – of survivors. Their lives, and deaths, have evaporated from history. Furthermore, the (presumably) murdered daughter of Józef and Regina Klotz does not even have a name, a cherubic symbol of the countless murdered Jews who ceased to exist in the public records, or in the memories of any living human being.*

As for Józef himself, he had probably been dead for some time before Salomon's arrival in Warsaw. 'My father rarely shared his thoughts and stories with me, but he did tell me what he had heard about the circumstances of Józef's murder,' said Dekel. 'Apparently, when someone on a Warsaw street recognised Józef, they called the Germans. My uncle was forced to pull down his trousers [to reveal whether he was circumcised] and he was shot in the street.'

Andrzej Gowarzewski wrote that Klotz was probably shot in 1941 in a bombed-out ruin of a building on Ulica Nowy Świat, one of the main streets in Warsaw. Nowy Świat was outside the Warsaw Ghetto in which Jews were forced to reside. The automatic death penalty for Jews leaving their designated area without permission was introduced in October 1941.

Gowarzewski does not reveal the original source of his claim, while Dekel himself never visited the alleged murder site. 'I wasn't sure whether the information was reliable, and I didn't want to have to endure the emotional turmoil,' Dekel told me. 'Does it really matter if it happened on one street corner, or on another?'

* * *

Leon Sperling was still playing some friendly matches for Cracovia in

* Regina's father was Eliasz Witkowski, and the family was from Włocławek. According to the archives of the Institute of National Remembrance in Poland, an Eliasz Witkowski from Włocławek was murdered in the Vilnius ghetto in 1942, aged sixty-seven. Regina's brother was Mojzesz Michuel. A Mojzesz Michuel Witkowski also appears on a list of detainees in the Vilnius ghetto, presumed murdered. I could not find out what happened to Regina's mother Penina, or to her sister Hana.

1934, combining this now more informal pastime with his work as a clerk at Bank Małopolski in Kraków.

In February 1935, he got married in Kraków to Sara Perla Ettinger, aged twenty-six, from Jarosław, a town in south-eastern Poland.* The couple moved into a flat on Ulica Krowoderska, around the corner from where Sperling had lived with his family from birth.

Research of the Hebrew press of the time by the Israeli journalist Asher Goldberg reveals that Sperling twice had the opportunity to emigrate to British-controlled Palestine, but tragically refused both offers. In 1925, Maccabi Tel Aviv embarked on a tour of Europe, the first club from the Land of Israel to do so. The team was led by Shimon Ratner (he later changed his surname to the Hebrew word Leumi), the star footballer in the country at that time. Ratner was a native of Kraków who had previously represented the great Zionist team, Hakoah Vienna.

In September 1925, the team arrived in the city of Ratner's birth, to massive excitement among the Jewish community there. Ratner invited Sperling to lead a Maccabi training session and then to have dinner with the team back at their hotel. Sperling met there with the Maccabi team management, including Yosef Yekutieli, who later founded the Maccabiah Games, to this day often referred to as the Jewish Olympics. The top brass made Sperling a proposition. If he signed for Maccabi Tel Aviv, they would pay him a fair salary, help him to find a supplementary job and secure accommodation for him.

---

* Immediately after the Germans entered Jarosław on 10 September 1939, the synagogue was set on fire. Two weeks later, the vast majority of the 7,000 Jews in Jarosław (around one third of the total population) were forcibly deported to what had become Soviet-occupied territory after the Nazi-Soviet pact of the previous month. In the summer of 1940, many of these refugees were sent by the Soviet authorities to Siberia. Almost all those who remained in the former Polish territories were murdered after Nazi Germany invaded the Soviet Union in June 1941.

Sperling, who was still at the peak of his club and international career, declined the offer.

Twelve years later, the Holy Land came knocking again. This time, with governmental and popular antisemitism in Poland clearly on the rise, Sperling's refusal is more difficult to rationalise.*

In 1937, a representative team from another Jewish sports organisation in Palestine – Hapoel – travelled to Poland. The team included Romanian-born Gedalyahu Fuchs, who had captained the Palestine national team, the forerunner of the Israel national team, in its first-ever international in 1934.**

Fuchs and his teammates were very aware of Sperling's reputation as one of the greats of Jewish football and they too invited him to take one of their training sessions. Highly impressed with his ideas and energy, they offered him a job coaching Hapoel in Palestine. Sperling, now newly married and with his mother and several siblings still living in close vicinity, politely shook his head, unwittingly signing his own death warrant. The Hapoel squad returned home accompanied by Sperling's copious notes on tactical strategies and training methods, but fatefully, not by the man himself.

In 1939, Sperling finally got his chance to put his many footballing theories into practice, but not in the way he might have wanted. As the Nazis took over Kraków, he fled east to Lviv. In the now Soviet city, he took a job as coach of Piszczewik, a team that represented the collectivised food industry.

He was not the only Jewish footballer from Kraków to make the same journey. Indeed, a sort of ex-pat commune of fleeing Jewish

* Large-scale anti-Jewish pogroms took place around this time in Grodno (June 1935), Przytyk (March 1936) and Brześć nad Bugiem (Brest) (May 1937).

** All eleven players in Palestine's first-ever international team were Jews. In the 7–1 defeat to Egypt, the team's sole goalscorer was Avraham Nudelman.

footballers sprang up in Lviv in the two years before the Nazis eventually arrived. As we have already seen, it is thought that Zygmunt Krumholz also ultimately decamped there, as well as Roman Grünberg, a top Cracovia player from just before the war.

There is little doubt that Sperling would also have come into close contact with Zygmunt Steuermann. For all we know, he may have even featured in some way in the legendary death match at Janowska. Indeed, a brief paragraph on Sperling in the *Przegląd Sportowy* issue dated 19 July 1945 announced that he 'perished in a camp in Lviv' (Janowska was the only camp in the city). Given its proximity to the war's end, and the resulting freshness of the witness information used, this report cannot be discounted.

Stefan Żywotko was one man who witnessed Sperling's activities at close hand during the latter's time in Lviv. Żywotko grew up in that city and enjoyed a long and successful coaching career in Poland from the 1950s onwards. In an interview published to mark his one hundredth birthday in 2020, Żywotko chatted with the Polish sports journalist Michal Zichlarz about his long life. He recalled his time in post-1939 Lviv, where he played as a young man for the reserve team of Piszczewik and experienced Sperling's scrupulous training methods.

'The entire Kraków elite was there [in Lviv],' he remembered. 'Muniu Sperling was a quiet man who had many players to help, those who had fled with him to Lviv. He instructed, conducted training, and the usual championship matches continued. Muniu Sperling was the spirit of this group of refugees.' Żywotko's words are invaluable in building a more complete picture of Sperling's character. Putting various stories and descriptions together, we can conclude that he was proud of the heritage that he was to be murdered for, strong-willed, logical, thoughtful, hard-working, an unassuming leader of men.

We don't know whether his wife Sara was with him during these two years up to the Nazi invasion. In fact, I could not find any documents on Sara's fate in the Holocaust. She too vanished from history. There is no evidence that she and Leon had any children, but that does not mean much.*

My attempts to find out what happened to Sperling's family was hampered by my inability to locate any living descendants with the requisite knowledge. Here is what we do know. Leon's father Salomon Wolf died in 1915 when his youngest son was a teenager. In 1942, Leon's mother Ruchel, then aged seventy-nine, and his sister Helena were murdered in the Bochnia ghetto, forty kilometres east of Kraków. Chaim (Henryk), his eldest brother, was also murdered in 1942, probably transported from Kraków to either Auschwitz or Bełżec to be gassed.**

The historian Jarosław Rokicki investigated how Leon Sperling's own murder was recounted in post-war anthologies of Polish sport and sportspeople. He advances two overlapping versions but does not elaborate on their ultimate original sources. (I could not discuss the subject with him. He died in 2020, shortly before I started research for this chapter.)

Rokicki's summary does not mention Janowska or any camp, although as we saw with the accounts of Steuermann's murder, some witnesses did mistakenly believe Janowska to be simply part of the Lviv ghetto. The first version put forward by Rokicki is that Sperling was shot dead by the Germans in the Lviv ghetto between the 15th and 20th December 1941, the first to the sixth day of Chanukah that year,

* I could find no information either on what happened to Sara's older sister Mina, her mother Frania, or her father Israel, during the Holocaust.

** Leon Sperling had at least four other older siblings. Bernard Dov died in Israel in 1976. I don't know whether he survived the Holocaust, or whether he left Europe before the war. I cannot find any information on what happened to Leon's sister Amalia, or to his brothers Faiwel or Emil.

a joyous festival that he would surely have sought to celebrate in some way even amid the pervasive misery. The second version is that this great Jewish footballer was shot dead by a drunken Gestapo officer in the Lviv ghetto around 20 December 1941. Just like Klotz, he would have been forty-one years old.

Maybe the end actually happened on 18 December, twenty years to the day since Poland's first-ever game, when little Muniu Sperling marched proudly on to that snow-bound pitch in Budapest, and wove his inimitable magic once again.

CHAPTER 4

THE GERMAN PATRIOT

Matches between Germany and the Netherlands have a special resonance for the football fan of the modern era. We think of the 1974 World Cup Final in Munich, or Frank Rijkaard spitting at Rudi Völler in Milan at the 1990 World Cup, as the pair trudged off the pitch having both been sent off. Sports commentators tiptoe diplomatically around the patent root cause of the bitter rivalry between these two great footballing nations – namely, the German occupation of the Netherlands in the Second World War. The Dutch midfielder Willem van Hanegem, who left the Munich pitch in tears after his team's defeat, was rather less circumspect. 'They murdered my father, sister and two brothers,' he is reported to have said. 'I am full of angst. I hate them.'

The history of this evocative fixture dates back even further than the first of Europe's mass conflagrations of the twentieth century, back when the two neighbouring countries were just setting out on their illustrious footballing journeys. Among these early encounters, the most dramatic took place in the charming city of Zwolle, in the north-east of the Netherlands, in March 1912.*

* There were around 800 Jews in Zwolle before the Holocaust. The first mass arrests of Jews in the city took place in October 1941, five months after the German invasion. An unknown number of these Jews were transported to Mauthausen concentration camp where they were murdered. However, the bulk of the deportations took place from August 1942 until April 1943, when most of the remaining Jews of the town were sent to be murdered at death camps in Poland, mainly Sobibór and Auschwitz-Birkenau.

It was the first international match to take place there, which helps to explain the atmosphere of feverish and joyous anticipation that will be just as familiar to football fans of today. 'In Zwolle, there was a bustle everywhere that only a major football event can generate,' reported the Dutch newspaper *Arnhemsche Courant* the day after the game. 'As usual, the pubs were packed, while trams, carriages and cars carried groups of cheerful supporters through the city and to the ground. None of this happened quickly, because both the city itself and the road to the new sports stadium were swarming with laughing and singing enthusiasts.'

The match itself certainly lived up to the earlier excitement, a pulsating encounter which see-sawed both ways. On a difficult pitch rendered heavy by the incessant rain of the previous days, Germany went home with a creditable 5–5 draw, thanks largely to a late comeback inspired by their 19-year-old left-winger, Julius Hirsch.

Losing 5–3 with fifteen minutes to go, Hirsch had single-handedly rescued the game with two goals in four minutes. 'Hirsch suddenly breaks through the Dutch midfield and, after cleverly bursting past the two full-backs, scores Germany's fourth goal,' stated the *Arnhemsche Courant*. 'Hirsch then repeats the same feat four minutes later,' reported the correspondent from the German magazine, *Neue Sportwoche*, 'earning him a thunderous ovation from players and crowd at the end of the game.'

Hirsch scored four goals in all – the first time so many goals had been scored in one game by any player representing the German national team. The other German goal was scored by Gottfried Fuchs who, like Hirsch, was a Jew from Karlsruhe, a city in the south-west of the country near to what now constitutes the border with France. Which means – in case you happened to miss an obvious point – that all five of Germany's goals in this particular match against the Netherlands were scored by Jews.

Like van Hanegem's family, Julius Hirsch did not manage to get through the Second World War alive. Although van Hanegem understandably blamed the Germans for their deaths, his family was actually killed by British carpet bombing of the little harbour Dutch town of Breskens in September 1944, as the Allies sought to prevent the retreat of German soldiers in the area.

The demise of Julius Hirsch, however, had rather more intention behind it. The perpetrators were the ruling authorities of the country that Hirsch had represented with distinction in both sport and war. They deported him from Karlsruhe on a train that eventually picked up hordes of his fellow Jews along its long and winding route to the death camp of Auschwitz-Birkenau in Poland. Soon after arrival, four-goal hero Hirsch would have been forced to undress and then herded naked into a gas chamber with anything up to 2,000 other Jews. The guards would have eventually succeeded in locking the doors, having forced back Hirsch and the other Jews, who knew very well by then what was coming, with a ferocious barrage of whips and sticks.

'You would hear cries and shouts as the people within began to fight against each other and to beat at the walls,' testified Charles Bendel, a Jewish doctor from Romania, who witnessed similar such spectacles. 'This went on for two minutes. And then complete silence.'

Enter specially assigned Jewish prisoners, the Sonderkommandos, to untangle Hirsch's body from the others amid all the blood, urine and faeces, extract his gold teeth and collect any other valuables, burn all the bodies and dispose of their ashes.

* * *

How do we explain this most extreme and barbaric of all turnarounds? It would be remiss to recount the life of Julius Hirsch without at least grappling with that question.

It might be comforting to think – and many in Europe still do want to think it – that what ultimately took place can be attributed to a temporary and unforeseeable bout of insanity. But although Jews of Hirsch's generation kept on telling themselves, often until it was too late, that they were as German as they come, you could argue that the red warning lights had been flashing, equally persistently, for many long years. 'Ideas about Jews that were pervasive in Germany, and had been for decades,' concluded Daniel Goldhagen in his book *Hitler's Willing Executioners*, 'induced ordinary Germans to kill unarmed, defenceless Jewish men, women and children by the thousands, systematically and without pity.'

Ludwig Robert was a visitor to Hirsch's home town of Karlsruhe, situated on the northern edge of the Black Forest, way back in August 1819. Robert, from a well-to-do Jewish family and a successful playwright and librettist, had converted to Christianity only a few weeks before his visit, stating that he thought it unfair to place the 'burden' of Judaism on his children's shoulders.

Robert's mind was clearly preoccupied with this burden, which he no doubt felt and perceived because of his own life experiences. Indeed, his recent play *Die Macht der Verhältnisse* ('The Power of Circumstances'), a major hit with audiences, had focused on an antisemitic incident and the vulnerable position of Jews in German society. However, the scenes he was to witness in Karlsruhe were a shock even to a man who had just abandoned thousands of years of heritage in a bid to protect his family from the disdain and venom of German society.

Anti-Jewish pogroms, known as the '*Hep! Hep!*' riots after the perpetrators' rallying cry, had started in the Bavarian city of Würzburg at the beginning of that month. The frenzy soon spread far and wide, including to Karlsruhe around 150 kilometres away – then home to only 670 Jews, around 4 per cent of the population. For two whole days, Robert heard the cries reverberating in the streets 'amid loud laughter': *Hep! Hep! Jude Verreck!* ('Hep! Hep! Death to the Jews!') Notices on walls throughout the city bayed for a massacre against the tiny and terrified minority.

In his eyewitness account, Robert recorded that the streets were strewn with rubble, indicating that much Jewish property had been destroyed. He was struck by how the Jew baiting and beating were simply regarded as part of everyday life, and therefore unworthy of any comment or condemnation.

'Children were playing in front of the doorsteps, laughing and giggling; they recounted the day's events with childish interest,' he wrote. 'But none of the men or women admonished them or even engaged them in serious conversation. And there was even less chance of seeing a priest (to reproach the crowds).' A little more than a century later, there was once again plenty of opportunity to view this mixture of feverish violence, amused gawking and blasé indifference.

The anti-Jewish ferment in 1819 was in no way limited to the circles of the poor and downtrodden. In many German cities, the educated middle class, including students and university professors, were prominent among the rioters. 'There was no indignation expressed at these incidents, not even in the official newspapers,' lamented Robert. When it came to the Jews, much of the intellectual elite and the masses were now marching in lockstep, marking the start of a long and deadly marriage.

Nevertheless, by the time Julius Hirsch entered the world on 7 April 1892, German Jewry was convinced that its world had changed immeasurably since the *Hep! Hep!* riots. In the 1820s, Jews in the Grand Duchy of Baden, of which Karlsruhe was the capital, were permitted for the first time to practise law and medicine. By 1862, the Jews of Baden had attained complete emancipation and could even settle in cities from which they had been previously excluded. In 1871, all restrictions on the Jews' right of residence, acquisition of real estate and choice of profession were abolished throughout the newly formed German empire, otherwise known as the Second Reich, when the twenty-five German-speaking states, city states and duchies came together as one.

Socially, too, Jews believed that they had been fully accepted. Assuming that antisemitism in Germany would only apply to Jews who looked or sounded foreign, they had embarked on a campaign to adopt the appearance and habits of the host population, to be more German than the Germans.

For example, some followers of reform or liberal Judaism – whose adherents formed the majority among German Jews by the late nineteenth century and certainly numbered the Hirsch family among them – would even celebrate the sabbath on a Sunday, rather than the traditional Saturday. For many, the Jewish festival of Chanukah was effectively merged with Christmas. Around the time of Hirsch's birth, German Jews reacted with horror to the arrival of thousands of *ostjuden* – the poor and traditionally religious Jewish immigrants from the Russian empire, fleeing from persecution, with their perceived primitive and unhygienic ways.

On the economic front, meanwhile, German Jews had flourished to a remarkable degree. At the beginning of the nineteenth century, the vast majority had been poverty-stricken, with many working as domestic servants and unskilled labourers. By 1871, however, only around one in four was still considered poor. Jews had become an overwhelmingly middle-class and urban population, with their participation in business, the professions and the arts far in excess of what their insignificant proportion of the overall population (around 1 per cent) might suggest. 'Theirs was perhaps the fastest and greatest leap any minority has experienced in modern European history,' writes Amos Elon in his book *The Pity of it All*, a chronicle of German Jewry.

But all the while, although the vast majority of German Jews diligently covered their ears, the alarm bells had nevertheless continued to sound. An economic crash two years after German unification unleashed the mania again, provoking familiar and widespread accusations that the Jews had been enriching themselves at other people's expense through alleged underhand and criminal dealings.

Opinion-forming writers added intellectual heft, seeking to codify the instinctive hatred of the masses with an explanatory ideology. By the end of the same decade, the influential journalist Wilhelm Marr had warned that 'the Jewish spirit and Jewish consciousness have overpowered the world.' He demanded resistance against 'this foreign power' before it was too late, claiming that soon 'there will be absolutely no public office, even the highest one, which the Jews will not have usurped'. Using for the first time a word that was to cast the darkest of shadows over the subsequent century, he formed an organisation, the *Antisemitenliga* ('The Anti-Semitic League'), to lead the assault.

Similarly hostile voices began to make inroads into the political system. One example was Adolf Stöcker, a well-known Protestant preacher and the official chaplain of the imperial court, who founded the overtly antisemitic Christian Social Party and won a seat in Parliament from 1879. 'If modern Jewry continues to use the power of capital and the power of the press to bring misfortune to the nation, a final catastrophe is unavoidable,' raged Stöcker. 'Israel must renounce its ambition to become master of Germany.'

Few Jews took Stöcker's threats of catastrophe seriously. They had little interest in the early Zionist movement, led by Theodor Herzl, who warned that Europeans would never allow the Jews to settle unimpeded in their continent, advocating an independent Jewish state instead. Overwhelmingly, and unquestionably including Julius Hirsch himself, Jews instead continued to place Germanness at the front and centre of their identity, right up to the moment that their world collapsed. To serve Germany was a sacred task, said Hermann Cohen, a leading philosopher and proponent of a reformed Judaism, 'like service of the divine'.

The crowd is not always right, however. And sometimes it can be hopelessly and tragically wrong. In 1896, as young Hirsch toddled around his prosperous home in Karlsruhe, an unknown Berlin doctor and Zionist by the name of Bernhard Dov Cohn published a pamphlet entitled *Before the Storm: A Serious Word of Warning to the Jews of Germany*. The German variety of antisemitism 'had method', Cohn cautioned, and was therefore especially dangerous. 'Between Jews and non-Jews in Germany there exists, in effect, a state of war,' he wrote. 'It is no longer a legal question. The demand is not for our defeat or submission – this they have already achieved – but for our destruction.'

No doubt viewed as self-evidently ridiculous and irrelevant, and undeserving of contemplation by great minds, Cohn's pamphlet was utterly ignored by the Jewish and general German media. He died in obscurity five years after the pamphlet's release. Nevertheless, his sharp insight into German society, and his courage in shunning the herd, would ultimately prove to be worth their weight in gold. Cohn's own children were clearly paying close attention at the family dinner table. Four of them emigrated to British-controlled Palestine in the 1920s, arriving in comfortable time before their father's casually dismissed prophecy became a devastating truth.

* * *

Julius Hirsch's upbringing in Karlsruhe was typical of many thousands of his German Jewish contemporaries. His father, Benjamin Berthold Hirsch, originally from the nearby village of Weingarten, owned the family textile company, Gerbrüder Hirsch, together with his brothers. (The Hebrew name Benjamin will have been reserved for an inner Jewish circle of family and friends, with the accompanying name of Berthold used to present a fully German facade to wider society.) No doubt as Berthold Hirsch, he had fought as a young man in the Franco-Prussian war of 1870–1 that culminated in the unification of Germany, and he subsequently inculcated his family with an ardent faith in the fatherland.

Julius's mother Emma (née Erlanger) hailed from Buchau am Federsee in the Upper Swabian region of southern Germany, and from such well-to-do stock that she took herself off to Paris as a young woman and trained as a hat maker.*

Like József Braun and Leon Sperling, Hirsch was the youngest sibling of a large brood. The two sisters, Anna (fifteen years his senior) and Rosa were the eldest, and then came the five boys – Hermann, Leopold, Max, Rudolf and Julius. With cousins galore living nearby, and a local Jewish community now numbering close to three thousand, the picture emerges of a warm, supportive and busy home.

To add the icing to young Julius's cake, his childhood coincided

* Only around forty Jews were living in Weingarten on Kristallnacht, the nationwide pogrom against Jews, in November 1938. Two teachers from the local school moved their classes into the synagogue and encouraged their students to desecrate and destroy the Hebrew books and scrolls, and then throw them into a nearby stream. A few days later, the synagogue was demolished. According to the memorial book for German Jews, a total of sixty-one Jewish residents who came from Weingarten or who had lived there for a long time were murdered in the Holocaust. In Buchau, meanwhile, the synagogue was made of such strong stuff that it was only partially destroyed on Kristallnacht. The Jewish community was therefore forced to pay for it to be blown up by explosives the following week. Of the 200 Jews living in Buchau before the war, four returned after it.

with the birth of football as a popular sport in Germany, first brought to the country by British tradesmen and merchants. Starting its rise in Berlin, it had spread further south by the early 1890s to the region of Baden and the city of Karlsruhe, where it proceeded to thrive and eventually dominate the nation's football. According to Uli Hesse, in his book *Tor! The Story of German Football*, 'the man almost solely responsible for making Karlsruhe into the football power that would one day overtake Berlin' was a Jew, Walther Bensemann.

Acting with the zeal of an obsessive missionary, Bensemann inspired thousands of enthusiasts, brought much-venerated English teams over to the country on tours, and founded football clubs wherever his itinerant life took him. As an eighteen-year-old student in 1891, he founded Karlsruher Fussballverein (KFV), a club that was to achieve major success in German football until the First World War.

Julius Hirsch cut his teeth playing in his free time with other football-mad youths on the pitch at Engländerplatz, a square named in honour of the sport's birthplace and situated only a few minutes' walk from the family apartment on Akademiestrasse in the centre of Karlsruhe. But it was at Bensemann's brainchild KFV that Juller, as he was to be known by family, friends and teammates throughout this life, was first to make his mark.*

Several English coaches had been plying their trade in Germany, with their knowledge and experience gratefully absorbed by passionate, ambitious pupils. If Burnley's Jimmy Hogan was József Braun's mentor a few years later, then the equivalent for Hirsch was William Townley from nearby Blackburn in England's north-west, a footballing hotbed both then and now. Townley was a former England international who had scored the first-ever hat-trick in an FA Cup final,

* Walther Bensemann fled from Germany in 1933. He died in Switzerland the following year, apparently penniless.

a record that merited demigod status among the young footballing fraternity in Karlsruhe.

Within a few weeks of becoming coach in January 1909, Townley had identified Hirsch's ability to cut through defences like a rapier with his speed and dribbling ability, and then finish off his work with a powerful left-foot shot, the Ryan Giggs of his era. Hirsch's talent was such that he broke through to the first team at an even younger age than Giggs, earning him the nickname 'Junior' from his Lancastrian boss.

His rise coincided exactly with the peak of football mania in a city which had become synonymous with the sport. Despite Karlsruhe's comparatively insignificant population, *Illustrierte Sportzeitung*, a Munich newspaper, described it in 1910 as 'Germany's football metropolis – if you ask where soccer is played in Germany, the insider will always mention the name of the Baden royal seat of Karlsruhe first and foremost'. A metropolis built by a Jew, creating the perfect stage for two more to display their wares to an adoring public in a newly emerging footballing nation.

* * *

By dint of the painstaking research of his German-language biographer Werner Skrentny, we can build a picture of Julius Hirsch's first steps into top-level football. On 6 November 1938, just three days before Karlsruhe's Jews were beaten and terrorised during the Kristallnacht pogroms that raged throughout the Reich, Julius's son Heinold wrote an essay at school, later to be preserved for posterity. It was entitled 'Mein Ahnen' ('My Ancestors'), his last such piece of work before being expelled from school for having a Jewish father. He was sixteen years old, the same age as his father when he hit the big time.

According to Skrentny, who interviewed Heinold before his death in 1996, Julius had recounted his career in detail to his son. Skrentny therefore presents the story of Hirsch's debut, in a 4–0 victory against FC Freiburger in March 1909, as if the recollections in the essay had been recounted in the first person.

'As you can imagine, I had a few heart palpitations when I played for the first time among such famous names, but I soon settled down … After the game, the coach at the time, Townley, said: "That left-winger will be a permanent fixture in the team now!"' A few weeks later, Hirsch repaid his coach's faith in youth by scoring his first goal at the top level in a 4–0 derby victory against Alemannia Karlsruhe.

Once settled into his new role as coach, William Townley planned his assault on the national German championship for his first full season, 1909/10. Winning this title was a mountainous and tortuous task. KFV competed in the Southern German championship, which itself was divided into North, South, East and West divisions. The winners of these sub-regional leagues then played off with each other to become the sole representative of Southern Germany in the deciding national knockout competition, to be fought out with the champions of the other regions throughout the country. (A national league, or Bundesliga as we know it today, was not introduced in Germany until as late as 1963.)

In his title pursuit, Townley was blessed with the then infamous Hirsch–Förderer–Fuchs attacking triumvirate, the most formidable forward line in the country at the time. Fritz Förderer, an inside forward who shared Hirsch's technical ability and explosive shooting power, had represented Germany in the country's first-ever official international match. Gottfried Fuchs, three years older than Hirsch and a close friend until the latter's death, was a stylish centre-forward whose goalscoring prowess would break records for Germany. The Fuchs–Hirsch partnership, in particular, tripped off the tongue of the local football fan, not least because their names mean the 'fox' and the 'deer' in German.

The three were known for their clever interplay in tight spaces, a technical accomplishment that still earns praise in the modern day and must have seemed extraordinary in an era when English-style brawn still ruled the roost. Sepp Herberger, who went on to become the coach of Germany's first-ever World Cup winning team in 1954, was then a teenager from Mannheim, a nearby city in the Baden region. 'Förderer, Fuchs and Hirsch had a legendary reputation at the time,' he recalled years later. 'They impressed me so much with their feats of skill and captivating combination moves that I can still recreate them in my memory today.'

KFV romped to the Southern German championship title that season, scoring more than 100 goals in their twenty-three games. As an example of the city's dominance, two Karlsruhe teams were involved in the ensuing national championship knockout tournament – KFV and FC Phoenix Karlsruhe, who had qualified for the final stage as the national champions from the previous year. The two arch-rivals were to be pitted against each other in the national semi-final, to be staged at KFV's Telegraphenkaserne stadium, the scene of Germany's first victory in international football the previous year.

Eight thousand spectators crammed into the ground, breaking the record for an attendance at any German football fixture. Such was the hype and enthusiasm that well over a century later we can log onto YouTube and watch the oldest surviving film of a football match in Germany, garnering a sense of the action, the crowd and the footballing idols of the time. In the two-and-a-half-minute video, we see ticketless fans perched on walls overlooking the pitch, the slightly crouched gait and left-footedness of Hirsch, and glimpses of the dark, handsome, debonair Fuchs.

KFV emerged 2–1 winners, qualifying to face underdogs and northern German champions Holsten Kiel in the national final in Cologne. Playing a highly defensive game to thwart the threat of the notorious forward line, Kiel held out gamely until the second half of extra time when yet another run from the tireless Hirsch was this time illegally halted in the area. Max Breunig, standing at six foot four and described by Jewish coaching legend Hugo Meisl as 'the most colossal centre-half of all time in both Germany and the continent' promptly smashed in the winning penalty. 'The Karlsruhe soccer club had finally and deservedly become German champions after many long years,' reported *Neue Sportwoche*.

The pride of Karlsruhe arrived back to an adulatory welcome in the city, greeted by masses of laudatory telegrams and whisked immediately from the train station to a gala banquet. Having just turned eighteen, Julius Hirsch had already won the first of his many accolades, both on and off the pitch.

* * *

Hirsch's stellar performances in the colours of KFV soon earned him representative honours, as both regional and national selection committees rushed to capitalise on the telepathic understanding of the club's exceptional forward line.

He first became a regular starter in *Der Kronprinzenpokal* (the Crown Prince's Cup, named after Crown Prince Wilhelm, eldest son of Kaiser Wilhelm, the very last German emperor), a knockout competition between the various regions of Germany. When Southern Germany ended up lifting the trophy in February 1912, the team's selectors could have been forgiven for sporting a smug smile during the post-match celebrations, after the opposition had utterly failed to cope with the cream of Karlsruhe.

In the semi-final against Central Germany, Hirsch and Fuchs scored both the goals in a 2–1 victory. And then 7,000 spectators in Berlin were treated to what must be one of the most thrilling finals of any high-level competition in history. With six KFV players in the starting line-up, Southern Germany edged past Brandenburg 6–5, with one goal from Förderer, two from Hirsch and a hat-trick from Fuchs.

These were Hirsch's halcyon days, the time in a top sportsman's life when he feels that everything he touches is turning to gold. Just five weeks after the *Kronprinzenpokal* triumph, he performed his career-peaking heroics against the Netherlands in Zwolle in what was his second appearance for the German national team. (His debut for Germany, a 4–1 defeat against Hungary in December 1911 in the first international match ever to take place in the future footballing powerhouse of Munich, had in truth offered little indication of the pyrotechnics to come, with Hirsch hardly getting a kick against superior opponents.)

Given his unstoppable displays in the spring of 1912, Hirsch was a shoo-in for the Germany squad of twenty-two chosen for the Stockholm Olympics that June. Indeed, such was Hirsch's prominence in German football that the editor of *Fussball und Olympischer Sport* even chose to lead with a photo of him in action on the front cover of the magazine published before the tournament. The text inside the cover explained the choice in glowing terms: 'The picture is typical of the eminently lively style of play of this nimble player. Hirsch is one of the masters of football today … Everyone is impressed by his extremely fast and remarkably energetic runs that are a danger to any opponent.'

The youngest player in the squad at the age of twenty, Hirsch made the starting eleven for the first-round knockout tie against an Austria team containing several players from the predominantly Jewish club DFC Prag.* The match was played not at the Olympic Stadium, where Józef Klotz was to write his name in the history books a decade later, but at the Råsunda stadium, the site of Pelé's triumph with Brazil in the 1958 World Cup final.

Unfancied Germany, 1–0 up at half-time, looked to be on course for an upset until the team's goalkeeper, Albert Weber, was badly concussed after a heavy collision. With no substitutes allowed, Weber tottered around not knowing what day of the week it was and completely incapable of stopping the shots flying past him. He later confessed that he thought he saw four different balls arrowing towards him all at once and could not work out which one to save. Germany lost 5–1.

In truth, despite their recent Karlsruhe-powered development, Germany was still at that stage some way behind its Central European neighbours, Hungary and Austria, not to mention Great Britain, who retained the Olympic football title with ease.

Nevertheless, the Germans could at least console themselves that others were even further behind. In a consolation tournament for

* At least one of the players who represented Austria that day qualified for selection for my team. According to the database of the United States Holocaust Memorial Museum, the former DFC Prag defender Bernhard Graubart (sometimes spelt Graubard), then aged fifty-one, was deported in October 1939 along with 1,300 other Jews from Ostrava in what is now the Czech Republic. The captives' task, to be carried out in appalling conditions, was to build a new concentration camp in Nisko, a Polish town on the River San. The project was abandoned, and little is known of the fate of the individual prisoners, except that almost all were never heard from again. On the German-language Wikipedia page devoted to him, Graubart's unknown date of death is introduced by a Christian cross, Europe's final obliteration of his identity. He was born in Bolechów, now known as Bolekhiv in modern-day Ukraine, the town from which my own name very probably emanates. It is never far from my mind that my own grandparents and great-grandparents managed to get a lot further away from Bolechów than Graubart did.

teams already eliminated, Germany were first paired with Russia. For reasons of fairness, the selectors selected the eleven players in the squad who had sat out the Austria game. Gottfried Fuchs, inexplicably omitted from the first game, scored ten goals in a 16–0 victory against a team that had reportedly been paralytically drunk on a boat trip around the Stockholm archipelago the night before.*

Germany came up short again in the consolation tournament semi-final, losing 3–1 to Hungary. In its post-tournament analysis of what had gone wrong for Germany, the magazine *Neue Sportwoche* lamented that 'Karlsruhe's famous three-man attack, on which great hopes had been built, failed completely', a rather odd assertion given that Hirsch, Fuchs and Förderer only played all together in the final consolation match. It seems that Germany's football journalism was as far behind Austria and Hungary as their football was.

* * *

After KFV had won the German championship in that 1910 final in Cologne, the club continued to occupy the highest reaches of domestic football for the next two years, exercising absolute hegemony over the Southern German championship. As an illustration of the club's dominance, the titans of the modern day, Bayern Munich, were dealt a footballing lesson in two matches in the spring of 1911, rolled over 5–0 and 3–1.

KFV were nevertheless to miss out narrowly in the next two national

* With his ten goals, Fuchs equalled the individual world record for goals scored in an international match set by Sophus Nielsen of Denmark in the previous Olympics in 1908. The jointly held record stood for almost ninety years, until Australia's Archie Thompson scored thirteen goals in a 31–0 defeat of Northern Samoa in 2001. It seems certain that the German national record for individual goals in one game will be forever held by a man who fled Germany for his life because he was a Jew.

championship play-offs. The pride of Southern Germany lost to VfB Leipzig in the semi-finals in 1911, at the end of which Townley left the club for financial reasons to join SpVgg Fürth, in Northern Bavaria.

In the 1912 national final, Holsten Kiel inflicted sweet revenge on KFV by engineering an exact reversal of the scoreline from two years previously, a 1–0 win by virtue of a penalty. The shock defeat owed much to the sub-par performance of the infamous Jewish partnership up front. Fuchs was considered so indispensable that he was selected to play despite a pre-existing knee injury that consigned him to ninety minutes of hobbling, while Hirsch blasted over the bar with a minute left on the clock when it seemed easier to score.

Meanwhile, 200 kilometres east of Karlsruhe, Townley was already getting busy in Fürth, calculating exactly how he was going to win a German championship with a second club. In the spring of 1913, he recruited two Jews to help him fulfil this ambition – Hirsch and Frigyes Weicz, a centre-forward from Hungary who had been impressing the footballing fraternity with his performances for a club in Frankfurt.* 'You can bet on us winning the championship next season,' was Townley's bullish prediction in a letter to a friend back in England.

He knew his football inside out and grasped that the combination of Hirsch's ability and his confidence as a previous league winner could supply the necessary catalyst in the dressing room, turning the team from nearly men into champions. Still just twenty-one, Hirsch had already built up a wealth of experience and know-how that he could pass on to his teammates. To exploit his leadership potential and

* Ten years later, in 1923, the future diplomat and Secretary of State of the United States, Henry Kissinger, was born in Fürth. Having played for the schoolboy team of SpVgg Fürth, Kissinger became a passionate supporter of Hirsch's former club and an ardent follower of football throughout his life. By 1938, he had fled Germany along with his family and many other Fürth Jews. Those that remained from the previously 2,000-strong community were deported to the east and murdered. Forty returned after the war.

footballing skills to the full, Townley immediately awarded Hirsch the captain's armband, while switching his on-field role from left-wing to inside-left, where he could exert a greater influence on the direction of the game.

Townley was not the only shrewd onlooker with a similar opinion on Hirsch's best position. After what it described as a 'brilliant individual performance' by SpVgg Fürth's new signing in Germany's 2–1 defeat to Switzerland in Freiburg in May 1913, the magazine *Fussball* nevertheless fumed that Hirsch was being criminally underutilised.* 'A man of his determination, shooting power and technique doesn't belong on the wing getting cold, when we have no one inside him who can score!' the magazine argued. 'Hirsch would be ideal as inside-forward.' Another publication, *Der Rasensport*, was similarly exasperated: 'To put Hirsch on the left-wing, only someone who doesn't know Hirsch can have this idea.'

Roared on by up to 10,000 spectators at the Ronhof stadium, then the largest capacity of any football ground in Germany, SpVgg Fürth stormed the Southern Germany championship in the 1913/14 season, with captain Hirsch justifying Townley's tactical switch by scoring seventeen goals in eighteen games. Three potential knockout games now stood between the team and the prized national championship. For sheer drama, they were not to disappoint.

* * *

In the quarter-finals, Fürth overturned a one-goal deficit at half-time to beat SpVgg Leipzig. 'The Fürth attack, with the ex-KFV player Hirsch and Weicz from Budapest, was the highlight,' reported *Fürther*

* SpVgg stands for Spielvereinigung, literally meaning 'Game Association'.

Zeitung. As for the semi-finals and final, if you think (as I did) that the golden goal rule in football was only introduced (and later abandoned) for international tournaments in the 1990s, then you should think again.

The Ronhof stadium was said to be filled to even more than its official capacity for the semi-final against Berliner BC 03, as 12,000 squeezed on to the terraces. After going two goals down this time, Weicz himself notched a brace to take the game into two fifteen-minute periods of extra time, as is still the norm nowadays for knock-out games. Fellow striker Karl Franz put Fürth in front, before the Berlin side equalised right at the end of extra time to make it 3–3. The rule in force was for two additional extra-time periods of ten minutes to be played at that point, and then another, but that the game would cease immediately should either team score during these periods. The golden goal came from Franz, in the 146th minute of the game.

Believe it or not, the final in Magdeburg at the end of May 1914 against reigning champions VfB Leipzig was an even longer affair, with the golden goal not coming until the 153rd minute, the second period of the third cycle of extra time. In modern football-speak, neither side left anything on the pitch in two and a half hours of blood-and-guts football. It was a bruising affair, and some players stepped over the line, Hirsch included. Desperate to get his hands on the coveted trophy once more, 'Hirsch was admonished at half-time by the chairman of the football association for his unfair play,' reported *Neue Sportwoche*.

Leipzig equalised an earlier Franz goal late in normal time. A Weicz free kick restored the lead in the 104th minute, only for Leipzig to level terms once again a few minutes later. The pitch resembled a battlefield by the end, with several walking wounded due to the prohibition on substitutes, one Leipzig player carried off completely incapacitated and one Fürth player dismissed by the referee. Eventually, Frigyes Weicz managed to limp down the left wing to get a cross over to Karl Franz, who duly converted to spark exuberant celebration.

Several hours later, the news of the victory gradually filtered back to Fürth, a city which had been in a state of nervous anticipation all day. 'On the street in front of our clubhouse, the crowd, which had grown to around one thousand people, began to pace up and down in their excitement,' recorded the 1914 SpVgg publication that commemorated the victory.

> All manner of uncontrollable rumours were circulating. Then, at about 7:15, it suddenly became quiet. A commotion became noticeable in the pub, and people said: we won 3–2! Boys with bicycles brought the victory news to the most distant parts of town. *We* have won – all of Fürth felt itself involved in SpVgg's victory.

The players were all awarded gold pocket watches at the city's official celebration ceremony that took place two months later, on Saturday 26 July 1914. Two days after that, the Austro-Hungarian empire declared war on Serbia, and Europe was soon sliding down the slippery slope to savage conflict.

Within a year of the championship triumph, the two goalscoring heroes of Magdeburg, Frigyes Weicz and Karl Franz, lay dead or mortally wounded on the battlefield. Towards the end of the war, in April 1918, Hirsch's elder brother Leopold was also killed, in Northern France. The tombstone marking his grave in the Jewish cemetery in Karlsruhe bears an inscription written by Julius Hirsch himself. 'Your life was faithfulness to duty and love of country. Your death set the seal.'

In that school essay from November 1938, Heinold Hirsch referred to his father's own experiences in that terrible war. Heinold's words testify to the principles of German patriotism instilled so relentlessly during his upbringing that he was still clinging to them amid the trauma that was now afflicting his family: 'Like thousands of his sports comrades, he then stood for four years in the field of honour to defend the homeland.'

* * *

As football was still an amateur sport in Germany, Julius Hirsch had earned a living as a salesperson while winning championships and playing for Germany. From the age of sixteen, he worked in a Jewish-owned leather goods shop in Karlsruhe called Freund and Strauss. On signing for SpVgg Fürth, he found employment in the neighbouring town of Nuremberg, working as a salesperson for Bing, also Jewish-owned and soon to become the largest toy manufacturer in the world. The two jobs were bisected, from April 1912, by a compulsory year of military service in an infantry regiment of the Prussian army, a constituent part of the forces of the German Empire, based in Karlsruhe.

Hirsch was clearly an able man. He spoke French to a very high standard, having studied the language at school and no doubt benefiting from his mother's time in the country by practising at home. According to a questionnaire he completed in 1939, later discovered by his biographer Werner Skrentny, he also spoke English to a reasonable level. The German army capitalised on these administrative and linguistic skills by stationing him behind the front line during the war, in a logistical unit of the Bavarian army (he was living in Nuremberg when he volunteered immediately upon the war's outbreak in 1914).

His mobile unit handled food, medical and ammunition supplies for combat troops and arranged the transport of wounded soldiers to field hospitals. In the questionnaire, Hirsch indicated that he had also performed duties as an interpreter during the war, very possibly involving the supervision and interrogation of captured enemy soldiers in France.

Whatever the precise content of the role, Hirsch distinguished himself and received due acknowledgement. In 1916, he was awarded the Iron Cross Second Class, an honour bestowed for a single act of bravery in the face of the enemy, or actions that were clearly above and beyond the call of duty. (A second such act would result in the award of the Iron Cross First Class.) The reason for this award is not stated, and we are left to speculate that he performed a heroic act to aid his fellow soldiers on the front line while under enemy fire. Three of his brothers – Leopold, Max and Rudolf – also received the Iron Cross Second Class. Both Rudolf and Julius's friend and teammate Gottfried Fuchs were even awarded the First Class variety.

These men formed part of a much larger and what now seems a pitifully tragic story. Less than a couple of decades before the onset of their destruction, Jews in Germany had bent over backwards to demonstrate their patriotic credentials. Up to 100,000 of them served in the German army in the First World War, of whom 12,000 were killed in action and 18,000 awarded the Iron Cross. The Jewish community might have hoped that such extensive self-sacrifice would serve to dispel any lingering repudiation of their claim to Germanness.

Not a bit of it. As the war started to go against Germany, the government was besieged with complaints that the Jews were shirking their military duty and that hostilities were only dragging on for Jewish profiteers to get rich. The army high command responded by initiating the *Judenzählung* (Jew census) to determine whether Jews were indeed using their connections and wiles to position themselves far away from the sharp end of the war.

Although it is highly likely that the survey results comprehensively disproved the hypothesis, they were never actually published, feeding more conspiracy theories that powerful Jews were manoeuvring behind the scenes to suppress the truth. When soldiers re-entered civilian life after the war, the festering resentment of alleged Jewish cowardice and self-interest only intensified. Jews were denied entry into the *Der Stahlhelm, Bund der Frontsoldaten* (The Steel Helmet, League of Front Line Soldiers), the nationwide veterans' association formed in 1918. Instead, Vizefeldwebel (vice-sergeant) Julius Hirsch joined the *Reichsbund jüdischer Frontsoldaten* (the RjF, or Reich Federation of Jewish Front Line Soldiers).

In the minds of RjF members, Germans had only failed to embrace the Jewish minority within their midst because they lacked access to the facts. Once presented with persistent proof of Jewish commitment to the fatherland, all that would surely change. 'The RjF sees the basis of its work as complete allegiance to the German homeland,' reads its foundational document. 'It has no goal and no ambition outside of this German homeland and opposes in the strongest possible terms any attempt to place us German Jews as outsiders in relation to this German homeland.'

A 1920 leaflet issued by the RjF depicts a weeping mother sitting by a war grave. 'Christian and Jewish heroes fought side by side and rest side by side in a foreign land,' it read. 'German women, do not allow a Jewish mother to be scorned in her grief.'

They were talking to themselves.

* * *

Despite the gathering storm clouds, life for Julius Hirsch returned to a semblance of normality. In 1920, soon after returning from the war, he got married. Back in 1912 in Karlsruhe, he had met Ellen Hauser, a Protestant daughter of an innkeeper. The couple had maintained their long-distance relationship during Hirsch's years in Bavaria and his subsequent war service. Two children followed – Heinold in 1922 and daughter Esther in 1928.

Just as he did before the war, Hirsch combined his footballing and business activities – only this time, given the passage of time and the inevitable impact of not playing at the top level for several years, with rather less emphasis on the former.

Some more discerning footballing minds had identified a slight waning of his abilities even before the outbreak of hostilities. 'He has undoubtedly passed his peak,' reported the *Norddeutsche Sportzeitung* after his seventh and final appearance for the national team, a 6–2 defeat against Belgium in Antwerp in November 1913. 'His former penetration and shooting ability are gone.'

The rather portlier Hirsch that returned to the colours of KFV in 1919 could still show flashes of his former brilliance, even earning him a couple more appearances for Southern Germany, but he was in truth a long way from the player he was. 'Hirsch is still fast and can play a nice pass, but one has the impression that he can no longer summon his former energy,' commented *Fussball* magazine in 1919.

He soon entered a realm familiar to modern-day football fans – the ageing star who strolls around the pitch as if playing an exhibition match, inspiring affection and sentimental recollection of previous exploits. 'The only player I would like to single out is old Juller Hirsch, who produced an excellent game, especially in the second half,' reported the Swiss version of *Fussball* after he had made a guest appearance for a team in St Gallen in 1922.

Meanwhile, Julius and his brother Max gradually took over the reins of the family business, now specialising in sports goods, complete with a logo of a stag's head to reflect the meaning of their surname. As a sure sign that things were going well, he and Ellen moved into an apartment on Kaiserallee, a prestigious address in the upmarket Karlsruhe suburb of Weststadt. Just like his father, on Saturday mornings he would visit the liberal (non-Orthodox) synagogue on Kronenstrasse, a picture of a prosperous and contented family man, an archetypal German Jew in the last years before the incompatibility of those two words was confirmed for good.

In 1924, a few years before their respective deaths, Hirsch's parents, Benjamin Berthold and Emma, held a celebration for their golden wedding at the kosher Nassauer Hof hotel in Karlsruhe. One can only imagine their overwhelming sense of achievement and pride as they surveyed their burgeoning family in that happy function room. The menu card, subsequently preserved by the family, reveals a sumptuous feast. Rabbi Julius Cohn from the family synagogue was invited to address the elderly and respected couple.*

It never pays for Jews to get too comfortable, however. Within a matter of years, the synagogue, the hotel, and Julius Hirsch's life, would all lie in ruins.

* * *

* By November 1938, Rabbi Cohn was working as a rabbi in the city of Ulm in south-western Germany. On Kristallnacht, he was taken from his home and violently dragged with other Jews through the streets of the city to the blazing synagogue. There he was thrown into a dry fountain and his beard set alight. His face was severely burned and he was confined to hospital for four weeks. A few months later, he fled Germany for England, planning for his wife Dorothea to join him shortly afterwards once they had gathered enough money to pay the exorbitant emigration tax for a second time. However, the exit door soon shut for good. Rabbi Cohn died in London in March 1940, still suffering from his injuries. Dorothea Meth-Cohn was murdered in Auschwitz-Birkenau in October 1944.

In the space of a few weeks in the wake of Kristallnacht, 23-year-old Ulrich Alexander Boschwitz wrote a novel entitled *Der Reisende* ('The Traveller'), now marketed in its English-language translation as *The Passenger*.

The central character, Otto Silbermann, is a successful and assimilated German Jewish businessman, married to a non-Jewish wife. The story charts Silbermann's increasingly irrational behaviour as it begins to dawn on him that his lifelong beliefs about Germany, and about Jews' place in that society, had proved to be completely false. In a state of growing panic, he criss-crosses the country by train in a frenzied and vain attempt to find a means of escape from the hell that engulfed him, the chaotic journey reflecting his profound inner confusion.

Boschwitz's novel kept entering my head when researching the last years of Julius Hirsch. Whereas Silbermann's fictional realisation was sudden – perhaps unrealistically so – Hirsch's psychological journey was gradual and possibly incomplete, even up to his last moments. As well as being beset by the burden of his financial tribulations as the noose tightened, Hirsch was slowly driven to despair and severe mental illness as cold reality undermined his most cherished convictions. The demands of this huge mental leap, which some German Jews did indeed manage to accomplish sooner or later, completely overwhelmed both Silbermann and Hirsch.

Things actually started to go downhill for Hirsch even before the Nazis seized power. The onset of the Great Depression in 1929 hit Hirsch's company badly. Sigfa Sport, as the company was now known, soon ceased its own factory production and instead concentrated solely on wholesale trade. New investment was sought to see the company through its difficulties, but the stay of execution was only temporary. Following several years of loss-making activity, bankruptcy proceedings were initiated on 10 February 1933, just eleven days after Adolf Hitler had become chancellor of Germany.

A couple of months later, insult was added to injury. After a meeting in Stuttgart, the various clubs that comprised the Southern Germany Football Association, including SpVgg Fürth and KFV, released a statement to the local press. 'The undersigned clubs joyfully and resolutely place themselves at the disposal of the national government in the field of physical training and are ready to cooperate with full commitment,' the statement read. 'In the spirit of this cooperation, they are willing to reach all necessary conclusions, especially with regard to the question of the removal of Jews from sports clubs.'

Hirsch immediately and furiously thrashed out a resignation letter to KFV, typed on the stationery of his now defunct company, its contents the epitome of naivety and pathos: 'I do not wish to leave unmentioned the fact that among the scapegoats of the German nation, who are so hated today, there are also German Jews who are decent people and whose national loyalty is evident in their actions and in the blood they have shed.' He then goes on to list the war medals awarded to him and to his brothers and details the fate of his brother Leopold, 'fallen on the field of honour' just fifteen years before.

At this point, Hirsch abruptly switches tack from passionate protest to everyday pragmatism as he recalls that he is struggling to put food on his family table: 'I am currently in an economically precarious situation, so may I ask the honourable club management to waive the amount still owed by me, because I have never received any monetary benefits from KFV?' Continuing with the now conciliatory tone, he signs off with 'sportsman greetings'.

As he endeavoured to make ends meet, Hirsch turned first to what he knew best – football. He moved with his family to Strasbourg, just across the border in France, and took over as coach of fourth-tier FA Illkirch-Graffenstaden on the outskirts of the city. As well as achieving some respite from Nazi rule, Hirsch no doubt saw this modest

József Braun, the greatest Jewish player, sits on the far left, next to his friend and fellow prodigy, György Orth.

Courtesy of the Hungarian Olympic and Sports Museum

ABOVE Serial champions MTK, pictured in 1921. Standing fifth from right is József Braun. The fourth player from the left is Antal Vágó. Standing between the two is Béla Guttmann.

Courtesy of Attila Kapási

LEFT Now a top coach, Braun is pictured (standing fourth from left) with his FTC Fiľakovo team in 1937. A little more than five years later, he was murdered as a slave labourer in the European Holocaust.

Courtesy of Vladimír Cirbus

Zygmunt Steuermann, the charismatic goal machine, standing on the far left, together with his Hasmonea Lwów teammates in 1924. Courtesy of Adam Musial

Steuermann, the player standing on the far left, representing a Lwów (now Lviv) city team in a clash with Breslau (now Wrocław) in 1926. Steuermann inevitably scored in a 4–1 victory. Courtesy of Maciej Lisicki

The Poland team before the historic game against Sweden in Stockholm in 1922. Centre-back Józef Klotz (left) and wing wizard Leon Sperling (right) are sitting on either side of the goalkeeper. Courtesy of Adam Musial

The Jutrzenka Kraków team in 1921. Józef Klotz sits on the right of the bottom row. His younger brother Janek is kneeling on the left of the row above. Courtesy of Danny Dekel

Józef Klotz's wife, Regina, together with their daughter, whose name is not known. The Holocaust fate of Regina and the daughter is also unknown. Courtesy of Danny Dekel

Leon Sperling, standing fourth from right, with his Poland teammates before the 1924 Olympics.
Courtesy of the Polish National Digital Archives

The elder statesman: Sperling (right), captain of Cracovia, tosses up before a game against Legia Warsaw in 1932.

Courtesy of the Polish National Digital Archives

Julius Hirsch (sitting on the far right) with his Karlsruher FV teammates in 1909. Hirsch had just broken through to the first team at the age of sixteen.

Courtesy of the Karlsruhe City Archives

Hirsch in action at KFV's Telegraphenkaserne ground around 1912, the year he scored four goals in one game for the German national team.

Courtesy of the Karlsruhe City Archives

ABOVE LEFT Árpád Weisz as a Hungary international. By this stage, Weisz had already spent several years as a prisoner of war in Italy.

From *Dallo Scudetto ad Auschwitz* by Matteo Marani (Diarkos)

ABOVE RIGHT Weisz pictured around the time he became the youngest coach to win the Italian league, a record he still holds today. Italy expelled him from the country a few years later. Courtesy of Bologna FC

LEFT A signed photo of Max Scheuer, the dogged little fighter of Hakoah Vienna. Courtesy of the Jewish Museum Vienna

BELOW Champions of Austria: Scheuer stands on the far left of the victorious Hakoah team in 1925. His business partner Richard Fried is pictured third from left.

Courtesy of the Jewish Museum Vienna

Otto 'Schloime' Fischer, standing third from left, with his Hakoah teammates before a game in Riga in 1926.
Courtesy of Raimonds Kaže

Fischer went on to become a brilliant and innovative coach, masterminding the 'Barcelona of the Baltics'. Courtesy of Robert Beig

Paul Goldberger, third from right wearing the cap, pictured with his Freiburger FC teammates in 1907, the year they won the German championship. Courtesy of Eintracht Frankfurt

Goldberger with the Hungary team and their opponents from Bohemia on his sole international appearance, in 1908. Goldberger is third from right among the players sitting or kneeling.
Courtesy of Attila Kapási

LEFT The Jewish Iniesta: Antal Vágó at the 1912 Olympic Games.
Courtesy of Attila Kapási

BELOW Vágó as chauffeur, pictured in 1927 with his employer, friend and fellow Jew Alfréd Brüll in the front passenger seat.
Courtesy of György Rudas

Henrik Nádler (left), ever the entertainer, in action for the Hungary national team in a 5–0 win against Switzerland in 1925. Courtesy of Richard Panchyk

The boy about town: a dapper Nádler as a young man. Courtesy of Richard Panchyk

Nádler (left) in a labour camp in 1944. Within a few months, Nádler was murdered at the Bergen-Belsen concentration camp.

Courtesy of Richard Panchyk

appointment as a first stepping stone to greater things in football. But the ambition came to nothing. Having been trumpeted in the local media as 'a student of Townley, the best English coach that ever worked on the continent', he was back in Karlsruhe by the summer of 1934, at the end of his first season in charge.

With the family now in a more modest apartment, Hirsch set himself up as a travelling fabric salesman, journeying across Germany to eke out a living. At the same time, he tried to keep himself sane by coaching and even playing (he was now well into his forties) for Turnclub Karlsruhe 03, one of two Jewish sports organisations in the city that had been suddenly inundated with new members expelled from other clubs. (The alternative, the Zionist club Hakoah Karlsruhe, would surely have been a bridge too far for Hirsch.)

From May 1937, he was employed as a payroll accountant and assistant office manager at a Jewish-owned paper factory, Vogel and Bernheimer, just outside Karlsruhe. Less than a year later, however, the company was 'aryanised' (the prevailing Nazi term for the seizure of property from Jews and its transfer to non-Jews), and Hirsch was subsequently cast aside by the new, purer-blooded owners.

He applied for a coaching job at a Swiss first-division side, but his résumé would certainly have paled in competition with those of other top-level Jewish coaches from Central Europe eager to ply their trade safely out of the Nazis' reach. His next idea was to find work in Paris. After all, he spoke fluent French and his sister Rosa lived there with her husband. But, again, he got nowhere. On 3 November 1938, three months after his arrival in the French capital and six days before Kristallnacht, he gave up the ghost and started his journey back to Karlsruhe.

It was at this point that the life of this great Jewish footballer started to unravel at breakneck speed. Six weeks after he boarded the train in Paris, there was still no word of Julius Hirsch.

* * *

As his family sat at home sick with worry, their husband and father was recuperating in a psychiatric hospital. Hirsch had not arrived home as expected because he had disembarked from the train in north-eastern France and opted instead to try to kill himself. Rejected, ostracised, bewildered and poverty-stricken, he had sunk into a deep, psychotic depression.

'Hirsch apparently left Paris in a pathologically altered state of mind,' read a later medical report. 'In the hallucinatory delusional belief that his wife and children were dead, he attempted suicide in a quarry near Commercy … He received first aid in the hospital of Commercy and was transferred from there to the local lunatic asylum in Fains-les Sources on November 4, 1938.' He had apparently been found all alone in the quarry with a knife in his hand and wounds to his body.

It was not until mid-December that a rambling letter from Hirsch arrived at the family home, detailing his whereabouts. Such was the seriousness of his condition, however, that his doctors only allowed Ellen to take him home after more than three months of treatment.

The atmosphere back in Germany was hardly a pick-me-up for a sick man, having become notably bleaker in the six months he had been away. On Kristallnacht, 500 Jews in Karlsruhe were arrested and deported to the concentration camp at Dachau. All known Jewish shops and the Nassauer Hof hotel were ransacked. The Orthodox synagogue was destroyed. The Hirsch family synagogue on Kronenstrasse was laid to waste and set alight. 'A large crowd crowded in front of it,' recalled Kurt Witzenbacher, an onlooker who was then eight years old. 'SA men carried out Torah scrolls and a still smouldering upholstered chair and threw everything on a pile.'

The fire at the synagogue was only extinguished because there were concerns that the adjacent petrol depot of a car company would be affected. The Jewish community was therefore ordered to demolish the synagogue at its own expense the following week.

On 30 January 1939, with Hirsch still in the French hospital, Adolf Hitler celebrated six years in power by informing the Jews that they had seen nothing yet. He told an adoring Parliament:

> During the time of my struggle for power it was in the first instance the Jewish race which only received my prophecies with laughter when I said that I would one day take over the leadership of the state, and with it that of the whole nation, and that I would then among many other things settle the Jewish problem. Their laughter was unrestrained, but I think that for some time now they have been laughing on the other side of their face. Today I will once more be a prophet: if the international Jewish financiers in and outside Europe should succeed in plunging the nations once more into a world war, then the result will not be the Bolshevisation of the earth, and thus the victory of Jewry, but the annihilation of the Jewish race in Europe!

At the beginning of May 1939, Hirsch was admitted to another psychiatric hospital, this time in Achern, fifty kilometres south of Karlsruhe. The treatment in the institution was brutal, reflecting the prevailing scientific assumption that patients could be jolted out of an episode of mental illness. Hirsch regularly had convulsions and comas intentionally induced with the aid of cardiazol and insulin. Understandably, he was not keen to stick around. With rain sheeting down one day, he temporarily escaped wearing only felt slippers and tried to steal a bicycle to ride back to Karlsruhe. In the end, he was not permitted to return home until late September, after a lengthy five-month spell of detention, although the doctors still maintained in a discharge note that he was 'unhealed'. By this time, Germany had invaded Poland, the war had begun in earnest, and emigration was an even more distant dream.

Already down on the canvas, Hirsch was kicked some more. German Nazi propaganda routinely depicted Jewish intellectuals and merchants as lazy parasites who shied away from an honest day's work. The opportunity to teach them a lesson, to humiliate them, promised an exhilarating thrill. Now denied employment in their own fields, such Jews were often forced to undertake unskilled labour in miserable or hostile conditions. From 1939 until his eventual deportation in 1943, former Germany international and Iron Cross bearer Julius Hirsch, now a severe depressive with proven suicidal tendencies, would travel to the outskirts of Karlsruhe to work in a rubbish dump.

* * *

In the context of the Holocaust, Jews in Germany fared significantly better than in other parts of Europe. Although it became increasingly difficult to leave Germany after 1933 and to gain permission to live in another country, many Jews did manage it. However, in those areas that Germany invaded after the war had started, Jews were often trapped, contributing to much higher murder rates (often around 90 per cent) among pre-existing populations.

In January 1933, there were 523,000 Jews in Germany. By 1939, approximately 282,000 had emigrated, mostly to countries that turned out be safe for them, such as the United States, British-controlled Palestine and the United Kingdom, but many also to neighbouring states, such as France, Belgium, Netherlands and Denmark, where they were soon caught up in the maelstrom. In Karlsruhe itself, the Jewish population reflected the general trend, more than halving in size in the space of six years from its 1933 figure of around 3,200 (the reduction also included the forced deportation of 165 Karlsruhe Jews with Polish citizenship back to their country of origin in October 1938).

The close family and friends of Julius Hirsch offer some examples of this pattern. His brother Rudolf fled to Colombia, while his sister Rosa went to France where her husband Louis Einstein was ultimately murdered in 1944. His friend and teammate Gottfried Fuchs moved with his family to Switzerland, then Paris, where he met Hirsch for the last time during the latter's stay there in 1938. In May 1940, with German troops already in France, the Fuchs family somehow managed to get hold of a precious lifeline – some extremely rare visas to Canada (only 5,000 desperate Jewish refugees were allowed into that vast country from 1933 to 1948).

For those remaining in Karlsruhe, Hitler's self-fulfilling prophecy of extermination was soon staring them in the face. In October 1940, 895 Karlsruhe Jews were deported to Gurs internment camp in southwestern France, operated by the French Vichy government. Conditions were appalling, disease was rife and most of those who did manage to survive were subsequently sent to be murdered in Auschwitz-Birkenau in November 1942.

Only between 400 and 500 Jews were left in Karlsruhe after this transport to Gurs and the pressure on those remaining was unbearable. Members of so-called mixed families (one Jewish and one non-Jewish spouse) had been spared that deportation, but how long before they too would be consigned to an unknown fate? In September 1941, Julius, Heinold and Esther were all compelled to wear a yellow Star of David on their outer clothing, further cementing their sense of alienation and impending doom.

By early 1942, Ellen Hirsch was being repeatedly urged by her non-Jewish family to do what was necessary to save her children. She hatched a plan. She would request a legal annulment of her marriage due to her husband's 'racial affiliation', and to the resulting 'unbearable' exclusion of both her and her children from the *Volksgemeinschaft* (national community). According to Skrentny's research, Hirsch fumed privately about his wife's scheme but chose not to contest her wishes in court. One assumes, anyway, that the opinion of a Jew in a German court in 1942 would have been a complete waste of breath.

The judge was sceptical. He argued that Ellen must have been fully aware of the problems posed by her husband's race ever since the Nazis came to power almost a decade previously, and consequently rejected her application. No doubt recognising Ellen's true motivation, he also noted as an aside that 'the sought-after annulment of the marriage as such would not change the children's blood affiliation and the fact that they are considered Jews according to prevailing conditions.'

The case was heard on 3 March 1942, around a year to the day before Julius Hirsch was gassed. Less than three weeks after the hearing, he left the family apartment, probably as a concession to Ellen's continued determination to demonstrate to the authorities that their relationship was over. He moved into the so-called *Judenhaus* (Jew house), a sort of dosshouse for Jews with nowhere to go, and situated on Kronenstrasse, a few doors down the road from Hirsch's now ruined synagogue.

With Hirsch now gone, Ellen was in a stronger position to file for divorce by citing a breakdown of the marriage. Both Ellen and Heinold both testified to this effect in court, although the latter admitted that he spent the rest of his life regretting his involvement. Revealingly, the court stated that allegations about the marriage breakdown 'are to be evaluated with caution according to the special circumstances of the case', reflecting the belief that Ellen was primarily interested in saving her children. Nevertheless, on 2 December 1942, the court registered the divorce.

Ellen's gamble was certainly ill-conceived, and it could also be convincingly argued that it backfired to a dramatic extent, with tragic consequences. As the judge of the first hearing intimated, she fundamentally misunderstood German Nazi ideology, overemphasising the importance of the religious antisemitism that had been prevalent in Germany and throughout Europe for centuries, and downplaying the more modern breed of racial antisemitism, based on Jews' supposedly inferior genetic characteristics.

As they had two Jewish grandparents, Heinold and Esther were *mischlinge* (mongrels) of the first degree according to Nazi classification. Whereas *mischlinge* in Nazi-occupied Eastern Europe were treated as Jews and condemned to death, the policy towards them throughout Germany (and Western and Central Europe) was inconsistent and complex, reflecting some disagreement within the hierarchy. Some argued for their integration, others for their ostracisation, sterilisation or liquidation, with a harder-line stance gaining more sway as the war progressed. But one thing was for sure – the religion that any given *mischling* professed to follow was more or less irrelevant in determining their fate.

On the eve of the festival of Passover, 18 April 1943, and after Julius Hirsch had already been dead for six weeks, Ellen succeeded in getting her children baptised. Whereas the divorce arguably turned out to be counterproductive, the baptism was merely pointless.

In February 1945, with the war hurtling towards defeat but with the thirst for Jewish blood nevertheless remaining unquenched, 22-year-old Heinold and sixteen-year-old Esther were deported to Theresienstadt, sixty kilometres north of Prague, a cross between a ghetto and a concentration camp, in which 33,000 Jews were murdered and from which a further 90,000 were sent to be exterminated further east.

Heinold and Esther formed part of a group of seventeen deportees from Karlsruhe, comprising only Jewish partners of mixed marriages and *mischlinge* of the first degree. Among the group was Max Hirsch, the older brother and former business partner of Julius, who was himself married to a non-Jew. Thanks to the proximity of the end of the war, all seventeen managed to survive and returned safely to Karlsruhe in June.

A few years before her death at the age of eighty-four in 2012, Esther wrote some recollections about her stay in Theresienstadt. 'If father had still been married,' she suggested bitterly, 'he would have come to Theresienstadt with us on the same transport and would have been liberated with us by the Russians.'

After the war, Esther's mother Ellen reverted to the surname Hirsch, lived a very secluded life and apparently never spoke about these events again.

* * *

While in Theresienstadt, Heinold and Esther would not yet have known what had happened to their father. Perhaps they even harboured some dream that they would encounter him there.

Hirsch was one of twelve Jews ordered to report to Karlsruhe train station on 1 March 1943 for an 'emigration transport'. Hirsch was number six on the list, his entry complete with the middle name Israel, an obligatory addition for all Jewish males in Nazi Germany with a non-Jewish first name. Four people did not show up, including a family of three who had gone into hiding.

His daughter Esther accompanied him to the station. More than sixty years later, in an interview with Skrentny, her memories of that fateful early morning were still vivid. Her heart-rending description also offers an invaluable insight into her father's personality, confirming the impression of a gentle, trusting and straightforward family man.

> It was a radiantly beautiful day. Even today, I can't believe that the sun could shine on that day! We did not believe that we would never see him again … My father had not thought that the Germans could do anything to him. He could not have imagined this as a front-line fighter and as a well-known national football player. He was attached to Germany, he was for Germany – just like his brothers in the First World War. He never thought he would be treated like this. How humiliating it was for him to work as a forced labourer on a Karlsruhe rubbish dump. He was a kind man and always full of understanding. I loved him very much and am grateful for his affection. I am still grateful today. He was always for a friendly and loving coexistence.

The train arrived in Dortmund the following morning. The deportees then spent the night in a hall next to the city's main station. From there, Hirsch managed to send a postcard addressed to Esther, whose fifteenth birthday was to be on 3 March. It read, 'My dears! I landed OK, things are going well. Going to Upper Silesia, am still in Germany. Warm greetings and kisses from your Juller.' By the time the postcard arrived, Hirsch was dead.

After the train had stopped at various pickup points, more than 1,500 German Jews were aboard. Survivor testimonies about the same transport, compiled by the cultural foundation of the German Football Association in 2021, detail the conditions that Julius Hirsch would have had to endure during his last hours on earth.

'Family members screamed when their loved ones collapsed and were later pronounced dead,' said Ernst Lion from Dortmund. 'Children screamed, thirsty and disoriented ... With a few stops in between, the train moved steadily for a night and then a whole day.' The memories of Justin Sonder from Chemnitz were little different. 'During the journey to Auschwitz and before, we received no food or drink,' he told a war crimes trial in 1987. 'We had to defecate in a bucket that stood in a corner of the wagon. During the entire journey, the doors of the cattle cars, which had only one air flap, remained closed.'

Hirsch's train arrived at Auschwitz-Birkenau at a similar time to a transport of around 1,750 Jews from Berlin. On 4 March, the likely date of the registration of the two arrivals, at least 535 men and 145 women were newly selected for slave labour at the camp.* The remainder of the passengers on the two transports – children, pregnant women, the disabled, the sick and any other adults deemed insufficiently fit for gruelling work – were sent immediately to the gas chambers, their names unrecorded.

The proportions sent to their respective fates on that day were typical at the camp – 20 per cent to precarious life as a slave labourer, and 80 per cent for instant liquidation. As there is no record of Julius Hirsch's arrival, we are left to assume that he was selected for the latter category.

Living out his life in the safety and comfort of Montreal until his

* Deportations of Jews during this very week demonstrate the broad geographical sweep of the European Holocaust. Among those setting off on a transport from Berlin to Auschwitz-Birkenau on 2 March 1943 was a group of 158 Norwegian Jews who had been brought over by boat and train from their home country to the German capital in order to be sent to the death camps. On 4 March, a round-up also commenced of 4,075 Jews living in the Bulgarian-occupied region of Greece – around 3,000 kilometres from Norway – to be deported to Treblinka death camp. The murder rate of Jews in that region was 97 per cent.

death in 1972, Gottfried Fuchs never returned to Germany and evidently never stopped thinking about his teammate. 'My grandfather was a very humble man, and spoke little about his past,' said Fuchs's grandson, Julian Heller, in an interview. 'I do remember him saying, however, that he would never forgive them for how they had treated his friend Hirsch, and would never forgive them for what they did to him.'

What about Fritz Förderer, the final member of the feared KFV, Southern Germany and Germany front three, and like the other two, a native of Karlsruhe? What did he make of it all, a man who trained, travelled and played with Hirsch and Fuchs for many years, and owed much of his footballing success to his excellent on-field understanding with the two Jews?

The historical record speaks for itself. In 1939, the city of Weimar in eastern Germany appointed Förderer as administrator of the municipal sports facilities and as a sports teacher. He joined the Nazi Party and coached a team of SS guards at Buchenwald concentration camp, near Weimar, in which 11,800 Jews were murdered.

In 2012, Ernst Otto Bräunche, the head of the Karlsruhe city archive, wrote an article about Förderer, in part detailing his experiences in Soviet-occupied Weimar in the immediate aftermath of the war. 'He was probably not a convinced National Socialist,' suggested Bräunche, 'because after the war, after a short break due to staff cutbacks in the city, he regained his position as groundsman by order of the Russian occupying power, and in 1945 also coached the football team of the Russian soldiers stationed in Weimar.'

I think that Bräunche is rather too keen to rehabilitate this son of Karlsruhe, downplay his Nazi credentials and ignore the sickening moral abandonment of his teammates. In Germany today, we see the now ubiquitous memorialisation of the Holocaust, including all the speeches, statues, plaques and prizes so belatedly devoted to Julius

Hirsch many decades after the German state gassed him to death. But Bräunche's words indicate to me that much dissembling nevertheless continues in that country behind the facade, a deep-rooted dysfunction that even now prevents genuine understanding of the forces that took this great Jewish footballer from object of admiration to victim of brutal murder in the seeming blink of an eye.

CHAPTER 5

THE EMPEROR OF ITALY

Matches against foreign opposition have always held a certain mystique and allure for European football fans, with their heroes testing their mettle against unfamiliar opposition. Before the World Cup was introduced in 1930, friendlies and the Olympic Games served to quench the thirst for competition between national teams. And before the European Cup started in 1955, club supporters had to make do with various lesser alternatives: occasional foreign tours; the Mitropa Cup involving the best that a select group of countries could offer; and various standalone tournaments that attracted much media and popular attention.

One such tournament was Le Tournoi international de l'Exposition Universelle de Paris, held in May and June 1937 to coincide with a major art and technology exhibition taking place in the French capital. Eight teams were invited to participate, including such leading lights as Olympique de Marseille and FC Sochaux, winners of the French league and cup respectively in 1937; Austria Vienna, Mitropa Cup winners in 1936; VfB Leipzig, 1936 German cup winners; and Slavia Prague, winners of the Czechoslovak league in 1937.

There were even representatives from England, a footballing culture which still habitually turned its nose up at foreign opposition, viewed condescendingly back in Blighty as inferior Johnny-come-latelies to the sport. The team in question, Chelsea, had only finished thirteenth in the English league that year, which begged the question of how many others had already rejected the invitation, believing the tournament to be beneath them. But being an English team that also contained several internationals, many seasoned observers still fancied the London club to win the knockout tournament with ease, especially after they disposed of Olympique de Marseille and Austria Vienna to reach the final.

Between Chelsea and the trophy stood Bologna, who had already dismissively swotted aside FC Sochaux and Slavia Prague, winning 4–1 and 2–0 respectively. Sitting in Bologna's dugout was a Jew, Árpád Weisz, a former Hungary international. An obsessive thinker about football and a fearless innovator, Weisz had already masterminded three title wins in Italy, a country whose then peerless quality of football was to be demonstrated by two successive World Cup triumphs during the 1930s.

Seven years before the tournament, in 1930, a 34-year-old Weisz had led Ambrosiana (the temporary name of Inter Milan) to his first *scudetto*. Hired by the Bologna board in 1935 with the clear brief to smash what had latterly become the Juventus hegemony in Italian football, he repaid his bosses by presenting them with back-to-back championships.

If there was to be any complacency in Chelsea's approach to the game, they would soon learn that they were dealing with the wrong team, and the wrong man. Meticulously prepared and organised as always, Bologna tore into their opponents, with a hat-trick from winger Carlo Reguzzoni helping the team to a crushing 4–1 victory. It was not just Chelsea that were blown away; the attending press corps was unanimous in its verdict that something extraordinary had taken place right before their eyes.

The Italian newspaper *La Stampa* praised a performance of

'marvellous verve, speed and technique' in attack, while at the other end of the pitch, the Bologna defence was like 'an unbreakable wall impossible to penetrate'. The French press was just as effusive. 'Bologna imposed themselves physically and with a ferocious desire to win,' reported *Le Figaro*. 'But they also boasted a solidity which thwarted the British side ... It would be foolish to doubt the quality either of this team or of Italian football.' Meanwhile, *Le Matin* enthused that 'Bologna is a great and beautiful team that deserved victory in the exhibition tournament. Against Sochaux, Slavia and Chelsea, the team displayed tremendous fair play and the best sporting spirit, not to mention a technique and method that render it the top team in Europe.'

At that moment, Weisz was unquestionably the most sought-after coach in the strongest footballing country in the world. Even with such success, however, he was always going to be skating on thin ice. At least, that is, if the past was anything to go by.

At various points in its centuries-old history, the Jews of Bologna had been expelled from the city four times, forced to pay crippling taxes, confined to a ghetto, obliged to wear a distinguishing badge on their clothing and seen their religious books publicly burned. In 1858, a matter of decades before Weisz's arrival, the Bologna authorities had attracted worldwide attention by kidnapping a six-year-old local Jewish boy by the name of Edgardo Mortara from his broken-hearted parents and placing him for the remainder of his life under the protection of the Pope.

Weisz himself opted to baptise his own children soon after their birth, presumably seeking to shield them from the rather unpleasant consequences of being a European Jew. All to no avail. A little more than a year after his magnificent triumph in Paris, the Italian government banished him and his family from the country. The wily fox of football was hounded across Europe until his hunters eventually caught up with him, precipitating a one-sided contest that even the master of strategy was always destined to lose.

* * *

It was in Solt, a small scenic town lying seventy-five kilometres south of Budapest, that Árpád Weisz made his first appearance, on 16 April 1896. The birth certificate from the day tells us that the proud parents were Lázár Weisz, a 40-year-old veterinarian, originally from Hejőszalonta, a tiny village in north-eastern Hungary; and 29-year-old Zsófia (née – conveniently – Weisz), 'the housekeeper of the town veterinarian', from Szécsény, in the north of the country near the modern-day border with Slovakia.*

Gábor Andreides, who wrote a book about Árpád Weisz and the many others who made the journey from Hungary to Italy to play and coach, recalls reading somewhere that Árpád had a sister. However, neither he nor I have found any evidence of her existence. What is certain is that Weisz arrived in Budapest as a young boy, as a 1908 list of veterinarians had Lázár living in Hölgy Street in the capital city's Kőbánya district. Three years later, the family had moved around the corner, to Füzér Street.

Andreides surmises that Weisz came from an assimilated Jewish family. The assumption rings true, for four reasons. First, whereas the young József Braun grew up in the Orthodox Jewish community

* The Jews of Szécsény, numbering approximately 300, were packed into a ghetto in the town in early May 1944. Many of the able-bodied men were immediately drafted for slave labour service. One month later, the remaining Jewish population, predominantly women, children and the elderly, were led to the railway station for deportation, ultimately to Auschwitz-Birkenau. According to survivor Katalin Loffler, the local population lined the streets as the Jews were led away, some clapping and cheering.

of Putnok, the few Jews of Solt attached themselves to the Neolog community in Kalocsa thirty kilometres away.* The Neolog ideology sought integration into Hungarian society, defined Judaism in religious terms only and denied that the Jews also constituted a distinct nation. Second, the name Árpád is heavily associated with the Magyar Grand Prince and national hero who established a dynasty that ruled Hungary for four centuries from 896 CE, exactly 1,000 years before Weisz's birth. The name was no accident – Lázár and Zsófia were making a statement. Third, the family chose to settle in Kőbánya, a Budapest district that had far fewer Jewish residents than the areas of Terézváros or Erzsébetváros, which by contrast were brimming with Jewish life and activity. And fourth, Weisz later appeared to have had little compunction in baptising his young children, a decision likely to have been a step too far had it run completely counter to the ethos of his upbringing.

By the time Weisz was fourteen, he was playing in the youth team of Kőbánya's local club, Törekvés. The club was enjoying the most successful period in its history around this time, hovering near the top of the Hungarian first division in the years immediately before and after the First World War. Weisz started out as an inside left, but *Sporthirlap* soon reported that 'expert eyes have discovered that his real place is on the left wing'. By seventeen, he had made his breakthrough to the first team in his now favoured position.

However, just as he was getting his feet under the table at Törekvés, war erupted. The hostilities put Weisz's career on hold for several years

* There were 511 Jews in Kalocsa prior to the Holocaust. At least 393 of them were murdered. The population of Kalocsa now numbers 18,000. There are no Jews. The database of the United States Holocaust Memorial Museum reveals no evidence of Jews living in Solt directly before the war. The only sign of Jewish life in Solt today are the dead Jews in the cemetery.

at a critical stage of his footballing development. Fate does, however, work in mysterious ways. His wartime experiences were to play a crucial role in his eventual rise to stardom and greatness.

* * *

Enlisted in the 32nd Budapest Infantry Regiment of the Austro-Hungarian army, Weisz was dispatched in 1915 to fight on the Isonzo Front, a stretch of territory mostly located in modern-day Slovenia. The enemy was Italy, which had just joined the war on the side of the United Kingdom, France and Russia.

There were twelve separate battles on the front, with the two sides bogged down in a bloody stalemate for two and a half years. The cost in human life was extremely high for so little military gain. The Austro-Hungarian army alone lost 200,000 men at Isonzo, one sixth of its total number of casualties in the First World War.

A good job then that Weisz had the sense to get captured early on. On 28 November 1915, aged nineteen, he was taken prisoner during the Fourth Battle of Isonzo in the Alpine mountain region of Mrzli Vrh. From there, he was sent to sit out the rest of the war in the relative comfort of a prisoner-of-war camp in the Sicilian city of Trapani.*

The circumstances of his captivity in Trapani are not known. Nevertheless, it seems that Weisz gave us all a lesson in how to derive advantage from adversity. He used the period of inactivity to master Italian, a skill that without doubt helped him to generate contacts and accelerate his coaching career several years later. 'He is the foreign coach who best speaks our language, whose subtleties he knows

* The only Jews in Trapani during this period would have been Weisz and some of his fellow prisoners. The 2,000 Jews of Trapani, then constituting one quarter of the population, had been expelled in 1492 by the then Spanish rulers.

thoroughly,' observed the magazine *Il Calcio Illustrato* while Weisz was working his wonders in the 1930s.

He must have kept himself in shape in the Sicilian sunshine too, because the now 23-year-old managed to establish his reputation as a top player soon after his return to the Törekvés line-up during the 1919/20 season. Already by February 1920, he had caught the attention of the *Sporthirlap* correspondent after inspiring his team to a 3–1 victory at Budapesti Torna Club: 'Weisz, originally from the youth team, promises to be a genuine force. His through balls and shots both deserve praise.'*

Wind the clock forward a year, and seasoned commentators had started to clamour for Weisz's inclusion in the Hungary national team. 'Törekvés had the best man on the field, left-winger Weisz, who merits the attention of the selection committee,' argued *Nemzeti Sport* after a home draw against Budapesti Atlétikai Klub in April 1921.

The inevitable call-up eventually arrived. In an interview with Weisz shortly before his international debut in a home game against Switzerland in June 1922, the *Nemzeti Sport* journalist focused on the natural footballing intelligence that defined him as a player and eventually became the hallmark of his illustrious coaching career:

> Árpád Weisz, nicknamed 'Csili' and from Törekvés, is twenty-four years old [he was actually twenty-six], and plays a very sensible, thoughtful and calculating brand of football.** He can be deployed

* I have found evidence of several games during that 1919/20 season where Weisz appeared in the same Törekvés team as Béla Guttmann, who was also brought up in Kőbánya, before the latter's transfer to MTK Budapest during the following season. They also travelled together to Paris as part of the Hungary squad for the 1924 Olympics (although they were never selected for the same Hungary XI). We can therefore presume that the two most successful Jewish football coaches of all time knew each other well.

** The nickname is said to derive from Weisz's habit of jangling coins in his pocket. The Hungarian verb *csilingel* means to tinkle.

in all positions across the forward line, crosses the ball very accurately, and is also a confident goalscorer. He has recovered from four years in Italian captivity and is in better condition than ever. He is reluctant to talk about the upcoming matches, but he says he will fight hard and strongly believes that people will not be disappointed.

* * *

At least as far as his first game was concerned, Weisz was wrong. People were very disappointed, and they made no attempt to hide it, either. In a team captained by Vilmos Kertész, one of three Jewish brothers who all played for the Hungary national team, Weisz was paired next to his club colleague and another debutant, the inside left Ferenc Hirzer. 'We know very well that Weisz and Hirzer only made the team by forming an excellent unit, but individually neither of them is an international level player,' reported *Nemzeti Sport*, adding the scathing observation that Weisz played a 'scared, timid, anaemic game'.

He was dropped for the remaining three internationals of the summer, but a bright start to the following season for Törekvés earned him a recall in front of 65,000 spectators in a Central European face-off against Austria in Vienna, a game marked by the return of the great József Braun after a year out through injury. This time, Weisz was not paralysed by the hype and made his mark in a 2–2 draw. He even managed to extract praise from the normally brutal *Nemzeti Sport* journalists: 'We had expected little from Weisz, but he surprised us ... showing speed in his running and great intelligence in his passing.'

In this way, a pattern was set for the six games of Weisz's international playing career. Spanning only eleven months in total, his performances fluctuated wildly and never fully convinced the doubters. His footballing brain and his pace had initially piqued the interest of the selectors but press descriptions from the time repeatedly suggest that he lacked the physical robustness, aggression and competitiveness to establish himself at the very top level for a sustained period in an era unsuited to more dainty, technical players. 'I attribute Weisz's inconsistent form to … his timid nature which means he is deeply affected by any strong criticism,' speculated *Sporthirlap*.

In the Vienna game, he had been so good that he 'attracted the interest of Austrian clubs', according to the same newspaper. But in the return fixture two months later, a 2–1 defeat, his 'timidity prevented him from doing anything significant'. In a goalless draw against Italy in Genoa the following March, participating for the first time in top-level football in the country of his one-time captivity, he once again looked 'scared'. But in a comprehensive 6–1 victory against Switzerland a week later, 'he was the perfect winger at times … he showed in Lausanne that he is the best left-winger in Hungary.'

The selectors' patience finally evaporated after a 1–0 away defeat in Vienna in May 1923. 'The Hirzer-Weisz pair played today as if they were playing in a national team for the first time, apprehensive and impotent,' reported *Sporthirlap*. 'This is especially true of Weisz, whose display was completely naive.' *Budapesti Hirlap* chimed in with the general chorus of condemnation, remarking, 'Weisz, whose great speed predestined him for the left-wing position, was so slow yesterday that his Austrian opponents dispossessed him most of the time.'

Although he was chosen in the 21-strong squad (including at least eight Jews) for the 1924 Olympics in Paris, he never appeared on the pitch for the national team again. In a book about the top Hungarian footballers of the past, published in 1969 around twenty-five years after Weisz's murder, authors Zoltán Antal and József Hoffer delved into the archives to provide an apt summary of his playing career: 'The lightweight, very capable "Csili" played sensibly by making use of his technique. He ran energetically, passed carefully and – although quite rarely – shot at goal with great power. Agility was also one of his virtues. Courage – less so. He conspicuously avoided physical confrontation.'

Weisz, it seems, was a whole lot more brain than brawn.

* * *

In the intervening year between his last cap and his selection for the Paris squad, Weisz spent a season with Maccabi Brno in the Moravian region of Czechoslovakia.* Football-mad Jewish textile industrialists from the city had invested enough funds for the Zionist club to go out and recruit some top players from the high-quality Hungarian league.

Of all the Jewish clubs of that era, only Hakoah Vienna surpassed Maccabi Brno for achievement and international reputation. For a couple of years, Maccabi spent much of their time travelling around Europe earning large appearance fees, a sort of Jewish Harlem Globetrotters with a couple of guest non-Jewish stars thrown in, such as Weisz's long-time teammate Ferenc Hirzer.

During that 1923/24 season, with Weisz on the left wing, Maccabi embarrassed Austrian champions Rapid Vienna, a club historically associated with antisemitism, beating them 4–1 in front of 30,000 baffled supporters; drew 3–3 with soon-to-be champions Slavia Prague in the Czechoslovak capital; and overcame Juventus 2–1 in Turin. Such was the team's reputation that they were even invited to take on the

* In October 1941, there were 11,102 Jews in Brno. In November, the first transport of 1,000 Jews was deported to Minsk, where they were shot, murdered in gas trucks or starved to death. Between December 1941 and July 1943, 9,064 Brno Jews were sent in eleven transports to Terezin concentration camp near Prague. Some were murdered there, but most were later sent for extermination in the death camps in Poland. Only an estimated 684 Jews survived.

Italian national team in an Olympics warm-up in early May 1924, drawing 1–1 in Bologna.

Maccabi's Hungarian contingent was hit from two angles after the Olympics. They were firstly subject to a thinly veiled antisemitic onslaught from politicians and journalists back home after Hungary, with four players from Maccabi Brno and one from Hakoah Vienna in the squad, crashed out to unfancied Egypt in the second round. 'The fiasco of the Hungarian colours was caused by the players who returned from abroad bribed by money and without Hungarian awareness,' commented the nationalist newspaper *Magyarság*. 'Their accomplices are those who, instead of [selecting] honest and worthy Hungarian players, built a team in Paris from foreign, Czech-Jewish clubs.'

If this torrent of abuse wasn't enough to make the players think twice about continuing to play for Maccabi, the Czech Football Association then pitched in by forbidding Jewish clubs from employing Christian players, allegedly because the leading domestic clubs did not take kindly to the competition in the transfer market. The top Jewish players, such as Weisz, József Eisenhoffer, Lajos Fischer and Rudolph Nickolsburger, resolved to leave in solidarity with their departing Christian teammates.

As Weisz considered where to move next, Italy must have loomed large as the obvious option. He spoke Italian fluently and was familiar with the national culture. Meanwhile, Hungarian players were all the rage in Italy after a Braun-inspired national team had thumped Italy 7–1 in April 1924. Lured by the higher wages and standards of living, these players were only too happy to take up the offers being thrown at them. Indeed, by the 1925/26 season, there were fifty-five players from Hungary in the Italian Prima Divisione (the top league was only restructured with the name Serie A in 1929), of whom nineteen were full Hungarian internationals.

The first stop for Weisz was Alessandria in Northern Italy, equidistant from the major cities of Milan, Turin and Genoa.* Weisz had turned out for Maccabi Brno against Alessandria on the Czech club's European tour a few months previously, and he had perhaps received an offer at that point. It appears that he performed well enough at his new club for twice national champions Internazionale, commonly referred to as Inter Milan, to come calling at the end of his first season there. It was to be the start of an on-off but highly fruitful love affair that lasted for the best part of a decade.

Almost all his time at Inter was spent in the dugout. Weisz made just eleven appearances in the 1925/26 season for the *Nerazzurri* (black and blues) before a knee injury intervened to put a stop to his playing days at the age of thirty.

Throughout a career curtailed at either end by war and injury, Weisz had been a good footballer. 'Good' would not necessarily be the first word one might use to describe him as a coach.

* * *

Fascinated by team organisation and preparation and bursting with new ideas, Weisz hungrily seized an opportunity to learn more about the coaching trade, first taking on a role as assistant to Augusto Rangone back at Alessandria. Rangone was a highly respected football man, steeped in the technical aspects of the game, who would later serve as coach of the national team.

---

* Jews had been recorded living in Alessandria from the late fifteenth century. In 1938, there were 101 Jewish residents of the city. On 13 December 1943, local Italians attacked the synagogue, destroying or stealing the silver objects and throwing holy books and scrolls into a huge bonfire in a city square. In total, forty-eight Jews were deported from the region in 1943 and 1944, mostly to be murdered at Auschwitz-Birkenau.

Within a few months, Inter had brought Weisz back to the club for the 1926/27 season, this time as head coach. It was a huge show of faith from such a leading club in someone so young, and a testament to the deep impression he must have made on the hierarchy in his short time as a player there.

Weisz was a pioneer from the outset, abandoning the smart jacket and tie beloved of his coaching peers and donning a football shirt and shorts to give clear instructions and practical demonstrations next to his players on the training pitch. Coming from a generation of Budapest footballers heavily influenced by the Jimmy Hogan school, he drummed home the importance of diet and lifestyle. 'Alcohol in particular crushes a player's hopes of reaching peak performance,' he wrote. To foster team togetherness and focus, he introduced the concept of the *ritiro*, whereby players stayed together in the same hotel the night before a game.

On the tactical side, he was among the first to bring to Italy a variation of the W-M formation attributed to the highly successful English coach Herbert Chapman and later employed to power Italy to two successive World Cups in the 1930s. It was a system which strengthened defence and facilitated more fluent counter-attacks, with inside forwards deployed deeper to support the midfield and the centre-half pushed back into a three-man back line.

Taken together, it was a coaching philosophy and approach that Weisz codified in his 1930 book *Il Giuoco del Calcio* ('The Game of Football'), tellingly introduced with a foreword by Vittorio Pozzo, coach of the victorious Italy team of the subsequent decade. In those days, newspaper columnists might analyse the strengths and weaknesses of players, but they were less likely to discuss the approach of the coach, whose impact on team success was less accepted than it is today. For someone like myself, seeking to understand Weisz one hundred years later, the ideas expressed in his book therefore become invaluable.

As well as exploring the roles and responsibilities of each position within the team, Weisz debates the respective merits of what was then known as the English style of play, involving dribbling, constant running and long balls, and the Scottish style of play, focused on passing and possession of the ball. He advocates a mixed pragmatic method that combines the importance of possession with sudden switches to attack, making use of long passes when necessary – now a standard compromise formula in top-level modern football.

He decries the notion, again well ahead of his time, that there is any necessary connection between being a top player and a successful coach. He also stresses in the book that the coach must not only possess expertise in tactics and technique but also the emotional intelligence to grasp the psychological make-up of each player. In his view, the coach's insight into human nature was the key to effective people management, motivation and the fulfilment of individual and team potential.

Indeed, Weisz was not one for bellowing orders or issuing chastisements. His managerial style reflected his personality – quiet, thoughtful, discerning and diligent – summoning, perhaps, a comparison with the modern-day great, Zinedine Zidane. If he had a disagreement or dispute with a player, he would invite them for dinner and try to iron the problem out.

His musings on the connection between players' mental and emotional make-up and their achievement on the pitch, recorded in a 1934 article in *Il Littoriale*, stand out for their poetic eloquence: 'There is no performance without passion, no passion without interpersonal connection, no interpersonal connection without friendship, no friendship without sincerity, but what defines the atmosphere is the harmony of the team.'

Crucially for a coach, Weisz had a keen eye for a player and what each individual could potentially contribute to the team unit. In September 1927, he plucked the seventeen-year-old striker Giuseppe Meazza out of the youth team and threw him into the fray in a pre-season tournament in Como. One of the all-time greats, Meazza is still the second highest goalscorer ever for the Italian national team, winning the World Cup twice (once as captain) and regularly appearing on football journalists' lists of the top ten greatest players in the tournament's history.

In 1980, the San Siro stadium in Milan was officially renamed as the Stadio Giuseppe Meazza in his honour. The fans of Inter, who have shared the stadium with rivals AC Milan since 1947, still often refer to the San Siro by the name of their former idol. In this way, one of the most celebrated landmarks in world football, scene of World Cup matches and European Cup Finals for almost an entire century, is closely linked to Árpád Weisz.

But it is not the only way. The stadium built on meadows on the western outskirts of the city was inaugurated with a friendly game between the two Milan rivals in September 1926. The festival match did not quite work out as the then sole tenants AC Milan might have wished. The visitors spoiled the party with a resounding 6–3 victory.

If AC Milan were hoping for a celebratory launch of their spanking new stadium, they hadn't counted on a young Hungarian Jew – to be known in future years throughout Italy as *Il Mago* ('the magician') – weaving his spell from the sidelines in one of his very first outings. If you look closely at the bottom of the Inter team sheet that day, you will see the words *Allenatore* (Coach): Weisz.

* * *

Weisz's first stint at Inter was solid, though it gave little indication of the fireworks to come. The league was then divided into two sections, with the top few teams in each section qualifying for another round-robin tournament. Inter qualified for the final stage in both 1926/27 and 1927/28 but did not come close to pulling off a title win.

Inter and Weisz parted ways at that point, albeit, it later turned out, only temporarily. In September 1928, an announcement appeared in *Sporthirlap* back in the country of his birth: 'Árpád Weisz, who has been coaching in Italy until now, will take over as manager of Sabaria. An agreement was reached between the trainer and the Szombathely club yesterday.'

He spent just one year at the Hungarian First Division club close to the Austrian border, but it was certainly a formative one. From December 1928, Weisz took his team on a three-month tour of Cuba, Mexico and finally the United States. In the concluding leg of what had previously been a highly successful tour, Sabaria lost 3–0 to the Jewish team New York Hakoah, which included Béla Guttmann and Weisz's former Maccabi Brno teammates Nickolsburger and Eisenhoffer. The game ended in a mass brawl between the players, a crowd pitch invasion and the intervention of riot police to bring an end to the bedlam.

As well as availing himself of this international footballing education, Weisz met his future wife during this season in Szombathely – Ilona Rechnitzer, a local Jewish woman twelve years younger than him. They were married in the city in September 1929 and immediately moved as a couple to Milan. Sabaria were in a financial mess, and Inter, clearly believing that there was much more to come from Weisz, had invited him back for another crack at the title.

Except, by this stage, they weren't called Inter anymore. Benito Mussolini's fascist authorities inevitably disliked the name Internazionale – a name which derived from the ambition of the club's founders to recruit some of their players from outside Italy's borders – and forced a name change to the more patriotic Ambrosiana in honour of the patron saint of Milan. As another sign of an increasingly inhospitable environment, foreign players had by now also been banned from competing in the Italian championship.

(The powers that be still permitted foreign coaches such as Weisz, however, if clubs could show that 'they cannot find anybody suitable in the Motherland'. Despite the hostile environment and bureaucratic hurdles, seven of the sixteen coaches in Serie A by 1935 were Hungarian, compared to five Italians, showing the continued appeal of the perceived maestros from Central Europe.)

Weisz repaid his bosses' renewed faith in spades in that 1929/30 season. Ambrosiana's march to the championship, the club's first *scudetto* in ten years, owed much to Meazza's remarkable goal ratio of thirty-one goals in thirty-three games. The twenty-year-old had flourished due to Weisz's strict regime, which involved a steak diet to build him up physically and relentless practice kicking a ball against a wall with each foot until he became equally proficient in both. He was now the complete forward – a lethal finisher, a powerful header of the ball, a brilliant dribbler and with the vision to assist others to score with a perceptive final pass that no defence could see coming.

It was Meazza who saved Ambrosiana's skin in the nerve-jangling final stage of the season. The third-last game took place at the club's home ground of Campo Virgilio Fossati against second-placed Genoa, only four points behind and breathing down their necks.

The fervent home crowd filled the rickety grandstand far beyond its natural capacity, causing it to collapse before the game with dozens taken to hospital with injuries. When the match did kick off, the shaken Ambrosiana players succumbed to an early 3–1 deficit. But Meazza then composed himself to score two late goals, earning a hat-trick for himself and a vital point for his team. Two weeks later, in a game hastily switched to the San Siro, Ambrosiana clinched the title with a 2–0 victory over third-placed Juventus.

Árpád Weisz, now aged thirty-four, had placed himself firmly on the footballing map. The Jewish coach remains to this day the youngest ever to win Serie A.

* * *

This was a golden period for Weisz. Two weeks after lifting the championship, his first child Roberto was born in a Milan hospital. Just as with Árpád's Hungarian name a generation before, the choice of an Italian name was a clear signal that Roberto's parents were determined to integrate into society and avoid the growing popular antipathy towards foreigners. By this time, Ilona had also Italianised her own name to Elena.

Although Mussolini's regime did not enact its antisemitic legislation until several years later, the couple also saw fit to baptise both Roberto and his younger sister Clara, born in 1934. As with many Jews throughout Europe in this period, they sensed the way the wind was blowing and acted accordingly to avoid unpleasantness and obstacles to career progress. In their home country of Hungary, for example, the number of Jewish conversions to Christianity jumped fifteen-fold in the year 1919 in response to the antisemitic pogroms of the government-instituted White Terror.

The Serie A title earned Ambrosiana a tilt at the Mitropa Cup, founded in 1927, a cross-border competition and precursor of the

European Champions' Cup introduced almost three decades later. In 1929, Italian entrants saw fit to join the existing representatives from Austria, Hungary and Czechoslovakia. Juventus and Genoa both crashed out in the first round that year. Their failure was a sign of the footballing strength of the three other competing nations, which all either reached the semi-final or final of the 1934 and 1938 World Cups but have since disappeared from the top echelon of world football.

Ambrosiana therefore faced an uphill task after being paired with Mitropa Cup holders and Hungarian champions Újpest in the first round – or quarter-finals – of the eight-team tournament in 1930. The confrontation did not disappoint, conjuring something of a footballing extravaganza for the ages. After a 6–6 aggregate draw in the home and away legs, and another stalemate in a first play-off, Ambrosiana eventually ran out 5–3 winners in the fourth match.

With the benefit of hindsight, we can also see more than just great games of football. A surviving grainy film of the first leg of this all-time classic encounter between the champions of Weisz's home and adopted countries, both of which would soon come down firmly on the wrong side of history, shows the Ambrosiana players lining up before the kick-off to perform a fascist salute with their Jewish coach looking on. And on the day of Ambrosiana's eventual triumph in the tie, 14 September 1930, Adolf Hitler's Nazi Party dramatically increased its vote in the German federal election, establishing it unequivocally as a potent political force in the country.

Modern-day football pundits often criticise what they regard as over-hasty managerial sackings, harking back to the day when coaches were supposedly handed more time to iron out blips in form. Along with other misguided preconceptions about the distant footballing past – involving, for example, docile and chivalrous spectators or gentle and scant media coverage – this is a myth that does not stand up to closer examination. After exiting at the Mitropa semi-final stage to Sparta Prague, and falling to fifth place in Serie A, a ruthless board dispensed with Weisz's services at the end of the 1930/31 season, barely a year after he had brought the title to Milan.

Fortunately, the directors at Bari were just as fickle, sacking the coach who had just won them promotion to Serie A and inviting Weisz to replace him on the Adriatic coast in the south of the country. However, at the end of his one and only season there, Bari teetered on the brink, finishing level on points with Brescia and consigned to a play-off to decide the second relegation spot.*

The game, played on the stage of Weisz's future glories, the Stadio Littoriale in Bologna, had all the tension and drama of end-of-season play-offs of the modern era. Brescia took an early lead, but two late goals from Dario Gay, known as *il toro* (the bull) by supporters because his heading power resembled a goring, secured Bari's top-league status and prompted dramatic scenes at the final whistle.

Players wept with joy, winger Armando Massiglia passed out on the pitch amid the emotion of it all, and fights broke out between rival travelling fans outside the stadium. Back in Bari, on the Piazza San Ferdinando, locals listened to live commentary on a loudspeaker and embarked on a procession of joy through the streets after the stirring comeback. On the team's triumphant return, his many local admirers carried the understated and reserved Weisz on their shoulders from the centre of a tumultuous town all the way back to the quiet of his home.

* The Bari Jewish community of the Middle Ages was subjected to repeated bouts of punitive taxation, forced conversion to Christianity and violent pogroms before being permanently expelled in 1540. The history of Brescia Jewry in northwestern Italy was remarkably (or perhaps not so remarkably) similar, although the community managed to get to 1572 before being expelled.

* * *

A new president – the industrialist Ferdinando Pozzani – had meanwhile been appointed back at Ambrosiana. He made two quick decisions. First, to win over a fanbase that did not appreciate the break with tradition, he changed the name of the club to the compromise formula Ambrosiana-Inter. Second, he brought Weisz back for the 1932/23 season for his third stint at the club.

In a further two seasons there, Weisz improved the club's position considerably, lifting them from sixth place in the season before he rejoined to successive second-placed finishes behind serial champions Juventus. Moreover, his team went one better than their last attempt and reached the final of the Mitropa Cup in 1933.

Ambrosiana-Inter overcame First Vienna in the opening round, before getting their revenge over Sparta Prague in the semi-finals. Weisz's team was now arguably stronger than their title-winning predecessors, with new additions alongside Meazza such as centre-forward Virgilio Levratto, nicknamed *Lo Sfondareti* (net-ripper) owing to his thunderbolt shots, and the creative talents of the two naturalised Italians from South America, Francisco Frione and Atilio Demaría. However, they were still rank underdogs for the two-legged showdown against opponents Austria Vienna, who had comfortably dispatched Juventus in the semi-final.

The fact that the *Nerazzurri* narrowly failed to cause an upset can be attributed to two factors – some questionable refereeing decisions and the genius of Matthias Sindelar, the so-called 'Mozart of football'.

Ambrosiana-Inter took a 2–1 first-leg advantage to Vienna, where 58,000 packed into the Prater stadium, used less than a decade later to detain many of the city's Jews before they were transported east to their deaths. However, the Czechoslovak referee František Cejnar, dubbed by *La Stampa* as 'the fat dictator of whistle blowing', first awarded a penalty to Austria Vienna that surprised even the home players and then saw fit to dismiss both Demaría and defender Luigi Allemandi. The desperate nine-man rearguard was no match for Sindelar, who completed a hat-trick to secure a 3–1 win and the coveted trophy.

Weisz left Milan for good at the end of the following season. The trigger-happy Pozzani, who ended up firing eight coaches in his eleven years as president, could not stomach the Juventus dominance, nor Weisz's typically studied remark that it would take another two years of patient team-building and expert coaching before Ambrosiana-Inter could reach the summit of Italian football.

One man's loss, however, is another man's gain. In January 1935, no sooner had Weisz demeaned himself by accepting a job at lowly Novara in Serie B than Bologna's dynamic new president Renato Dall'Ara turned up at his door to bring him back to the big time.

* * *

Although Bologna had been champions in 1929, they had since fallen well behind serial champions Juventus. The club's start to the 1934/35 season, losing five of the first eight games, had compounded the prevailing misery at the club. The ambitious Dalla'Ara set Weisz a clear goal – to replicate what he achieved at Inter, recover the club's fortunes and secure the precious *scudetto*.

There was certainly no shortage of talent already at the club to help him get there. It just needed someone of Weisz's coaching acumen to light the blue touch paper. The home-bred striker Angelo Schiavio had scored the winning goal for Italy in the World Cup final the previous year, while the native Uruguayan midfielders, Francisco Fedullo and Raffaele Sansone, effortlessly interchanging on the pitch and brimming with playmaking flair and inventiveness, had also gone on to represent their adopted country.

Soon after Weisz's appointment, centre-half and future fulcrum of the team Michele Andreolo was another to arrive from Montevideo, fresh from back-to-back Uruguayan title wins with Nacional. Despite being an inveterate womaniser and gambler, the larger-than-life Andreolo would go on to play for Italy too, a member of the World Cup-winning team in 1938.

Weisz's first full season, 1935/36, saw a highly competitive, see-saw title race. Bologna flew out of the blocks, winning seven of their first eight games and drawing the other. But looking down from the top gave the team mid-season jitters, and Juventus resumed their customary position, taking the helm at the halfway stage. Torino led for much of the second half of the season, with Bologna, Juventus, Ambrosiana-Inter and even Triestina breathing heavily down their necks.

I Rossoblù (the red and blues) of Bologna managed to drag themselves back up the table, and had managed to secure a one-point advantage over their rivals before the final weekend of the season. Weisz's team therefore just had to beat Triestina at their majestic home ground, the Stadio Littoriale, officially opened by Mussolini a decade before when the corpulent dictator made his spectacular entry to the arena on a horse.* Andreolo's first-half strike settled the team's nerves, and the second period was a victory procession, with goal-poacher Schiavio and an own goal giving the ecstatic crowd permission to celebrate early.

Without mentioning him by name the following morning, *La Stampa* summed up Weisz's achievement:

There were not many who gave Bologna a chance of victory at the

* The ground is now called Stadio Renato Dall'Ara, after Weisz's boss.

> start of the season. The team had finished in a lowly sixth place last year, and did not appear to have improved its squad at all since the previous championship. It had acquired a new centre-half of Uruguayan origin, Andreolo, but had lost a full-back of the calibre of (Eraldo) Monzeglio.

Indeed, all Weisz had done in terms of personnel had been to integrate Andreolo and replace the Roma-bound World Cup winner Monzeglio with the twenty-year-old Dino Fiorini, a fast and strong defender moulded to perfection by his coach. The title can therefore only be ascribed to coaching alchemy – some reorganisation and technical improvements here, some cajoling there, as well as the invaluable experience gleaned from his previous nail-biting title run-in with Inter that had taught Weisz exactly how to calm and reassure the players.

Weisz liked to work with a small squad, believing that this prevented the dressing-room tensions caused by either constant rotation or persistent omission of players in a larger roster. Indeed, in that season, he used only fourteen players in total in the thirty games played. There were no wholesale changes for the following campaign either, only unruffled tinkering. When veteran goalkeeper Mario Gianni decided to call it a day, Weisz simply returned to his old hunting ground in Milan to snap up Carlo Ceresoli. And when Schiavio entered semi-retirement, he exhorted Carlo Reguzzoni to supply more goals to compensate, a request he duly obliged.

The second title was won at a comparative canter. Bologna led the table from just after halfway through the season and sealed the triumph with two games to spare at the beginning of May 1937. A few weeks later came the demolition of Chelsea in Paris, attracting the attention of footballing connoisseurs throughout the continent. Little now appeared to stand in the way of Weisz, still only forty-one years of age, from building a dynasty of sustained success.

But history, it always pays to remember, has a habit of throwing Jews off their perch.

* * *

Bologna started the 1937/38 season strongly, beating eventual champions Ambrosiana-Inter and remaining well in contention at the halfway stage. However, they couldn't build up a head of steam in the title run-in, and ended up finishing fifth in a closely contested race, a disappointing outcome after the highs of the previous two years. Was there something playing on the mind of their brilliant coach?

While Weisz had been enjoying his time in the sun, Mussolini and his antisemitic fascist regime had been busy laying the groundwork for the exclusion of Jews from society, a time-honoured practice in the Italian regions over many centuries and thus a policy that threatened little popular resistance. Antisemitic propaganda had ratcheted up in the media from the mid-1930s onwards. 'Both the announcer and justifier of antisemitism,' declared *Il Popolo d'Italia* in late 1936, 'is always and everywhere the same – the Jew himself. Especially so when he exaggerates, which he often does.'

By late 1938, the authorities had finally tired of the bleating, manipulative Jews of the antisemitic imagination. Between September and November, a comprehensive series of racial laws were enacted to put them firmly back in their place. The 47,000 Jews of Italy (0.1 per cent of the population) were banned from jobs in government, banking, insurance, education, the entertainment industry and the practice of law; Jews were prohibited from attending all educational institutions; marriage between

Jews and non-Jews was outlawed; Jewish property was confiscated and Jewish businesses were forcibly expropriated and handed over to non-Jews.

Most significantly for Weisz, all Jews who had arrived in the country from 1919 onwards were told that they had to leave the country by 12 March 1939, or instead face expulsion. It is unlikely that Weisz needed such an explicit law to tell him he was not wanted. Eight-year-old Roberto had been kicked out of school, his baptism failing to offer any protection against this new breed of racial, biological antisemitism. And Weisz would have had to have been blind and deaf not to sense the frostiness and menace all around him.

'With regards to the world of football ... there is an area in which, we believe, a fair amount of foreign Israelite representation has been transplanted – that of coaches,' declared *Il Calcio Illustrato* in September 1938.

> Well, we don't really regret the fact that these people – who all came among us after 1919 – have to pack their bags within six months, since in this way they will stop selling smoke with that art of salesmanship typical of the race, and will leave their places open for many ex-players of Italian race, who are very capable of doing the job, and who in comparison with the foreigners mentioned above are only inferior in one respect: the facade!

'As their Jewish neighbours were persecuted, it was the rare non-Jewish Italian who spoke up for them,' reflects David Kertzer, a historian who has written widely on Italian antisemitism.

> More commonly, former friends crossed the street to avoid having to greet them ... Italy's antisemitic campaign ... can properly be placed alongside the antisemitic campaign in these years in Germany (and elsewhere in Central Europe) as a crucial step in the process

that would make the Holocaust possible. Before people could entertain the idea of sending Jewish children and other defenceless Jews to their death, simply for being Jewish, they first had to rob them of their humanity, to cast them as dangerous enemies. This the Italians did with the imposition of the racial laws.

Weisz's last involvement in what might be termed elite football was Bologna's 2–0 home victory on 16 October 1938 against Lazio. Ten days later he had left his post, the departure of the three-time champion accorded one dismissive line in *Il Calcio Illustrato*. 'As for Veisz [sic], it seems that he will leave Italy at the end of the year.' Five years later, in the autumn of 1943, 114 members of Bologna's small Jewish population were to follow him out of the country, sent on a hellish journey of more than 1,000 kilometres to be gassed at Auschwitz-Birkenau.

The great coach's journey to the same destination, however, was rather more circuitous.

* * *

Plotting in detail how to win a highly competitive league in a premier footballing country was one thing. Now the master schemer was faced with his most challenging puzzle yet. Where to go? He had to balance the security and well-being of his young family with his professional ambition and the need to find an income from somewhere. And all the while, he and Ilona had to hide their sense of rising panic from their children.

Going back to Hungary might at first glance have seemed the obvious choice. After all, it was the country in which both he and Ilona were brought up, which he had represented at international level and which was still very much a leading footballing nation (Hungary had reached the World Cup final just a few months before when they were beaten by Italy).

Although Árpád's parents Lázár and Zsófia had died by this point, in 1917 and 1934 respectively, Ilona's parents Samu and Malvin and her younger sister Katalin (the only sibling whose existence I could substantiate) were all still alive and well in the family's home town of Szombathely. Wouldn't it be lovely for Roberto and Clara to spend more time with their grandparents, while every day conversing and being educated in Hungarian, a language in which they presumably felt very comfortable?

Lovely and logical for people in a normal situation, perhaps, but not for Jews being chased from pillar to post in the Europe of late 1938. They might have lost to the same opposition in the World Cup final, but independent Hungary had beaten independent Italy to passing its own anti-Jewish laws earlier in that same year, severely limiting Jewish employment in the country's economy. Ferenc Sas, the only Jew to have played for Hungary in that World Cup final, had now fled to Argentina, while the Jewish captain of the national team at the 1934 World Cup and later the Újpest coach, László Sternberg, had upped sticks to the United States.

Moreover, Weisz had seen with his own eyes the explosion of anti-Jewish violence in Hungary during the White Terror straight after risking his life for the same country (and being incarcerated for several years for doing so) during the First World War. In their strategic yet highly anxious deliberations in front of a big map of the world, it would not have taken long for Árpád and Ilona to dismiss their birthplace as a potential destination.

Thanks to the detective work of Weisz's Italian language biographer, Matteo Marani, we discover that he instead tried his luck in Paris, where he had attracted so much attention just eighteen months before in *Le Tournoi*. He made precious little headway however, no doubt because there was precious little love for the Jews in France either.

In December 1938, just before the Weisz family arrived in the City of Light, the French foreign minister Georges Bonnet had been busy telling his German counterpart Joachim von Ribbentrop that France had accepted more than enough Jewish refugees from the latter's country and sought his help to find 'a solution to the Jewish problem'. Independent France even raised the possibility of deporting several thousand Jews to Madagascar, a plan investigated by independent Poland for its own Jews the year before.

In February 1939, however, Weisz was eventually offered a lifeline by FC Dordrecht in the Western Netherlands. Although the appointment would have come as a huge relief, it is difficult to overstate the extent of the professional demotion it represented after his exploits in Italy, a very public example of the marginalisation of Jews from European society. A modern-day equivalent might be a move from a highly successful stint at Real Madrid or Barcelona directly to a provincial club with no international renown and desperately fighting relegation in a much weaker national league – a poorly performing small-town club in Norway or Switzerland, perhaps.

In terms of the bigger picture, moreover, the entirely rational decisions taken by the Weisz family in these months sealed their eventual fate. Weisz's fellow Hungarian Jew, Ernő Egri Erbstein, was also forced to leave his job at Torino at a similar time. Erbstein managed to secure the promise of a new role at Feyenoord in Rotterdam. He, his wife and daughters sought to travel to the Dutch destination through Germany, rather than treading the Weisz family's path via France.

By this stage in early 1939, however, the German-Dutch border had been recently closed to Jews, many thousands of whom had already sought refuge in the Netherlands in the preceding years and had been seeking to do so in increasing numbers after the shock of Kristallnacht in November 1938. The Erbsteins returned instead to Budapest, where their chances of being murdered turned out to be high, but not as high as in the Netherlands. They survived.*

As I researched and wrote this chapter, one of Erbstein's daughters, Susanna, was still alive. She was born in 1926, four years before Roberto Weisz and eight years before his sister Clara, who have both been dead for more than eighty years. Millions of Jews throughout Europe played a similar game of Russian roulette at the time. But unlike with the actual game, most ended up with a proverbial or literal bullet in the skull.

* * *

In his stint as coach at FC Dordrecht, Árpád Weisz demonstrated human resilience, consummate professionalism and a persistent striving for excellence, his very considerable personal attributes withstanding even the most inauspicious of circumstances. This was not a man to feel sorry for himself, even with the most powerful justification to do just that.

The Dutch league was then divided into various regions, with the top team in each division then playing against each other to compete for the championship title. The Western region, in which FC Dordrecht played, contained so many teams that it was itself split into two. When Weisz arrived midway through the season, the team was rooted

* According to the testimony of Béla Guttmann, he and Ernő Egri Erbstein survived the Holocaust by escaping together from a slave labour camp in the environs of Budapest in 1944. Erbstein returned to Torino, before being killed together with his team in an air crash in May 1949 when on the verge of clinching the title.

to the bottom of the ten-team Eerste Klasse West II (First Division West II).

In comparison with the cathedrals of Italian football, FC Dordrecht's home stadium of Markettenweg was decidedly ramshackle, with a tiny grandstand and a capacity of 5,000 (one tenth of the capacity of the Stadio Littoriale). There was no Meazza, Schiavio or Andreolo to work with. But Weisz continued in the only way he knew how, stubbornly adhering to impeccable standards as if he were still top of the tree.

Matteo Marani, whose book *Dallo Scudetto ad Auschwitz* ('From the championship to Auschwitz') was first published in 2007, managed to interview former FC Dordrecht player Nico Zwaan, still a teenager when Weisz joined the club. 'He would make us work in rain or snow,' Zwaan recalled. 'He forced everyone to maintain a sporting lifestyle. But the thing that amazed us most, at least in the beginning, was his knowledge of how to prepare as an athlete. He himself was leading the training on the field.'

Weisz managed to haul his team to a few victories, earning a potential lifeline with an end-of-season relegation play-off at home against UVV Utrecht in June 1939. A second-half recovery in that game saved the club's status in the Eerste Klasse, securing what *The Dordrechtsche Courant* described as a 'completely deserved' victory. The report continues: 'The red-and-whites demonstrated that they still have something to offer, that the lessons that coach Weisz has taught them in a few months have not been fruitless.'

Given the resources at his disposal, the following 1939/40 season could be regarded as one of Weisz's most successful in relative terms, as his team climbed to a mid-table fifth-place finish in their regional league. In his short time at the club, Weisz had apparently managed to instil a close bond between the home supporters and the team, an undervalued achievement for any coach. Markettenweg was turned into something of a fortress, with FC Dordrecht winning six of their nine home fixtures that season, and drawing two more. Even mighty Feyenoord, the eventual national champions that year, were sent back to Rotterdam with their tails between their legs after a 1–0 defeat.

Time for a well-earned rest at the end of the campaign, to enjoy a cigar and a glass of wine and reflect on a job well done? Could he bask in the welcome warmth of May, as so many football coaches in Europe have done after a season of exacting targets painstakingly attained through skill and sweat?

Not this May.

* * *

German paratroopers landed near Dordrecht on the morning of 10 May 1940. The aim was to secure control over strategic bridges in the area and thus facilitate an advance to Rotterdam and The Hague in the heart of the Netherlands. The invaders met stout but short-lived resistance. Within five days, the country had capitulated.

The details of what happened to Árpád Weisz and his family after the German occupation was pieced together by Arie Heijstek, an archivist and former chairman of FC Dordrecht. Heijstek was working on a history of the club, due to be published in 2008 on the 125th anniversary of its founding, when he came across Weisz's name for the first time. He later speculated that any discussion of the Jewish coach had previously been 'silenced' by the club. In the club history published soon after the war, for example, there was no mention whatsoever of Weisz, who had left the club only a few years before and had enjoyed such a stellar reputation throughout Europe.

According to Heijstek, little changed for Weisz in the first months after the invasion. Remarkably, football continued during the 1940/41 season as before. Weisz duly continued to walk from the large family apartment on Bethlehemplein to take training sessions, ultimately leading the team to another creditable fifth-place finish in the regional league.

Outside this surreal bubble of normality, however, the wheels of ostracism and oppression were gaining speed. In August 1940, Jewish ritual slaughter of animals was banned, complicating the observance of a kosher diet. In October, more than 200,000 Dutch civil servants were obliged to declare whether they were Jewish or not, through a so-called 'Aryan declaration'. Just 0.01 per cent of all civil servants refused to sign; all Jewish civil servants were subsequently sacked. All Jewish business people had to register their companies with the authorities, making them vulnerable to punitive measures and ensuring that they could not be easily sold at the owner's discretion.

In January 1941, all Jews had to register themselves as Jews. In May, Jews were banned from visiting swimming pools, beaches and markets. On 1 September, all Jewish children were forced to leave their schools, thus earning Roberto the distinction of being expelled in two countries for the same reason.

Four weeks later, FC Dordrecht received a letter from the local police:

> Regarding what had been stated to you in words about the FC Dordrecht coach, the opinion of the Attorney General of the Court in The Hague has been requested. I therefore inform you that, on the basis of the order of September 15, 1941 on the public conduct of Jews, Arpad Weisz, coach of your club, is forbidden to be on a ground where matches open to the public are organized. Furthermore, I strongly advise you not to employ or keep in the service of

> your club any Jew, because under the present circumstances it could have very harmful consequences for your club.

A month later, Weisz was banned from attending training. By November, FC Dordrecht had found a replacement coach and he was cast out of work, living in a flat with no income, his active brain now solely devoted to educating his own children.

In January 1942, all Jews were ordered to have their passport stamped with a 'J'. In May, all Jews more than six years of age were obliged to wear on their clothing a yellow six-pointed Star of David with the word Jew clearly visible.

At 7am on an otherwise sleepy Sunday morning, 2 August 1942, the Weisz family were awoken from their slumbers by a loud knock on the door. The subsequent arrest is accorded a passing mention in the daily police logbook, sandwiched between the report of a fine for cycling without a front and rear light, and the news that police officer De Leeuw was absent from duty that day because his wife had given birth. 'The house was sealed by order of the German police. The inhabitants were taken away.'

Three months later, two Dutch bureaucrats named Dankmeijer and Pijl compiled an inventory of goods in the now empty home, a standard procedure in the Netherlands before the stolen contents were shipped to Germany. Among the many items listed for 'Room 1' was a 'wall cabinet containing children's clothes'.

By that stage, the children themselves were already dead.

* * *

Arie Heijstek laments that he found no evidence to suggest that the wealthy local businessmen running FC Dordrecht did anything to hide the Weisz family, or avert their deportation. 'It's amazing that everyone let him be picked up so easily. That there was no resistance at all.'

Not so amazing, perhaps, if other accounts of the mass deportation of Jews in the Netherlands are anything to go by, or if we take the necessary time to analyse the bald statistics.

Aside from one notable exception, reported the survivor Hannah Pick-Goslar,

> none of our other non-Jewish neighbours (in Amsterdam) came out of their front doors to see how we were or ask why we were being taken away like criminals, though as we left our apartment building, we saw, above us, some neighbours peering out to get a better look at the unfolding spectacle, their freshly poured morning coffee next to them on their windowsills. I also caught sight of some people on rooftops with binoculars watching us Jews being taken away.

There were approximately 140,000 Jews in the Netherlands in 1941, out of a total population of 9 million (98.5 per cent non-Jews, 1.5 per cent Jews). Around 102,000 of them ended up being murdered, a higher proportion (73 per cent of the total number of Jews) than in any other Western country. The death toll was boosted not just by widespread popular indifference, but by the active, even enthusiastic, compliance of the Dutch civil authorities.

'In their preparations for the extermination of the Jews living in the Netherlands, the Germans could count on the assistance of the greater part of the Dutch administrative infrastructure,' wrote Manfred Gerstenfeld, an expert on antisemitism and the Holocaust, who himself survived the Holocaust as a young child by hiding in Amsterdam.

> The occupiers had to employ only a relatively limited number of their

> own. Dutch policemen rounded up the families to be sent to their deaths in Eastern Europe. Trains of the Dutch railways staffed by Dutch employees transported the Jews to camps in the Netherlands which were transit points to Auschwitz, Sobibor, and other death camps.

The impressive Dutch collaboration even prompted a smiling Nazi leader Adolf Eichmann to remark that the smoothness of the transports had been 'a pleasure to behold'.

The Weisz family were first dispatched to the main transit camp in the Netherlands, Westerbork, situated in the northeast of the country. Before the Nazi invasion, the Dutch government had built Westerbork to intern Jewish refugees from Germany, and had promptly sent the bill of 1.25 million guilders for the camp construction to the local Jewish community.

Árpád, Ilona, Roberto and Clara waited there for the inevitable. 'Westerbork was another word for purgatory,' wrote Abel Herzberg, who arrived at the camp the following year. 'Desperation, total and absolute, seized everyone ... Deportation to Poland might at best be postponed – for a week, perhaps, or for a few weeks at most. Husbands were powerless to protect their wives; parents had to watch helplessly as their children were torn away from them for ever.'

As they waited, life was as bleak as imaginable. 'The wash-houses were dingy, the barracks lugubrious and overcrowded, the sleeping accommodation insalubrious and rudimentary,' reported Herzberg. 'The lavatories and latrines were disgusting, the overcrowding unbearable ... and the camp as a whole was hideous beyond description.'

In the period from June 1942 to August 1944, 112 trains in total departed the Netherlands with its Jews on board, mostly destined for Poland. Each train from Westerbork squeezed in approximately 1,000 Jews. In aggregate for this sterling work, the Dutch national rail company invoiced the Germans for the modern-day equivalent of 3 million euros.

Approximately thirty Euros per Jew.

* * *

After two months in the Westerbork purgatory, the four members of the Weisz family were duly sent on their way from nearby Hooghalen to Auschwitz-Birkenau (120 Euros). According to the Westerbork records, the date was 2 October 1942, Clara's eighth birthday. Space was being cleared in the camp for the imminent arrival of thousands of Amsterdam Jews rounded up on that very day, later to be known as 'Black Friday'. We can imagine the sounds and sights of the Weisz family's departure by reading the diary description of a similar episode in Westerbork by Dutch Jewish journalist Philip Mechanicus, himself later shot dead in Auschwitz-Birkenau:

> The transports are as nauseating as ever. Men, quiet, stony-faced; women, often in tears. The elderly – stumbling, faltering under their burden, tripping on the bad road, sometimes into pools of mud ... Whoever hesitates, whoever dawdles, is being assisted, sometimes herded, sometimes shoved, sometimes beaten, sometimes punched, sometimes persuaded by a boot, quickly shoved aboard the train ... When the cars are full, the prescribed number of deportees having been loaded, the carriages are sealed ... The commandant signals the departure: a wave of the hand. The whistle sounds ... a heart-rending sound is heard by everyone in the camp. The grungy snake, now fully loaded, crawls away.

Willem Polak, one of the very few survivors of the 2 October transport, recalled the conditions on the Weisz family's train in his 1947 testimony to the Netherlands State Institute for War Documentation:

> We travelled in closed freight cars; each car held 55 persons, as well as each person's luggage, which was not insignificant. You can imagine the circumstances under which we travelled. We were not allowed to use the toilets in the German stations. A bucket was left inside the wagon where men, women and children had to relieve themselves. There was no hygiene … Our provisions from the Netherlands were put on our transport, but we saw almost nothing of them. During the entire journey, which took two days, we had to share one loaf of bread with seven persons … The worst thing was that not even one drop of water was provided. One father of twins aged six and a half months asked one of the guards at a station to fill a feeding bottle with water ... He took the bottle, but instead of filling it with water he smashed it against the wagon. We did not receive one drop of water during the journey.

A registry of Jews deported from Westerbork to various camps, compiled in 1959, confirms that Roberto and Clara, as with almost all young children arriving at the death camps, were among the 652 deportees from the transport to be immediately gassed. The date of death is given as 5 October 1942. Ilona, approaching her thirty-fourth birthday, was murdered alongside them.* Less than two years later, in

* Although minimal, the Weisz family's chances of survival were still higher than if they had been sent to Sobibór, the main alternative destination for Jewish deportees from the Netherlands. From Westerbork, 34,313 Jews were sent to Sobibór. Only eighteen of them survived until the end of the war, including sixteen who were immediately transferred to work in other slave labour camps on arrival in Sobibór. So, in truth, two survived, both women – Selma Wijnberg and Ursula Stern. After the war, Wijnberg was threatened with deportation by the Dutch authorities as she had married a Polish Jew – with whom she had escaped from Sobibór in the Jewish uprising of October 1943 – and should therefore be considered a citizen of Poland rather than the Netherlands. The couple moved to Israel, and then the United States. Stern moved to Israel and changed her name to Ilana Safran.

July 1944, her mother, father, younger sister and the other 3,000 Jews of Szombathely walked the same steps to the same fate.

According to a list found among the documents held by Hanns Albin Rauter, the most senior SS officer in the Netherlands, some of the deportees on this 2 October train were converts to Catholicism. On their official entry documents to the Netherlands in 1939, Roberto and Clara had been registered by their parents as such (even though Árpád and Ilona were recorded as Jews). We can therefore be confident that they were among the stated converts on this Westerbork transport, with their parents still hoping against naïve hope, until the literal death, that repeatedly emphasising the baptism of their offspring might persuade the authorities to spare them.

What about Árpád Weisz himself? According to a death registration completed by the Dordrecht city authorities as late as 1951, Weisz was murdered 'in the area of Oświęcim (Auschwitz)' on 31 January 1944, aged forty-seven. The above 1959 list of Westerbork Jews reaffirms this date and place of death. The source of the original information we do not know.

Marani suggests, convincingly, that Weisz was taken off the train at Cosel, where up to 300 men on the 2 October transport were ripped from their families to be distributed among a regional network of slave labour camps that supported massive construction projects in aid of the German war effort. From August to December 1942, deportation trains from Westerbork, Drancy in France and Mechelen in Belgium, were stopped for this purpose in Cosel (now known as the city of Kędzierzyn-Koźle), 100 kilometres northwest of Auschwitz.

'During this so-called Cosel period,' writes Susanne Barth in her academic study of the subject, 'nearly 9,000 able-bodied men aged between sixteen and fifty-five were made to step out, while the elderly, the women, and the children rode on to Auschwitz, where they were murdered in the gas chambers almost immediately.' These Jewish men constituted on average one third of each transport. Not more than 700 of the 9,000, or 8 per cent, survived.

Piecing together survivor testimony, Barth describes how the men from the Westerbork transports were selected at Cosel. The picture she paints is doubtless very similar to the last memory held by Ilona, Roberto and Clara of their husband and father before they were themselves murdered:

> The SS commanded the men to get off, and immediately encircled them ... The Germans searched the trains for recalcitrant younger men, pulled them out, and knocked them down with rifle butts. Then the men had to collect their luggage. Those trying to say goodbye to their families were viciously maltreated. Finally, they had to kneel on the station platform ... Those finding it hard to keep kneeling with an upright upper body were beaten by the Germans. These scenes were witnessed by the women and children on the train waiting in the station.

The women and children were inconsolable. 'It was the last time I would see my mother,' said one male survivor of a Cosel selection from a Mechelen transport. 'I still remember the last image I have of her. She was pushed back sobbing in the wagon ...That's when I understood the spirit of Germany, the psychological and physical destruction of the Jews.' Another, deported from Drancy, recalled the events almost fifty years later in a video testimony: 'The cries of the children screaming for their fathers are still in my head'.

For men such as Weisz on the Cosel platform, some of whom left Westerbork with the fanciful notion that their alleged relocation to Eastern Europe would not be so terrible, the sudden appreciation of the terrible reality was overwhelming. 'The traumatising experiences in Cosel diminished the selected men's will to persevere, and they rapidly succumbed to the murderous conditions prevailing in the camps,' writes Barth. 'Men who had thus given up on themselves virtually died of the longing for their wives and children they rightly assumed dead.'

Many of the men perished from sickness, starvation or beating in the first brutal winter they had to endure. With the torturing knowledge embedded deep inside his brain that his wife and two young children had already been gassed, Weisz managed to survive for sixteen months. I wonder whether he ever got into conversation during this period with his fellow Jewish slave labourers and managed to tell them that he had won the last of three Serie A titles just a few years before. Or is that not the sort of thing one talks about when freezing and starving to death?

Barth says that those rendered unfit for work at any stage were sent to be liquidated at Auschwitz-Birkenau. We therefore do not know how Weisz was eventually done away with – whether he just expired where he was, or whether, when gravely ill, he was shipped off to be gassed.

* * *

When asked what first triggered his curiosity about Weisz, his biographer Matteo Marani recounted an interview he once conducted with Enzo Biagi, one of the most prolific and celebrated Italian journalists and writers of the twentieth century. Biagi was brought up in the Bologna area and happened to mention to Marani 'in a rather casual and superficial way' the coach of his local team during his teenage years, a man his interviewer had never heard of. 'I think his name was Weisz, he was very good but also Jewish and who knows how he ended up?'

Setting aside what is to me the rather pressing question of why, over a period of several decades, it never occurred to a journalist with Biagi's standing, skill, experience and contacts to try to establish the fate of such a prominent figure in his home community, we do now have a fairly clear idea of how this Jewish international footballer and great Jewish coach did end up.

And what we can say is that Árpád Weisz, more than any other member of my team of eleven, was the victim of a highly productive transnational collaboration, an impressive demonstration of what Europe can achieve when its constituent parts are all pulling together in the same direction.

CHAPTER 6

THE LIONS OF JUDAH

'A crowd numbering many thousands of people gathered at Westbahnhof [Vienna West train station] this morning,' reported the newspaper *Die Stunde*.

> The square in front of the station resembled the reception for a potentate in the days of the monarchy. Only on closer inspection would an observer realise that this must be an event related to football, because familiar leading figures from the leather-ball game could be seen here and there in the densely packed crowd.

The heaving multitudes were straining to catch a glimpse of their heroes, who had made history in London just a few days before. On 3 September 1923, the Zionist team Hakoah Vienna had taken on West Ham United at their home ground, Upton Park. It was said at the time that no English team had previously been beaten on their home ground by foreign opposition. You could say that the record remained intact after Hakoah's visit. Because West Ham were not beaten. They were destroyed.

By a scoreline of five goals to nil, Hakoah routed a team that had qualified for the FA Cup Final just four months before, a showpiece event that marked the first football match ever played at the soon-to-be world-renowned Wembley Stadium. No wonder that the Zionists of Vienna were bursting with national fervour, ecstatic that their club with its loud and proud Jewishness was making waves throughout a continent indelibly stained by centuries of Jew hatred.

'As the train entered the station, a band played the Jewish national anthem [Hatikvah],' continued *Die Stunde*. 'And then to roaring cheers on their victorious return from England, the Hakoah players and their travelling companions emerged. A huge convoy of cars, decorated with the blue and white of the Jewish national movement, then proceeded to cause a sensation everywhere, moving along Mariahilfer Strasse and the Ringstrasse to [what was known as] the Hakoah clubhouse, the Café Atlashof.'

Hakoah had left behind many admirers in the home of football. The experienced international referee for the game, George Simmons, was awestruck by what he had seen, remarking that each of the visiting players was worth a £5,000 fee. Indeed, the Zionist Jews had staggered the English onlookers with the speed, movement and technical precision of a passing game that stood in sharp contrast to the aimless long-ball approach favoured by the home side. 'Hakoah had a special style, a style that many of our teams could learn from,' commented *The Daily Mail*.

Accosted by journalists on the team's arrival in Vienna, Hakoah's veteran full-back Max Scheuer alluded to this possession-based football that had so mesmerised the West Ham players and fans. 'In my twelve-year playing career at Hakoah, I have never seen the boys work as wonderfully as they did in London,' said Scheuer. 'In the first fifteen minutes we were very nervous and it almost looked like it was going to be a debacle for us. But after Nemes scored the first goal, the team settled down, everything went well, and the English couldn't get the ball for minutes on end.'

This chapter is devoted to two players from Hakoah Vienna, a club whose story is still largely neglected despite, in my view, having no equal for drama, passion or tragedy in the long annals of the world's most popular and talked-about sport.

The two players under my spotlight represent two ends of a spectrum. One is Scheuer, Mister Hakoah himself, the club's longest-serving player, whose innumerable appearances on the blue-and-whites' many tours made him one of the most well-travelled men in Europe. The other, Otto Fischer, was perhaps more typical, a Jew whose prodigious footballing talent drew him to Hakoah for a limited period, before the club's fortunes and finances could no longer satisfy his ambitions.

Whereas several of their teammates used their global footballing contacts to avoid the fate of their more parochial Jewish peers, both Scheuer and Fischer committed the mistake of failing to act on one of the central tenets of the Zionism that fanned Hakoah's flames – namely, that without the ability to defend themselves, the days of European Jewry were numbered. Scheuer went west, Fischer went east, but both ended up the same way, two further statistics demonstrating the now unarguable accuracy of the Zionist prognosis.

* * *

In the 1930s, Erich Sinai represented the Hakoah Vienna handball team, one of several sports in which the club participated and often excelled. After the Anschluss – the Nazi invasion of Austria in March 1938 – he managed to avoid being murdered by fleeing east and eventually being imprisoned in a Soviet camp.

Interviewed as a very elderly man seven decades later, Sinai could not quite fathom how his younger self could have been quite so self-destructively dim: 'There were plenty of signs. [But] what we believed was … nothing will happen to us. And it is not going to be so bad … I cannot understand now that people at the time could not see what was going to happen. ... But people did not see it, or did not want to see it.'

Sinai's confidence had been founded on quicksand. The signs that he mentions not only emanated from the prevailing atmosphere during his youth, but from the recurrent patterns of history.

For several centuries before Sinai was born, Vienna had been known in Jewish folklore as *Ir Hadamim* (the City of Blood). During the Easter holiday of 1420, a rumour spread that the Jews had been busy desecrating Communion wafers and generally spending their days ridiculing Christianity. Wealthy Jews were arrested, tortured and had their property expropriated, poorer members of the community were dispatched on rafts on the Danube without oars and children were taken from their parents and sent off to Christian institutions for forced conversion.

Less than a year later, the remnants of the community – ninety-two men and 120 women – were dragged to the pyre in the Erdberg district of Vienna and burned alive. 'The flooding of the river Jordan cleansed bodies of pestilence and evil,' reads a centuries-old and celebratory Latin plaque in the Judenplatz, once the focal point of Jewish life in the city. 'Thus did the flames of hate rage through the entire city in 1421 and punish the terrible crimes of the repulsive Hebrew dogs.'

Alternating cycles of tolerance and persecution, familiar to all the Jews of Europe, followed until the middle of the nineteenth century. However, in a period of far-reaching liberalisation between 1848 and 1867, things suddenly started to look much more encouraging for the Jews of the Austrian, and later the Austro-Hungarian, empire. They were handed unprecedented privileges, such as the rights to live wherever they pleased, to enter professions and to own property, all factors which encouraged the growth of the community in Vienna.

In the 1850s, there were only around 6,000 Jews in the city. By the

1920s, their number had exploded to more than 200,000, making it the sixth largest Jewish population in any city in the world. When people talk of the golden age of Viennese Jewry, of its colossal and astonishingly disproportionate contributions to the arts, science, business and the professions, of Mahler, Freud, Zweig and Schönberg, perhaps they should also point out that it lasted around the average lifespan of a human being in the contemporary Western world.

The Jews flooding into the capital came from elsewhere in the Austro-Hungarian empire. Many were from Bohemia, Moravia and Austrian Silesia, known collectively as the Bohemian Crownlands, territories that now more or less make up the modern-day Czech Republic. Seeking work opportunities and to be part of a sustainably large Jewish community, the German-speaking families of Max Scheuer and Otto Fischer both moved to Vienna from this region.

Scheuer was born on 2 September 1895, in Schaffa, a small village now known as Šafov and right on the modern-day Czech-Austrian border. He was the only son and the fourth and youngest child of Elkan Ignaz, a horse dealer, and Karoline (née Fürst).*

Around the time of his birth, the Jews of Schaffa had entered hard economic times. The community had previously dominated the surrounding regional market in the sale of cloth, linen and leather and in the trading of raw materials such as sheep's wool, flax and hides. But the emergence of an advanced rail network made it possible for factory products to be sent directly to towns and markets, and for factories to obtain necessary raw materials from distant areas more easily. Local

* Once again, we see evidence of the bridge generation between Jewish tradition and greater assimilation. The name Elkan will have been used among close family and friends, and in religious services and ceremonies, whereas Ignaz would have been reserved for interaction with non-Jews and the authorities.

Jewish traders were therefore cut out of the equation, sucking the life out of the local economy.

The Jewish community dwindled as a result, from around 450 shortly before Scheuer's birth (40 per cent of the total population) to just sixty-eight at the time of the Anschluss.* Elkan Ignaz and Karoline (known as Lina) were part of this exodus. By 1910, they had decided to take young Max and his three elder sisters to the big city and try their luck there instead.

Otto Fischer, meanwhile, was born in Vienna on 1 January 1901, more than five years after Scheuer, to parents who had already arrived from the Bohemian Crownlands some years before. The fifth and youngest child of Heinrich, a salesman, and Netty (née Pokorny), Fischer was known from earliest childhood and throughout his life, even in newspaper reports and team sheets, as Schloime. It is a nickname which tells us a lot.**

It suggests that the Hebrew name given to him at his circumcision ceremony was Shlomo, translated in English as Solomon, after the famously wise king of Israel who commissioned the building of the First Temple of Jerusalem. Given the story I am about to tell, it is a fitting name. The casual use of the Yiddish nickname also indicates that Fischer and his family were happy to advertise their Jewishness

---

* According to varying estimates, between one third and one half of the tiny Jewish community of Schaffa managed to emigrate from Austria after the Anschluss, although it is not clear how many of these refugees survived in other countries. Those who did not leave were murdered.

** Heinrich was from Gewitsch, now known as Jevíčko; Netty was from Swietla, now known as Světlá nad Sázavou. Both towns are in the modern-day Czech Republic. During the Holocaust, the once significant but by then tiny Jewish communities in these towns were liquidated. Their precious religious and centuries-old artefacts were among the 140,000 such items sent to the Jewish Museum in Prague, an institution allegedly envisaged by the Nazis as the host to a permanent exhibition of an extinct people.

at a time when many Viennese Jews, and Central European Jews in general, were desperately trying to play it down.

As we see time after time in the stories recounted in this book, pre-Holocaust Jewish Europe was often sharply divided between these two camps – between discomfort and pride, assimilation and separateness, camouflage and openness, submissiveness and defiance. And nowhere was that schism more evident than in the football stadiums of Vienna.

* * *

For centuries, in the absence of any obvious alternative, the Jews of Europe had taken all the bitter blows, picking themselves off the canvas before soon getting pummelled once again. But in the second half of the nineteenth century, the Zionist idea emerged and ultimately revolutionised Jewish psychology.

The movement was turbocharged by two events. A few months before Scheuer was born, Captain Alfred Dreyfus, a Jewish officer in the French army, was convicted of treason for passing on military secrets to Germany. The evidence was both flimsy and concocted, but Dreyfus was forced to spend several years in barbaric isolation before the miscarriage of justice and subsequent cover-up were fully exposed.

The Zionists were quick to point out that the unjust victimisation of the Jew was not some random anomaly. It had widespread public support, and this in a country said to lie at the pioneering forefront of European tolerance and liberalism. 'French society, both openly and covertly, abandoned itself in great measure to a multiform antisemitism,' writes the historian Pierre Birnbaum about the prevailing atmosphere of the time.

A few years later, when Fischer was a toddler, hundreds of Jews were murdered, raped and maimed in the Kishinev pogrom, in what is now

Moldova, during the Easter weekend of 1903. Coming at a time when the Dreyfus affair was still raging, the globally publicised massacre further strengthened the claims of the Zionists, who rounded on the perceived passivity of the Jewish masses in the face of the braying mob.

It was high time, they insisted, to draw a line in the sand. From this moment on, resounded the new message, you do not have to lie down and take it. You can stand tall, stick your chest out and fight. And in the sporting arena, Hakoah Vienna was the prime manifestation of this growing determination to rewrite the script, to break once and for all with a long-suffering history of victimhood.

The writer Friedrich Torberg became a passionate Hakoah supporter at the age of ten. Having fled to the United States in 1940, Torberg later reflected on how the club had shaped his mindset and worldview during the impressionable years of his youth.

'It not only influenced my attitude towards Judaism, it determined it,' he wrote.

> I had the inestimable luck of growing up as a witness to Hakoah victories, of growing up together with Hakoah. I had the inestimable luck of never having to be 'ashamed' of my Jewishness, not for a single second. What should I have been ashamed of? Of the fact that the Jews scored more goals and swam faster and boxed better than the others? I was a child when I noticed all this. From childhood, I was proud to be a Jew. And this pride, which I would not give up for anything in the world, will remain forever connected to the name Hakoah.

Inspired by the formation three years earlier of József Braun's first club, VAC Budapest, Hakoah Vienna was founded in 1909. The club's membership was swelled in its early years by the recent arrival in Vienna of Jews from further east in the Austro-Hungarian empire than the Bohemian Crownlands. These were not so much economic migrants, but bruised witnesses to ferocious antisemitic violence, such as the attacks on 400 communities which raged across the western Galicia region surrounding Kraków in the spring of 1898.

Because of their recent experience, these Eastern Jews were more naturally drawn to the growing allure of Zionism, an ideology viewed as ridiculous by much of the established Viennese Jewish community, who saw themselves as cultured Westerners with no need for a separate Jewish homeland in the sweaty and primitive Middle East.

When the openly antisemitic mayor Karl Lueger presided over Vienna from 1897 to 1910, allegedly inspiring a young city resident by the name of Adolf Hitler, the Eastern Jews would have thought that they were experiencing more of what they had fled from, albeit in a milder form; much of the latter group, on the other hand, would more likely have convinced themselves that the Lueger phenomenon was either overblown or soon to blow over.

The bulk of the more assimilated mainstream was drawn to Wiener Amateure, later to change its name to the version known to modern-day football fans, Austria Vienna. This was a club very similar in character to several others throughout Central and Eastern Europe, such as Leon Sperling's Cracovia or Braun's MTK – open to players and members of any origin, yet nevertheless scorned by antisemites throughout the city as a Jewish club.

Hakoah, on the other hand, was explicitly and unashamedly exclusive, permitting only Jewish players and members (although non-Jewish coaches were allowed). Building on the initially small but tight-knit and highly committed core of Zionist players and members, Hakoah eventually managed to eke out success on the pitch. Having started out in the lower reaches of the Austrian league system, and with its progress then stalled by the First World War, the club had nevertheless achieved promotion to the top flight by the 1920/21 season.

Around this point, its popularity exploded. Instead of Zionism attracting people to Hakoah, suddenly it was now Hakoah acting as the recruiting sergeant for Zionism. 'As Hakoah's successes grew, so did its recognition among Viennese Jews,' recalled Fritz Baar, an early member who fled to British-controlled Palestine in 1938. 'It was only then that experienced athletes from other clubs and older, more affluent generations joined the club, and its following among Jews grew like an avalanche.'

Wearing a large Star of David on their blue-and-white shirts, and against a backdrop of unremitting hostility, Hakoah readied itself to take on Austria, Europe and the world. The club was to rise to the summit, only to tumble back down the mountain to destruction and oblivion, and all within less than three decades of its foundation. And, throughout this frenetic rollercoaster ride, Max Scheuer was right there in the thick of the action, as player, coach, administrator and believer.

* * *

Scheuer first appeared for the Hakoah first team in the autumn of 1912, having just turned seventeen, when the newly formed club was still languishing in the third division. By then, according to a later press profile, he had already been involved in Viennese football for more than two years. More or less immediately on his arrival in the city from Schaffa, he had founded the club Armania with like-minded youths in the heavily Jewish Leopoldstadt district where he lived.*

* The Jewish population of Leopoldstadt was close to 40 per cent of the total by the 1920s, earning it the nickname *Mazzesinsel* (Matzah Island), after the unleavened bread that Jews eat at Passover.

If it occurs to you that founding a football club is not necessarily what you would expect a fourteen-year-old to be doing, then you have made progress in understanding who Max Scheuer was, a footballing obsessive right from his early adolescence until his untimely end. An article in the *Neues Wiener Tagblatt* from May 1913, just after Scheuer had started playing for Hakoah, announces that he had been re-elected as an advisory board member at Armania. If he wasn't playing football, he was spending much of his time organising it or otherwise thinking or talking about it.

He began his career for Hakoah as a utility player, occupying several different positions. Scheuer's two goals from the attacking inside-right position against DFC in Prague in February 1914 were so imprinted on the memory of the club's former coach and administrator Arthur Baar, Fritz's older brother, that he was still eulogising the performance in his book about Hakoah published while living in Israel almost half a century later, in 1959. It was, Baar maintained, Scheuer's 'most famous match', granting him a hero status among diehard Hakoah fans that he was never to relinquish.

As with several of my team of eleven, war then arrived to break Scheuer's flying progress and rob him of some of his prime footballing years. According to his military records, he served for three years during the First World War with a specialist railway regiment stationed in the town of Korneuburg near to Vienna, a unit designated to build, repair or operate railway lines and associated infrastructure for the war effort.

On his return from duty, he soon slotted into the full-back berth that he was to occupy for more than a decade. It was one of two such positions in the common team formation of the time (Scheuer normally played at right-back), representing the last line of defence in front of the goalkeeper. Subsequent summaries of his career by former

Hakoah loyalists build a picture of Scheuer as a staunch defender, a warrior for the cause, a long-serving stalwart, a Zionist Carles Puyol.

'There were few defenders at the time who could match him in tackling, and doggedly pursuing and dispossessing the opposition,' wrote Arthur Baar. 'If he was "outplayed" by an opponent,' agreed Ignaz Hermann Körner, one of the founders of the club who also fled to Palestine in 1938, 'he clung to the opponent's heels and with gritted teeth, clenched fists and head down, did not rest until he regained possession of the ball.'

Scheuer was, according to Körner, the ultimate competitor, 'an insurmountable wall'. 'Even when he was injured, he played with the full force of his willpower until the final whistle. During the game, he would grumble incessantly and not exactly throw words of endearment at his teammates, but after the game was won, the grin would never disappear.'

Similar descriptions litter newspaper reports throughout a marathon career of around 600 games for Hakoah, spanning a remarkable nineteen years. 'Scheuer put in a magnificent performance,' declared *Wiener Sporttagblatt* after one game in June 1923. 'He is still not a wholly technically correct player, but an extraordinarily useful player who kept going until the very end, and this after his partner had become exhausted and could no longer play at his normal level.' Called up to the Austria national team a few months later, *Neues Wiener Tagblatt* applauded the selection, describing Scheuer as 'an honest and tough fighter who will certainly stand his ground'. In 1930, around a year before his eventual retirement at the age of almost thirty-six, *Der Montag* referred to him as 'indestructible', an 'old fighter'.

Everyone in football – teammates, coaches, fans, journalists – has always loved a scrapper. He was widely known by the diminutive nickname Maxl, reflecting not just his small frame but how well liked he was, a reassuringly familiar presence at Hakoah and a respected, recognisable personality throughout Jewish Vienna.

Indeed, references to his popularity kept cropping up as I combed the archives, particularly in later years after he began to acquire elder statesman status – 'the popular Hakoah captain' (*Wiener Sporttagblatt*, October 1927), 'the popular Hakoah international' (*Die Stunde,* September 1929), 'the most popular of all former players at the Krieau [Hakoah's stadium]' (*Wiener Montagblatt*, February 1937).

What explains the fighting spirit that made him so popular? It wasn't just sporting competitiveness and his deep love for football that drove Scheuer. It was also because, perhaps like Carles Puyol at Barcelona, what his club represented touched his heart and soul. Barcelona's famous motto is *Més que un club* (more than a club), because the team doesn't just exist to win and entertain, but to represent Catalan culture and nationalism.

The Austria-based authors of a book to commemorate the centenary of Hakoah's founding – in 2009 – thought along similar lines. They came up with the title *mehr als ein Sportverein*, a direct translation of the Barcelona motto. Quite right, but given what the club stood for and what happened to it, German is the last language I would use to convey the sentiment. To give Hakoah the much more appropriate Hebrew translation of the same phrase, they certainly were *yoter m'mo'adon*, and maybe more so than any football club in history.

And thanks to Körner's further recollections, we know that Scheuer was utterly devoted to that higher cause. 'The Viennese Zionists knew the favourite of the entire Hakoah club as a self-sacrificing campaigner in elections (for the Jewish National Party) and tireless collector for Zionist funds,' he wrote.

As with Friedrich Torberg, and even more so because he was there almost from the very start, standing shoulder to shoulder with all its most fervent advocates, Scheuer was moulded by Hakoah.

* * *

Scheuer's peak years as a player coincided with Hakoah's most successful period. After promotion to the top flight, the club soon emerged as regular front runners for the title. They just missed out in the 1921/22 season to the deeply antisemitic Wiener Sport-Club, a closely fought race between one football organisation that permitted only Jewish members, and another that permitted none.

By 1923, at the age of twenty-eight, Scheuer's consistently combative performances had finally led to representative honours. He turned out for the Vienna city select eleven in the home win against Prague in August of that year. The following month brought the famous victory against West Ham and the subsequent reward of an international cap for the game against Hungary in Budapest. A natural leader, he was even awarded the captaincy, tossing up before kick-off with another Jew, the Hungary captain Vilmos Kertész.

The press reacted to Scheuer's performance in a 2–0 defeat with qualified praise. 'Scheuer was excellent, but he didn't clear the ball quickly enough,' reported *Der Tag;* 'Although Scheuer … did a good job, he did not quite match his recent performances,' commented *Neue Freie Presse.*

He certainly merited another chance at the top level, but a Hakoah tour to Palestine and Egypt in the new year of 1924 coincided with the next Austria international game away to Germany. Given his now advancing age, he could not subsequently regain his place from strong rivals for the full-back position, such as the First Vienna pairing Josef

Blum and Karl Rainer. These two players went on to form the defensive backbone for much of the Wunderteam era, when the free-scoring team led by Jewish coach Hugo Meisl were widely considered the best international side in Europe.*

At club level, however, everything kept getting better for Scheuer. Hakoah had been greatly strengthened by the recruitment of top Jewish internationals from Hungary – the centre-half Béla Guttmann, winger József Eisenhoffer and strikers Alexander Neufeld (also known as Sándor Nemes) and Ernő Schwarz, all enticed by the club's burgeoning reputation and popularity throughout Europe. By the time of the start of the 1924/25 season, at which time the Austrian league became the first to turn professional in mainland Europe, Hakoah were primed for a serious assault on the title.

The circumstances of Hakoah's eventual triumph that season could not have been sweeter for their many fanatical supporters throughout Europe. First, they saw off a determined challenge from Wiener Amateure, the team backed largely by Jews with the conciliatory worldview held in contempt by many of the Hakoah faithful. Second, the pivotal victory came in dramatic fashion in Hakoah's third last game of the season against the antisemites of Wiener Sport-Club.

The game had been switched to a larger stadium, the Simmeringer Platz, more suited to handling the huge demand for tickets from the rival factions. The 25,000 in attendance were not to be disappointed.

* According to research by Eva and Hans Menasse and by the historian Alexander Juraske, Karl Rainer became a member of the Nazi Party after the Anschluss. In 1938, he profited handsomely from the forced aryanisation of the apartment belonging to the Jewish Menasse family on Haupstrasse in the Döbling district of Vienna. Also in 1938, Rainer took over the aryanised leather goods store of the Jewish owner Jakob Weigel on the same street. Weigel was murdered in October 1944. Rainer continued to run the business after the war, was celebrated for the rest of his days as a footballing legend, and died aged eighty-five in 1987, almost half a century after both Weigel and Max Scheuer were murdered.

Wiener Morgenzeitung's summary of the finale is as true now as it was in June 1925: 'The decisive goal for the Jewish team was scored in a sensational manner, probably the only one of its kind in the history of football.'

The big Hakoah goalkeeper Alexander Fábián was badly injured in the lead-up to Sport-Club's equaliser that made it 2–2 deep into the second half. With substitutes yet to be introduced into the rules of football, Neufeld opted to go in goal, while the jaded Fábián put on a sling and was told to hang around the opponents' penalty area. Just eight minutes later, and with six minutes left on the clock, the debilitated Fábián suddenly burst into life to convert Schwarz's cross and score the winner, a moment that neatly encapsulated the club's never-say-die ethos for the benefit of posterity.

By the time Hakoah took to the pitch for the next game against Simmeringer, other results had gone their way and the title was already assured. Scheuer revelled in the celebratory match, turning in one of those robust and reliable performances that had done so much to lift Hakoah from obscurity to the title in his thirteen years in the first team. 'Hakoah's Scheuer was by far the most impressive of the defenders … he was always well positioned, with some excellent tackling,' reported *Wiener Sporttagblatt.*

The old warhorse must have been brimming with satisfaction in the summer sunshine, enjoying the ultimate recompense for all his years of total commitment. He was a highly valued member of a team that had now achieved hero status not just in Vienna, but all over the globe.

* * *

Alongside their twenty games in that victorious 1924/25 league championship season, Hakoah also played twenty-four games against foreign opposition, twenty of them abroad. These were not practice games for reserve players, but full-blooded encounters involving Hakoah's first team, often taking place on consecutive days. A whole season played in parallel with their domestic commitments.

In November 1927, before a home game against Sportclub Wacker, Hakoah organised a special presentation for Scheuer to celebrate his fifteen years in the first team. To mark the occasion, the newspaper *Der Montag* published a detailed portrait of the man, his career and his achievements. The article also listed his footballing travels:

> He has been on all of his team's tours and it is quite interesting to hear about the important cities in the world in which Hakoah and its defender have already made guest appearances – in Czechoslovakia: Prague, Brno, Karlovy Vary, Ostrava, Teschen [Český Těšín], Bratislava; in Hungary: Budapest, Steinamanger [Szombathely], Raab [Győr]; in Romania: Czernowitz [Chernivtsi]; in Poland: Lemberg [Lviv], Stanislau [Stanisławów], Krakow, Przemysl, Warsaw, Lodz, Vilnius; in Latvia: Riga; in Lithuania: Kaunas; in Germany: Hamburg, Hanover, Braunschweig, Dresden, Leipzig, Zwickau, Plauen, Berlin, Frankfurt, Ludwigshafen; in Switzerland: Zurich, Aarau; in Belgium: Brussels, Antwerp; in France: Paris; in Egypt: Alexandria, Cairo, Port Said; in Palestine: Jerusalem, Tel Aviv, Haifa; in England: London; in the United States: New York, Philadelphia, Baltimore, Providence, Chicago, Detroit; in Canada: Toronto, Montreal, Winnipeg.

Hakoah travelled the world for various reasons: to raise much-needed income for the club and thus help meet the pay demands of the top European Jewish footballers they sought to recruit; to spread the increasingly resonant message of Zionism through the power of football; and to satisfy the hunger of thousands of fanatical supporters to see their heroes in the flesh.

'Hunger' and 'fanatical' are not hyperbolic words. The archives reveal the raw emotion and mass hysteria that greeted Scheuer and his Hakoah teammates on their travels, particularly when the club's star was shining at its brightest in the 1920s. Take for example the moment Hakoah arrived at Warsaw train station on the Sunday morning of 20 July 1924, to be greeted by a crowd estimated by the Polish press to number around 40,000. Let us try to put that figure in some sort of perspective. Many top clubs in the world in the modern era would be delighted to attract 40,000 to watch actual football matches, let alone turn up at a train station to register their devotion to the cause. Or, to come at it from an entirely different angle, 40,000 is around four times the number of Jews that now reside in the whole of Poland.

'As the train pulled into the station, we were met by a storm of shouts, cheers and applause,' reported Arthur Baar. 'On the platform, the crowd stood cheek by jowl. At first it was quite impossible for us to leave the carriage. When the waiting people saw us, there was an enthusiasm that cannot be described. The stewards had to work hard to get us out of the carriage.'

Then came the procession of fifteen vehicles carrying them to their destination to meet the great and the good of Jewish Warsaw. The surrounding scenes resembled those in Vienna after the West Ham victory – with a large blue and white flag at the front of the cavalcade, thousands craning their necks to catch a glimpse from balconies and windows, the main thoroughfare of Marszałkowska Street shut to allow the convoy through, police everywhere in sight, and the party eventually greeted by an orchestra playing the Jewish national anthem.

'Truly, there was not a member of Hakoah who did not have tears of emotion in his eyes,' said Baar. 'We were accompanied by a sense of Jewish togetherness that rang out in the fervent ovations.'

Tel Aviv had enjoyed a similar spectacle earlier in the same year. 'A great crowd of thousands of people gathered this morning at 8 o'clock at the Tel Aviv train station to welcome the members of Hakoah and the tourists who came with them,' reported the *Haaretz* newspaper. Meir Dizengoff, the mayor of the city that Jews had started to build from desolate sand dunes just fifteen years before, welcomed his fellow Zionists with rousing words.

'On your head are the laurels from your shining victories throughout the world, victories in which you showed that the blood of the Maccabees flows in your veins,' declared Dizengoff. 'And when you return to your homes, please tell our brothers in the lands of the Diaspora that a new life is taking shape here, a life of knowing the value of our nation and its honour.'

The next day, the adoring hordes came out in their droves to see Hakoah duly defeat Maccabi Tel Aviv. 'An enormous crowd gathered around the field, and a large number of groups stood on the roofs and balconies of many of the buildings near the playing field,' reported *The Daily Mail,* which devoted a long article to the stir Hakoah was creating in Britain's then colony.

Unbeknownst to them, however, Hakoah's popularity carried within it the seeds of the club's decline from its position near the summit of European and world football. The club embarked on an eleven-game tour of the United States in the spring and early summer of 1926, winning seven and drawing two in front of large crowds and attracting prominent media coverage.

The excitement was predictably intense in New York, home to 1.75

million Jews who still bore the scars of their former lives in Europe, making the city a fertile market for Hakoah's bold brand of defiance. The first game at the Polo Grounds stadium in Manhattan against a New York All Stars select team, at which the opposing teams paraded intertwined American and Jewish flags around the field before kick-off, smashed the record for a soccer game in the United States by 10,000. By the time the repeat fixture took place a week later, the buzz had reached fever pitch and a frenetic scramble for tickets ensued. This time, the game attracted 46,000, a soccer record that then stood for more than fifty years.

At the final tour game in New York a month later, Max Scheuer and his teammates had to be protected from the marauding fans desperate for a close encounter with their new-found heroes. 'The referee's whistle blew for a foul and the crowd swarmed on to the pitch thinking the contest was over,' reported the *New York Times*. 'It had a minute to go, however, and the police were busy pushing back the spectators when the final whistle blew.'

All this adulation was not lost on Jewish entrepreneurs in the city. They saw both football's growing appeal and the celebrity status of the Jewish players. Why not combine the two, and pay what is necessary to persuade some Hakoah players to sign contracts with New York clubs? The subsequent departure of ten players ripped the heart out of the Hakoah team, a devastating raid on the club's talent from which it failed to recover in the few years it had left.

* * *

Scheuer was not one of the departing players. Now thirty, he was several years older than the ten leavers, and thus unlikely to have been approached. In any case, I suspect that he would have rejected any offer that did materialise.

Ever since he returned from his First World War army service, during which time his father Elkan Ignaz had died suddenly at the age of fifty-six from appendicitis, Scheuer had been keeping his mother Lina company in their apartment on Darwingasse in Leopoldstadt. And as we shall discover, he was loath to leave anyone in the lurch. Loyalty to club, family and friends was his defining characteristic right until the very end.

Replacements clearly had to be sought to team up with Scheuer and the other remaining players. By far the most talented of the eventual newcomers could hardly have been more different from Scheuer as a footballing type. Otto 'Schloime' Fischer, a small, nimble, fast and technically gifted left-winger, had already established himself as one of Austria's foremost talents. Following on from Sperling, Hirsch and Weisz, he is the fourth player of a similar style in this same position in my team – clearly something of a Jewish speciality, continued in the modern era by the Israeli international, Manor Solomon.

Fischer emerged from the relatively down-at-heel Favoriten district in the south of Vienna, where Jewish workers, craftsmen and small-scale merchants such as his father Heinrich settled in small numbers in the last years of the nineteenth century. The precocious wunderkind was fortunate to have a first division club right on his doorstep. He joined the local Favoriten club, Hertha Vienna, and with his progress accelerated by so many older players fighting at the front, he made his debut in the top flight in June 1917 at just sixteen years of age.

Unusually for a player operating out wide, he was known from the start of his career not just for his ability to create opportunities for others, but as a prolific finisher too. 'Fischer from Hertha is one of the few wingers who scores in almost every game,' commented *Wiener Sporttagblatt* in March 1920. The journalist was not the only one to notice. The nineteen-year-old Fischer was snapped up later that same month by Heinrich Oppenheim, the Jewish coach of Karlsbader FK in the opulent spa town of Karlovy Vary in Czechoslovakia, a club bankrolled at the time by wealthy local businessmen.* **

By the time he returned to Vienna two years later, Fischer had matured in body and technique into a player ready to take the league by storm. He signed for First Vienna in the Döbling district in the north of the city, yet another Central European club with strong Jewish roots. The oldest Austrian football club, it was established in 1894 by gardeners working in the estate of Nathaniel Meyer von Rothschild, grandson of the founder of the eponymous bank. As gratitude for the start-up funding he originally provided, the club wear to this day the blue and yellow colours of the house of Rothschild.

Fischer did not take long to endear himself to his new team, with an explosive debut in October 1922 against Hakoah in front of 50,000 home fans. From the very outset of the encounter, his opposite number Max Scheuer was taken to the cleaners by what *Neue Freie Presse* described as Fischer's 'dazzling technique and brilliant runs … which decided First Vienna's victory in the first ten minutes.' He set

* Heinrich Oppenheim qualifies for my team. A defender for First Vienna, he played one game for Austria in May 1909, a 1–1 draw away to Hungary in Budapest. After leaving Karlsbader FK in 1922, he coached AC Milan for two years. A 1965 document from the International Committee of the Red Cross reveals that Oppenheim was first arrested near Ostrava in Czechoslovakia in April 1939, soon after the German invasion of the country. Released after six weeks, he fled to Lviv (where, who knows, perhaps he encountered Zygmunt Steuermann or Leon Sperling). In November 1941, the 52-year-old Oppenheim was deported from Lviv. Where the former AC Milan coach was murdered for being a Jew is not known.

** In the 1930s, the Jewish population of Karlovy Vary and its environs numbered more than 2,500. In 1938, the town and the rest of the Sudetenland region was annexed to Nazi Germany as part of the Munich Agreement. The magnificent Great Synagogue was torched that same year and then destroyed the following year. Almost all the Jewish population of the town fled into the interior of Czechoslovakia, which had not at that stage been taken over. Between 1942 and 1944, at least 90 per cent of these Karlovy Vary Jews were murdered.

up two goals early on and then notched one for himself in the second half in a 4–2 victory. His debut was only marred by having to come off the pitch late on, perhaps unsurprisingly 'injured by Scheuer'.

With twenty-eight goals in his eighty-one league appearances over four seasons, Fischer helped First Vienna to finish as runners-up twice to Wiener Amateure and never lower than fourth. His high goal ratio and overall contribution to a top-level team earned him the first of his seven caps alongside Scheuer in September 1923 against Hungary.

His two most notable performances in Hugo Meisl's national team came in the spring of 1925. In a 4–0 away victory in Paris, the France defenders suffered the same humiliating fate as Scheuer. 'Fischer launched a series of wonderful attacks,' reported *Wiener Sporttagblatt*. 'When he revealed his technical artistry, the opponents were lost.' *Illustrierte Kronen Zeitung* also honed in on the mismatch, suggesting that Schloime was toying with the French: 'Fischer took his opponents for a walk, however and whenever he wanted.'

A couple of weeks later, back in the familiar surroundings of Hohe Warte, First Vienna's home ground, he excelled once more in a 3–1 win against Hungary. *Neues Wiener Journal* declared it 'a victory for Fischer', describing some of his runs as 'so fabulous that they bordered on the unbelievable' and asserting that 'he dribbled in a relatively confined space with almost incomprehensible ease and precision'.

Illustriertes Sportblatt took a similarly effusive line:

> It must be said right away that only Fischer from the left wing decided the game for Austria … he got away from the Hungarian defenders, who were unable to stop him even by the most unfair means, which they used often enough. The three goals were like peas in a pod. In all three cases, Fischer dribbled to the goal line, unconcerned by all the kicks aimed at him, and then laid the ball to

his best-placed teammate in such a way that even a child could not miss the chance.

Max Scheuer was probably still suffering recurrent nightmares from Fischer's First Vienna debut more than three years previously when he faced the flying winger again at the end of March 1926, just before Hakoah set off on their long and ultimately fateful trip to the United States. On the boat that took them there, the veteran defender would have had some difficulty working out whether he was seasick or just still feeling dizzy from another Fischer runaround in a 5–4 victory for First Vienna. *Wiener Sporttagblatt* raved,

> The highlight of the first Vienna-Hakoah game was the fourth goal that Fischer, also known as 'Schloime', scored … A few metres past the halfway line, he set off into enemy territory and had to beat all Hakoah's men on one side of the pitch … He passed [Lajos] Hess as if he wasn't there.* Then it was Scheuer's turn. He went round him twice, because being content with once is not Fischer's style. When Scheuer had been dealt with, Fabian [the goalkeeper] rushed out of the box, and he was also outdone … Guttmann slid in, but he could only make Fischer stumble … Finally the crowning shot followed …The stands went wild with delight, and people even broke out into chants of 'Hoch Schloime!'

When it came to seeking reinforcements after the American tour, Hakoah's most senior player and recently installed captain Max Scheuer

* Lajos Hess emigrated to Palestine in the 1930s. He was the coach of the Israel national team when it recorded its first victory as an independent country, beating Cyprus 3–1 in 1949 in Tel Aviv.

would have been prominent in discussions. He would have had two motivations for recommending Fischer. First, his love for Hakoah – he surely would have wanted one of the top talents in Austrian football to play for his club. Second, self-preservation.

* * *

The 25-year-old Fischer, reluctantly sold by First Vienna in July 1926 for what was considered a substantial transfer fee, had to get used to an entirely new environment at Hakoah. For one thing, he was now playing for what had become a struggling team, whose departed stars had not been adequately replaced.

Nevertheless, there were some highlights, such as scoring one and setting up two in a 3–2 victory away at his former club First Vienna in February 1927. Fischer also got the opportunity to travel with the globetrotting Hakoah on the club's return to North America, starting in the April of that year. He played in all but one of the club's nineteen matches in a gruelling two-month tour of both the United States and Canada, including a 2–2 draw in front of 40,000 spectators against a New York Giants team that fielded three former Hakoah stars. (According to his German-language biographer Alexander Juraske, the Giants even tried to sign Fischer after the tour. However, Hakoah placed a prohibitively high price tag on their star winger, one of their few remaining talents.)

But without the quality of service he had enjoyed at First Vienna, the goals dried up, and he registered just four goals in twenty-nine league games in his eighteen months at the Zionist club. His scoring rate therefore plummeted from more than one in three at First Vienna, to just one in seven. The bald statistics did not escape the national team selectors. They overlooked Fischer during his time at Hakoah and opted instead for his arch-rival, the highly regarded Rapid Vienna winger, Ferdinand Wesely.

Playing in a weaker team was not the only drawback of Fischer's move. The other was being hated on a scale he had never previously encountered.

Throughout its short existence, Hakoah faced a constant undercurrent of animosity, a not entirely surprising piece of information given that the club's supporters and the rest of Viennese Jewry were to be humiliated, expelled and murdered with much spirited local support just a few years later. That background hum of contempt would regularly descend into outright violence, a precursor of things to come. Fischer was right at the centre of one such episode, in a match against the antisemitic Wiener Sport-Club in March 1927.

'Hateful scenes took place at Hohe Warte yesterday,' bemoaned *Wiener Morgenzeitung* the morning after the game. 'Acts of brutality, clashes between players and among spectators, indiscipline on the playing field, sendings off, and turbulent events on the terraces characterised yesterday's championship game.' Meanwhile, *Die Stunde* accorded the encounter its own special name – 'the riot game'.

A tinder box atmosphere was evident from the very outset. According to the *Arbeiter-Zeitung* newspaper, the entry on to the pitch of (presumably Jewish) referee Johann Neumann was enough to inspire cries of 'Yid!' and 'Off to Galicia, you Eastern Jewish pig.' However, as the journalist was keen to stress, 'that was just the beginning'. He continued, 'The game began and almost every action of the Hakoah players was accompanied by the howls of the anti-Semitic mobs: "Jewish bastards!", "Jewish morons!", "Off to Zion!", "Kick the Hebrew in the stomach!", "When they win, there'll be a pogrom!"'

When Hakoah broke the deadlock with less than twenty minutes left, the opposition protested furiously for offside and chaos reigned. 'After the Hakoah goal, several Sport-Club players rushed at the linesman, whom they attacked in a vulgar manner,' reported *Die Stunde*. '[Richard] Beer even snatched the flag from him.'

By the time the referee put himself out of his misery by blowing the final whistle, two players from either side had been sent off, including the diminutive Otto Fischer. The newspapers were at odds about who had initiated the confrontation, but there was no dispute that Fischer and Sport-Club defender Rudolf Hockauf had punched each other, leaving Neumann no option but to banish them from the field. 'A veritable fight between the supporters of both sides' soon erupted, and the police 'vigorously intervened'.

One hopes that Fischer managed to calm himself down and put some make-up on his facial bruises after all the excitement. *Illustrierte Kronen Zeitung* pointed out that his wedding to Ida Schwarz was to take place later that day.*

As for Scheuer – who had by then sported the offending Jewish colours for fifteen years rather than Fischer's six months – we can surmise that all the kerfuffle signified little more than another routine day at the office. A couple of years later, in March 1929, at the end of a game against Sportclub Neubau, the little fighter was even smashed over the head by a police truncheon after finding himself, rather predictably, on the front line of more violent mass disorder involving both players and spectators.

* Alexander Juraske conducted research on what happened to Ida Schwarz. She and Fischer divorced in 1933. She later stated that she married the non-Jewish Yugoslav Miroslav Rajkovic in Vienna in March 1938 in an attempt to avoid persecution. She nevertheless fled to Britain and worked as a domestic servant in Manchester during the war. She later divorced Rajkovic and returned to Vienna, where she died in 1986.

* * *

Hakoah finished a disappointing ninth in a thirteen-team league in Fischer's only full season at the club. And midway through the following season of 1927/28, Hakoah were forced to part ways with their expensive winger due to financial difficulties engendered by the second American tour.

Minus their former star players and with their reputation as world-beaters consequently undermined, the trip had failed to attract the same crowds as the previous year. And now with Fischer gone, the club suffered a fate that had appeared unthinkable when the league title was held aloft just three years before – relegation. Although Hakoah came straight back up in 1929, the club proceeded to yo-yo between the top two divisions, never again soaring to the heights.

Fischer himself benefited from his move, at least in the short term. After signing for his fourth club in Vienna, SC Wacker, his form improved to such an extent that Hugo Meisl recalled him to the national team for the home game against Switzerland in October 1928.

The summons proved more of a curse than a blessing. He was carried off in the first half with a serious knee injury, inflicted by a brutal challenge from the 'fierce' Swiss defender Rudolf Ramseyer, and was ruled out for the rest of the season. He rejoined Hakoah, attempting a comeback in September 1929 that lasted just a few minutes – against who else but bogey team Wiener Sport-Club – before he had to submit to the inevitable. At the age of twenty-eight, Schloime called quits on his playing days.

Max Scheuer's prodigious career, meanwhile, eventually petered to a halt in June 1931. His finale was a far cry from the dramas and noisy, packed stadiums that had sent pulses racing during the golden years.

He bowed out in front of 600 spectators in a meaningless end-of-season encounter at SK Viktoria XXI, as already promoted Hakoah succumbed to a 3–1 defeat in the second division.

Writing almost thirty years later, Arthur Barr reflected that Scheuer had been 'able to serve as a role model for countless players thanks to his fairness, fighting spirit and loyalty to the club'. In the modern era, only the likes of Manchester United's Ryan Giggs, AC Milan's Paolo Maldini and Roma's Francesco Totti have been longer-serving one-club men. His durability even sparked media interest in his diet. What foods had enabled him to play for all those years? 'My rule is simplicity – regular meals and moderate portions … on match days, I eat at least three hours before the match,' he told *Der Montag*.

Scheuer's love affair with Hakoah continued after retirement. He stepped in as caretaker coach in the latter half of the 1936/37 season, and acted intermittently as Sektionsleiter, or football director, from 1928 onwards (he was still playing when first appointed to the role).*

He was occupying this latter position at the bitter end. On 11 March 1938, the day before the Germans entered Vienna and three days before the club was forcibly shut down by the new authorities, the Zionist newspaper *Die Stimme* carried a short article detailing the proceedings

* I asked Gunnar Persson, who wrote a Swedish-language history of Hakoah Vienna, about this position. The role of football director, responsible for player recruitment and overseeing the club's general footballing strategy and operations, is a relatively new import to the top level of English football. It is often presented by the media as a sophisticated organisational upgrade on the old days, when the all-powerful manager with often archaic ideas was said to reign supreme. I had assumed too that the position had first started to emerge in continental Europe only in the last three or four decades, and was surprised that Scheuer had been appointed to this role around 100 years ago. 'In football,' Persson replied, 'nothing is new.' With every passing moment I spent researching the football side of this book, the truth of Persson's comment became ever more evident to me.

of Hakoah's general meeting earlier that week: 'The following gentlemen were elected: President Alexander Schwartz; Managing Vice President Oskar Menczel; Vice President Berthold Beer ... Head of Section (Sektionsleiter) Max Scheuer.' He was never mentioned in Austrian newspapers again.

In addition to his Hakoah duties, Scheuer continued to work in the rope goods trading business that he established together with teammate Richard Fried in 1925. Their office was located on Werdertorgasse in what was then Vienna's textile quarter, a thirty-minute walk across the Danube Canal from Scheuer's Leopoldstadt apartment.*

While Scheuer busied himself close to home, Fischer dedicated himself not to one particular organisation, but to his calling as a coach. His eventual destination may not have been as glamorous and fashionable as the Italy graced by Árpád Weisz, but his impact on club and country was every bit as significant.

* * *

As exponents of the Danubian school that espoused quick short passing combinations, constant movement and rigorous physical preparation, former players from Vienna were just as much in demand as their counterparts in Budapest.

It did not take long, therefore, before Otto Fischer picked up his first role, appointed in early 1931 as coach of FK Mačva Šabac, now one of the oldest clubs in Serbian football and then part of the Yugoslavian football structure. In his only season at the helm, Fischer steered the club to the top of its regional league, securing its first-ever

* Richard Fried managed to flee to the United States in 1939. His father Samuel, a prominent Vienna Zionist, was gassed at Treblinka in September 1942, aged seventy-eight.

qualification to the final stage of the national championship and the subsequent trips to the bright lights of Belgrade, Zagreb and Split.*

It appears that he managed to convey his deeply held footballing principles to inexperienced players in double quick time. Back in Vienna after a job well done, Fischer was interviewed about his experience in a lengthy profile in *Wiener Sporttagblatt*, entitled 'Schloime Fischer as educator'.

'It wasn't easy,' said Schloime.

> When I arrived in Šabac, I only found the very modest beginnings of a football team. There were a lot of highly talented youngsters, but each of them had one or other serious deficiencies, easily explained by the fact that they were basically 'wild' as players, without guidance or role models … But the Yugoslavs learned amazingly quickly. They grasped the value of ball control, they were eager to fill the gaps in their technique, and, above all, they showed an extraordinary appreciation of all tactical questions.

---

* Fischer would have been one of only seventy or eighty Jews in Šabac in 1931. In early 1940, their number was swelled by around 1,200 Jews, mainly from Vienna. The original aim of the refugees had been to travel to British-controlled Palestine and somehow gain access to the country despite not having immigration permits. However, during their boat journey, the Danube started to freeze over and the refugees were taken to the port of Kladovo in Yugoslavia until the weather improved. Strong British diplomatic protests persuaded the Yugoslav government not to allow the Jews to continue to their intended destination, and they were eventually brought to Šabac. Around 200 teenagers among them were finally given precious certificates for entry into Palestine, and were allowed to proceed by train. (Their good fortune is revealed by the statistics – for example, the British sprinkled just 5,265 such permits among millions of desperate European Jews in the period between April and September 1940, although in fact only 1,725 'legal' immigrants made it to the Promised Land during that period.) In April 1941, the Germans invaded Yugoslavia. In October 1941, the men among the remaining 1,000 Šabac refugees were shot into pits in a village just north of the city. In April 1942, the women and children were murdered in gas vans dispatched from Berlin for that precise purpose. Identifying any Jewish survivors has proven difficult.

Assisted by a recommendation from the hugely influential Hugo Meisl, Fischer's next project came at DSV Saaz in Czechoslovakia. Like his former stomping ground of nearby Karlovy Vary, the hop-growing town of Saaz (now known as Žatec) was predominantly German-speaking. Its football club therefore competed in the Deutscher Fußball Verband (DFV), a separate ethnic league within Czechoslovakia. In his one full season at Saaz, Fischer enhanced his reputation still further by qualifying for the DFV play-off finals and embarrassing mighty Austria Vienna and Rapid Vienna on those clubs' tours to the region in 1932.*

He was now starting to make waves among the chattering classes of Central European football. The Saaz success paid off with a move to the big city and a more prestigious club. HŠK Concordia from Zagreb had won the Yugoslav championship twice in recent years and boasted international players Zvonko Jazbec and Ivica Belošević.** Fischer performed creditably again, achieving fourth place in the national league and laying the foundation for his final, initially momentous but ultimately fatal, posting.

* * *

---

* In 1930, around the time Fischer moved there, the Jewish population of Saaz/Žatec was 760 (4 per cent of the total). In 1938, as part of Sudetenland, the town was annexed to Nazi Germany. A photograph shows packed streets of local people vying with each other to welcome the newly arrived German troops with Nazi salutes. 'The (Jewish) community,' the Encyclopaedia Judaica informs us, 'was destroyed.'

** In April 1941, the Independent State of Croatia was established, led by the Ustaše, the Croatian nationalist organisation. Six months later, the local Croatian mayor ordered the destruction of Zagreb's majestic synagogue. The demolition took six months, proceeding slowly so that the adjacent buildings would not be affected. The Jews of the city were sent either to Ustaše-controlled camps in Croatia or to Auschwitz. Community data estimates that 77 per cent of Zagreb's pre-war Jewish population of around 10,000 were murdered. Most of the remnants emigrated to the new State of Israel.

In 1936, when Otto Fischer arrived in Latvia, there were eight teams in the domestic first division. Seven were from the capital Riga. Fischer took the reins of the one provincial club, Olimpija Liepāja on the Baltic coast in the country's third largest city.

This was no low-quality, backwater league. We can reach this conclusion because the national team was easily getting the better of its Baltic state rivals, Lithuania and Estonia, and narrowly missed out on World Cup qualification in 1937, edged out 2–1 to strongly fancied Austria in the final play-off game in Vienna.*

Olimpija had won the league three times in the late 1920s, but during the following decade had been toppled by the best-supported club, RFK Riga, and the army team, ASK Riga. Fischer's assigned mission was to restore Olimpija's supremacy. He set about the task with an obsessive zeal reminiscent of Pep Guardiola seven decades later. He insisted that success would only come if the players bought into the footballing philosophy he first introduced in Šabac. It was to be the Schloime way, or the highway.

The detective work of a British author and documentary maker rescued the fascinating detail of Fischer's reign in Liepāja from obscurity. Vincent Hunt travelled there in 2015 to research a book about the brutal battles that raged in the region in the last phase of the Second

---

* Five Jews earned full international honours for Latvia between 1935 and 1938. Each played for first-division team Hakoah Riga, a Zionist club modelled on its Viennese forerunner. Iļja Vestermans, who was capped twenty-three times and scored thirteen goals for the national team, emigrated to the United States before the war. Zamuels Garbers and Villijs Kacs were killed fighting for the Soviet Red Army during the war. Nikolajs Levitanuss fought for the Red Army and survived. His brother Maksis Levitanuss escaped to the Soviet interior and survived. Harijs Lēvenšteins was a young Jewish player for Olimpija Liepāja under Otto Fischer, and was also a national boxing champion. Lēvenšteins represented the Latvia youth team and was destined for full international honours until the Soviets took over in 1940. He was murdered in Liepāja in 1941, aged twenty.

World War. In his discussion with the editor of the local newspaper and long-time sports journalist Andžils Remess, Hunt asked about the fate of the city's Jews. As an aside, Remess mentioned Fischer, whose success at Olimpija he had recounted in his book *Liepājas sporta leģendas* ('Liepāja Sporting Legends'), published in 1996. 'Fischer made Liepāja the pride of Kurzeme (the Western Baltic region of Latvia),' he had written.

Remess was not wrong. In Fischer's first season, Olimpija won the league without losing any of their fourteen games, making the 200-kilometre eastward journey to Riga to trounce both RFK and ASK on their home turf. It was to be the first of three successive league championship titles for the unwavering Jewish coach, with the bigger clubs from the capital singularly failing to lay a glove on his team.

Hunt was intrigued by what Remess had told him and did some more digging of his own. He found Zanis Musins, a 94-year-old emigré from Liepāja who had been living in England since the end of the war. Musins, an avid follower of Olimpija during his teenage years, vividly recalled the commotion Fischer had created in the port city.

'He was like a god around town,' reminisced Musins. '…If he ever turned up anywhere, people would be cheering him and carrying him on their shoulders. There wasn't much going on in Liepāja, but the football team was beating everyone. International teams were even coming to Liepāja and getting beaten – that was unheard of.'

High-brow football pundits of today argue that coaches must impose what they call an identity, a sustainable and effective system of collective play that does not solely rely for its success on individual talent and random moments of skill. We may regard this viewpoint as modern and cutting edge, until we learn that Fischer thought along exactly the same lines back in the sepia world of the 1930s. And not in Madrid or Milan either, but in a little-known corner of Latvia.

Musins described how Fischer dismantled Olimpija's previous long-ball style of play and its preoccupation with power and strength. 'Usually the full-backs would wallop it up the field and the strikers would be on their own, chasing and then dribbling once they got hold of it,' said Musins. 'But when Fischer came, all of a sudden the players were trained to pass the ball to a teammate.'

It is not for nothing that Hunt accords the label 'Barcelona of the Baltics' to the Olimpija team of this era. The first phrase Fischer apparently mastered in the Latvian language was, 'The team that plays on the ground never loses.' Players and spectators took time to adjust to this new possession-based method, initially complaining that it was monotonous to play and watch. Indeed, similar criticisms have accompanied Guardiola throughout his career. But it is amazing how a trophy or three can silence the grumbling.

In May 1938, Olimpija retained the title on their home ground by thumping closest challengers RFK 4–0. 'Greeted by ovations from the grateful crowd, Olimpija's champions left the pitch carrying their coach in their hands,' reported the *Libausche Zeitung,* the regional German-language newspaper. 'Olimpija had won this victory, and with it the Latvian championship, against the strongest opposition.'

In the eyes of the Olimpija faithful, Schloime Fischer could walk on the Baltic Sea.

* * *

Two months before this title win in Liepāja, there had been similarly ecstatic scenes in Fischer's native city of Vienna. His former teammate

Max Scheuer was on hand to witness the arrival of the German Nazis and their rapturous reception from the local population.

'The people in their worship of antisemitism are entirely at one with their brothers in the Reich,' wrote Sigmund Freud, who observed the mass unfurling of the red carpet at first hand. The rapport was not a fleeting one. Simon Wiesenthal, the post-war Nazi hunter, estimated that half the later crimes associated with the Holocaust were committed by Austrians, despite comprising only 8.5 per cent of the population of the Greater German Reich.

Within days of the Anschluss, the City of Blood was overflowing once more. On 16 March 1938, the *New York Times* conveyed a glimpse of the appalling new reality for Scheuer and the rest of the city's 180,000 Jews: 'This afternoon the Jewish quarter of Leopoldstadt was invaded by triumphant crowds that called families from their houses and forced them to kneel and scrub the pavements ... shouting "Perish Jewry", "Out with the Jews!"'

Jewish cemeteries were besieged, as hundreds of Viennese Jews made the astute judgement that things were only going to get a whole lot worse and found a way to end their own lives. 'Death [had become to the Jews] the kindest gift,' remarked the same newspaper.

The Jew baiting proceeded to gain steadily in momentum. The tormentors enjoyed inflicting their greatest indignities on Saturdays, the Jewish Sabbath revered for thousands of years as a day reserved for prayer, contemplation, family and rest. On Saturday 23 April 1938, also the last day of the festival of Passover, stormtroopers ran amok through the city, seizing mostly older Jews. They put them into lorries and drove them out to the Prater, Vienna's amusement park in the Leopoldstadt district.

The Prater amusement park was close to where Scheuer then lived, and adjacent to Hakoah's former Krieau stadium, where the team and its delirious fans celebrated their many proud victories. But this time, the sport on show at Prater was of the sadistic variety.

According to one witness, Jews were thrown to the ground and ordered to eat grass. While they ate, stormtroopers trampled on their hands, or made them climb trees and 'twitter and croak and gibber like birds'. Oswald Dutch, a Viennese Jew, recorded that many people, including pregnant women, were forced to run in circles until they fainted or collapsed, and then beaten until they got up and started running again. Others were strapped into the carriages of the amusement park's scenic railway and then driven at top speed until they lost consciousness. Several elderly Jews suffered heart attacks and died.

Six weeks later, on 10 June, Scheuer and his mother Lina left the apartment they had been renting together for twenty years. As almost two thirds of apartments inhabited by Viennese Jews were aryanised in the nine months after the Anschluss, we can safely assume that they were forcibly evicted by their landlord. (There was no law relating to Jewish tenants passed until almost a year later – in the meantime, Austrian landlords threw the Jews out because they wanted to.) Scheuer was relocated to Salztorgasse in the city's old town near to his office, in an apartment used to dump now homeless Jews.

Directly opposite the windows of his new residence was the delivery entrance to the Hotel Metropole, which had been requisitioned as the Gestapo's Vienna headquarters. Those arrested were brought through this entrance for the purpose of interrogation, torture and subsequent detention in concentration camps. On 23 June, Scheuer may well therefore have caught sight of his brother-in-law Hugo Hirsch, wife of his sister Rosa, on his way to Dachau concentration camp.

Emigration was the only obvious way out of this hell, and the clamour to leave was both widespread and desperate. At this stage, Jews could in theory leave Austria, provided that they paid an extensive array of taxes and fees, relinquished all valuable property and presented an entry permit from another country. They were allowed to take just thirty marks (later reduced to ten) out of the country in German and foreign currency.

Max Scheuer was one of those who succeeded in getting out. The records of the Vienna municipal archives state that he 'deregistered to U.S.A. on 10.11.1938', the second day of Kristallnacht. Due to the date of his departure, we can hypothesise that the devoted Scheuer had the opportunity to leave earlier but agonised about leaving behind his elderly mother or indeed his sisters, one of whose husbands was already imprisoned. It was only when the mass violence, arrests, arson and plunder erupted on Kristallnacht that his personal survival instinct may have finally won out.

As he left the city for the last time on that black day, Scheuer could only peer through the train window and watch his Jewish Vienna disappear in flames.

* * *

Through documents in Holocaust databases and post-war survivor testimony, we can try to piece together what happened to Max Scheuer after his Kristallnacht getaway. As with much information pertaining to that era, ambiguity reigns. Where necessary, we must read between the lines, place ourselves in the subject's shoes, imagine, speculate.

Despite what it says on his deregistration document, there is no record of any application by Scheuer for a United States visa. I was told by the relevant American authorities that 'the visa application-related records of posts ... are destroyed after their administrative use has expired'. Nor is there any surviving information about a visa application in the archives of the Central Office for Jewish Emigration in Vienna, which handled the relevant bureaucratic paperwork for thousands of anguished applicants.

Earlier in this chapter, I quoted Ignaz Hermann Körner's recollections of Scheuer as a player and as a Zionist activist. These come from his book *Lexikon jüdischer Sportler in Wien: 1900–1938* ('Encyclopaedia of Jewish Sportsmen in Vienna: 1900–1938'), written at some point between his emigration to Palestine in October 1938 (a few weeks before Scheuer himself left Vienna) and his death there in 1944. More than six decades after Körner wrote it, the Austrian historian Marcus Patka discovered his hitherto unpublished manuscript in the Israel-based archives of the Maccabi World Union, the international Jewish sports organisation.

In this book, Körner also wrote the following about Scheuer, a series of assertions no doubt gleaned from Hakoah colleagues who had left Vienna soon after both him and Scheuer: 'When Hitler came to power in 1938, Aryan former sports comrades advised him to leave Vienna and helped him across the border. He joined his old friend Eisenhoffer in Marseille and from there followed the Hakoahners Fleischer, Grunbaum and Kraus to South America.'

As we shall see, we now know that Körner was wrong on the South America front. However, he was right that Scheuer did indeed travel to Marseille on the French Mediterranean coast. And given that there is no evidence of an application for an extremely hard-to-come-by United States visa, and that Körner will have written these words soon after the events are alleged to have occurred, we must take seriously his claim that Scheuer was indeed spirited out of Austria without the requisite documentation by sympathetic non-Jews.

Indeed, it seems to me almost certain that the mention of the USA on his deregistration form may simply have reflected Scheuer's vague ultimate intention, rather than his immediate entitlement, to enter that country. Historians of that era assure me that when it came to the crunch, the Austrian border police were sometimes only too happy to see the back of any given Jew after a cursory check of documentation, perhaps with a bribe or two exchanging hands.

There are two reasons why Scheuer would have hit on the idea of Marseille as his destination. First, as was natural for someone who lived and breathed the club, it was the Hakoah connection that pulled him to the city. The tight circle in the city did not only involve his former teammate József Eisenhoffer, the highly successful player-coach of Olympique de Marseille, whom Körner namechecks.* Another Austria international, Friedrich Donenfeld, with whom Scheuer had played in the final stages of his career, was a fixture in Eisenhoffer's first team. It was Donenfeld who later provided important testimony about Scheuer's fate.**

The second factor commending Marseille to Scheuer was its function as one of the most important ports of departure for refugees seeking to flee Europe. Indeed, several thousand Jews from Germany and Austria had arrived there around that time, often without legal permission from a French state that was cracking down ever harder on Jewish migrants. Scheuer could at least try to keep his head down there and prepare for his next desired move, perhaps to the United States, or more likely across the Mediterranean to the Jewish homeland he

* József Eisenhoffer also appeared earlier in this book as a teammate of József Braun in the Hungary national team. He died in February 1945 from wounds sustained in a Soviet bombing raid on Budapest.

** Friedrich Donenfeld spent the war years working first for the French Resistance, and then after the Allied landing in Normandy, for the British intelligence services. He later became a highly successful coach, including two stints with the Netherlands national team.

had long fought for. But, as with so many other European Jews, tight American and British visa restrictions would have likely put paid to Scheuer's initial hopes.

How he managed to scratch out a living after his arrival, with no savings to fall back on, is a matter for conjecture. Before his departure from Vienna, he had filled out a form informing the Nazi authorities that he was relocating his rope goods trading business to France. Deprived of his local Viennese network, however, one can imagine that this plan bordered on the fanciful.

Living alone in temporary lodgings, with barely two francs to rub together, Scheuer would have soon discovered that his brother-in-law Hugo had been murdered in Buchenwald concentration camp, and his mother Lina had died shortly after from heart failure, no doubt induced by the stress of it all.

But at least he himself was safe and free. At least, that is, until he wasn't.

* * *

After the surrender of the French government to German invading forces in June 1940, the country was divided into two zones – one under German military occupation and one that remained under French administration.

The latter zone, which comprised the southeastern two-fifths of the country, included Marseille. The Vichy regime that presided over it, named after the spa city that became its seat of government, was led by the ageing but hugely popular hero of the First World War, Marshal Philippe Pétain. If Scheuer had thought that a French administration could not possibly be as bad for the Jews as the one he had left behind in Vienna, he was to be gravely mistaken.

The French acted swiftly, ruthlessly and independently, without instruction from the Nazis. 'Germany was not at the origin of the anti-Jewish legislation of Vichy,' Pétain's private secretary, Henri Moulin de Labarthète, later admitted. 'This legislation was, if I dare say it, spontaneous, native.'

In October 1940, two laws were published simultaneously. The first law defined who was a Jew and then excluded them from public service, teaching, journalism, theatre, radio and cinema. The second law gave local leaders the authority to intern foreign Jews or imprison them in forced labour camps.

Scheuer did not escape the resulting roundups. I found his name on a file of approximately 3,000 Jews who received aid packages from the Relief Committee for the War-stricken Jewish Population (RELICO), an organisation established in 1939 and principally funded by the World Jewish Congress. Written on the card relating to Scheuer are the words, '701 GTE Miramas'. Miramas was a small and still little-known labour camp around forty kilometres northwest of Marseille, while GTE is an acronym for 'Groupements de Travailleurs Étrangers' (Foreign Workers' Groups). The largest such group attached to Miramas was 701, comprising Spanish republicans who had fled their country following the Civil War and foreign Jews from the Marseille region, including Max Scheuer.

The limited survivor testimony about Miramas informs us that camp conditions were extremely harsh. Outgoing letters were censored, while incoming packages of food and other items were routinely confiscated by the French guards, whose unpredictable and vindictive behaviour could decide a prisoner's fate at any given moment. There were constant rollcalls, ensuring that prisoners were always reminded of their subservient status. There were no chairs, benches or tables in the barracks, so inmates were forced to eat standing up. Washing facilities for several hundred men consisted of one fountain and one tap in the courtyard. As a final flourish, the cost of the sparse food and cramped and unhygienic accommodation was deducted from the detainees' negligible payment for their labour.

There are no dates on his RELICO card to enlighten us further, but this is how Hakoah Vienna legend Max Scheuer lived for anything up to two years. The next relevant evidence we hear about Scheuer's travails in this French hellhole comes from Friedrich Donenfeld, whose post-war declaration reads as follows:

> Max Scheuer, probably one of the most loyal and self-sacrificing players of Hakoah, was in Marseille when the Germans overran France. Thanks to the support he received from the former Hakoah player Weiskopf, he managed to make contact with a Swiss footballer from the national team. He had already helped Moschkatz (Moritz) Häusler cross the Swiss border, and now he was prepared to do the same for Scheuer. Everything had already been arranged, but the loyal Max did not want to leave his long-time friend and fellow sufferer Benno Schechner-Aberbach behind. However, the latter did not turn up alone at the agreed meeting point, but had also brought his bride and her family with him. As a result, fourteen people made the difficult journey instead of the two that had been planned. The large group attracted attention and was caught by the German border guards. The friend was Scheuer's undoing! He was never heard from again.

This testimony was published, in 1961, in Arthur Baar's supplement to the book about the history of Hakoah he had first brought out two years before. The statement was signed by 'Frederic Donenfeld, Enschede'. Donenfeld was coaching in Enschede in the late 1950s, so we should assume he wrote these words at that point, around seventeen years after the events in question.

Such was the utter devastation of Jewish Europe that it took that long for any evidence to emerge about the fate of a Viennese celebrity such as Max Scheuer. The time lapse also helps to explain Donenfeld's comment that it was German border guards who apprehended Scheuer, when it would have been the French manning the border at the time of capture (most likely, as we shall see, in August or September of 1942).

It is as predictable that Scheuer would rely on the Hakoah network to help him escape as it is that, even in this desperate life-or-death moment, he would place loyalty to others above all other concerns. But after studying Donenfeld's testimony, I had as many questions as answers. Who was Weiskopf? How and why did Scheuer get out of Miramas to attempt this cross-border escape? Who was his friend Schechner-Aberbach? And what happened to them both after their escape was thwarted?

* * *

Edmond Weiskopf's story is the stuff of barely credible novels, a man who played fast and loose with death on a more or less continuous basis. Born in Budapest in 1911, he turned out on the left wing (where else?) for Hakoah Vienna under then coach Béla Guttmann in the early 1930s. He won the league with Olympique de Marseille in 1937, played for the France national team, fought in the Battle of France, got captured, escaped from a German prisoner-of-war camp and was still playing for Olympique de Marseille in the 1940/41 season, albeit now under the alias 'Edmond Virage' to avoid rubbing the authorities' noses in the fact that he was a Jew.

In late 1941 or early 1942, armed with his false papers, Weiskopf (Virage) was appointed as coach of FC Annecy, near the Swiss border. It was an ideal location from which to try to help people like Scheuer.*

Several months later, in August 1942, after negotiations between the French and German rulers, it was agreed that Jews from specific countries (including Austria) who had entered France from 1936 onwards were to be rounded up and delivered from the French zone to the occupied zone and hence to the death camps.

As rumours circulated in anticipation of this order, foreign Jews trapped in labour camps became increasingly anxious. Escapes were planned and sometimes assisted by sympathetic guards who had been alerted to the imminent deportation.

For example, Miramas survivors Jean Engel and Jules Stern later reported that on the evening of 2 August 1942, a guard announced that 'everyone still here tomorrow will be delivered to the Germans', giving prisoners time to disappear. I think it very possible that Scheuer escaped from Miramas around this point, subsequently managing to make his way to the Swiss border region and start scheming with Weiskopf and Schechner-Aberbach.

Benzion Schechner-Aberbach (the various Holocaust archives also refer to his surname as 'Aberbauch' or 'Auerbach', without the 'Schechner' prefix) was an Austrian citizen, five years younger than Scheuer. It is not apparent whether the two became friends in Vienna or somewhere in France. After being captured during their attempted escape to Switzerland, they were first sent together to Rivesaltes,

* Weiskopf subsequently managed to duck and dive his way through to liberation in 1944. His parents, stranded in Hungary, were both murdered in Auschwitz-Birkenau that same year.

a transit camp near the Spanish border housing Jews earmarked for extermination.

There they stayed for four days, before being sent on 5 October to Drancy, the camp in a northeastern suburb of Paris that performed the same function in the occupied zone as Rivesaltes did in the French zone. Drancy, which was also run at this time by French police, was the last point of departure to the death camps for 120,000 French and foreign Jews between 1941 and 1944.

After four weeks suffering the insanitary and overcrowded conditions at Drancy, Scheuer was sent on the last of his countless rail journeys during his adult life. He and Schechner-Aberbach were among the one thousand Jews from ten countries on Transport 40, which set off for Auschwitz-Birkenau at 8.55am on Wednesday 4 November 1942.

A heavy responsibility for the adults, amid the hunger, thirst, stench and filth of this long journey across Europe, would have been to console the 200 young children on board, many of whom were being deported without their parents. I feel strongly that Max Scheuer would have seen it as his duty to do just that.

Unlike the transport carrying Árpád Weisz a month earlier, there was no stop at Cosel to offer the faintest chance of reprieve. Arriving in Auschwitz on 6 November, 269 men and ninety-two women were selected for labour. Their number included Benzion Schechner-Aberbach, sent at some unknown later date to Stutthof concentration camp (600 kilometres north of Auschwitz), the probable location of his eventual murder.

There is no record, however, of Scheuer being similarly registered. Now aged forty-seven and worn down by the hard labour at Miramas, we must assume that this defiant and devoted Jewish patriot was among the 639 people from the transport selected for immediate liquidation in the gas chambers.

The records reveal that just four people from the transport, all adult men, were still alive in 1945.

* * *

By the time Max Scheuer was murdered, Otto Fischer had been dead for almost a year.

Following the Nazi-Soviet pact, the Red Army marched into Latvia in June 1940. Olimpija was temporarily disbanded and converted into an army club whose players were routinely withdrawn due to conscription. Fischer nevertheless remained at the helm of a much-diminished organisation.

A year later, on 10 June 1941, he married his second wife, Anna Lemkin, a thirty-year-old Jewish pharmacist. It was very possibly the last wedding of a Jewish couple in Liepāja before disaster struck. By the end of the month, the Germans had occupied the city. What soon transpired was the sort of cohesive teamwork that Fischer had sought to instil in his teams, as Germans and Latvians fused their considerable talents in the pursuit of a shared passion – the elimination of the Jews.

There were 90,000 Jews living in the country prior to the German occupation. Many fled before the invasion, leaving 70,000. Given that only 200 of them ultimately survived on Latvian soil, Jewish testimony about the era is like gold dust. One of the few written recollections comes from Bernhard Press, a Jewish survivor from Riga who presents us with devastating first-hand evidence of the scale of the local complicity in his book *The Murder of the Jews in Latvia*.

'A large part of the population was immediately willing to collaborate with the German execution squads,' he writes, 'while those Latvians who did not participate in the murder of their Jewish compatriots watched indifferently or with exultation as their friends and neighbours were driven to their graves.'*

There were 7,145 Jews in Liepāja itself in 1941 (around 13 per cent of the population), predominantly German-speaking like Fischer. They were soon dispensed with. On 5 July, a week after their arrival, the Germans ordered the Jews to sew yellow stars onto their clothing and confiscated much of their property. They prohibited them from leaving their house for most of the day, from walking on the same pavement as German soldiers or from using public transport. By the end of the month, the Arājs Kommando, a unit of the Latvian auxiliary police under the leadership of the Latvian SS officer Viktors Arājs and comprised of volunteers free to leave at any time, had carried out the mass shootings of around one thousand Jewish men in the city.**

It had been assumed that Fischer was one of the victims of this specific massacre. However, recent research by the Liepāja Jewish Heritage Foundation reveals that Otto and Anna were living at their

---

* On 30 November and 8 December, 1941, the Germans and their Latvian accomplices murdered approximately 25,000 Jews in the Rumbula Forest outside Riga, Latvia. Comparable in scale and intensity to the massacre at Babyn Yar in Kyiv in Ukraine, the Rumbula slaughter represents one of the largest mass shootings of Jews in the Holocaust. Most of the murdered were Jews from the Riga ghetto, as well as 1,000 Jews deported from Germany. Only three Jews who were taken to the Rumbula killing site survived the Holocaust.

** The Latvian Arājs Kommando was responsible for the murder of at least 26,000 Jews in Latvia, although the unit also participated in the murder of many thousands more in Belarus. Under the false name of Viktor Zeibots, Viktors Arājs later worked as an assistant in a printing company in Frankfurt, until being identified and found guilty of mass murder in December 1979. He died in a West German prison in January 1988, at the ripe old age of seventy-eight, having served one year for every 3,000 Latvian Jews he had murdered.

apartment on Dzintaru Street, a few minutes' walk from the Olimpija stadium, right until they moved to another residence on Brivzemnieka Street at the end of September 1941.

A popular story in Liepāja tells us that Fischer was granted a stay of execution because players and representatives from Olimpija pleaded with the Germans not to murder an honoured guest in the town. A lovely and heartwarming story, although history does point to the high probability that Fischer and his bride were eventually shot into a ditch with bullets fired by Latvians, some of whom, for all we know, may have carried the champion coach on their shoulders a couple of years before.

It is now thought likely that Otto and Anna were put to death at the Šķēde beach, several kilometres north of Liepāja, during a three-day massacre carried out by three units, two Latvian and one German, between 15 and 17 December 1941. By the end of the operation, in the middle of the normally joyous Chanukah festival and in a spot ordinarily reserved for romantic trysts and sandcastles, 2,749 Jews had been exterminated.*

Although the task may be distressing, I believe that we owe it to Otto Fischer to try to imagine how he probably spent his final moments, how he was rewarded, at the age of just forty, for the joy he had brought to the people of Liepāja. The task is made easier by twelve unbearable photographs taken by an SS officer that were later discovered and can now be viewed on the internet.

A ditch 100 metres long had already been dug in the sand dunes – a similar length to that of a football pitch. The Jews were first taken in groups of twenty to a site forty to fifty metres from the ditch, where they were forced to lie down with their face to the ground. Groups of

* Another great Jewish left-winger, Leon Sperling, was murdered during the same week.

ten were then ordered to stand up and remove their outer clothing. Marched closer to the ditch, they were then made to undress completely. Those who did not move to the ditch were whipped until they did.

The victims faced the sea, with their backs to their killers. Two shooters were assigned to each Jew. Children who could walk were treated as adults, but babies were held by their mothers and murdered with them. After the initial volley, someone would inspect the ditch and extinguish any sign of life with more bullets.

In 1956, Israeli citizen Daniel Lemkin took the short trip from his home in Rishon LeZion to the Yad Vashem Holocaust Museum in Jerusalem. His purpose was to complete a victim testimony for his sole sibling Anna, thus answering a global plea from the museum for more information about the millions of individuals murdered.

In the section on the form dealing with the marital status of the victim, he selected the answer *Ravak*, the Hebrew word for single. Fifteen years after her murder, and very probably for the rest of his life, Daniel Lemkin had no idea that his own sister had been married to the great Jewish footballer and ground-breaking coach, Otto 'Schloime' Fischer.

But, I suppose, why would he? There was no one left to tell him.*

* * *

Fischer's family back in Vienna were soon decimated. Fischer's mother Netty and two of his siblings, Hugo and Ernestine, were still alive at

---

* The parents of Anna and Daniel divorced in 1929. Their father Yitzchak died in 1933. Daniel's further testimony suggests that their mother Zisla was among the approximately 1,000 Jews of Kārsava, near what is now the Latvian border with Russia, to be shot into a mass grave in August 1941.

the start of the war.* Netty was murdered in Theresienstadt concentration camp in April 1943, aged seventy-three. Hugo, his wife Ilona and their 17-year-old daughter Gerda were deported to Auschwitz-Birkenau in July 1942, and murdered there. Ernestine managed to survive Thereseinstadt, but her husband Robert Tichy did not.

Although it might not seem possible, Max Scheuer's remaining siblings fared worse.** In early 1941, his two older sisters were both victims of the first phase of the mass deportations from Vienna, destined for resettlement in Jewish ghettos in occupied Poland.

Rosa, bereft of her already murdered husband Hugo, was transported in March 1941 on a train to Opatów and Łagów, two towns close to each other in the Kielce region of southern Poland. Jenny had already been sent the previous month to Kielce itself, alongside her husband Jakob (also Scheuer), their daughter Gertrud, and grandchild Denny, aged ten months. There is some confusion about Denny. Some documents say Denny was a boy, others a girl. Does it matter? I think it does. Anyhow, he/she was murdered.

In fact, they all were. Indeed, most of the passengers in these transports of February and March 1941 were eventually deported from their adopted ghettos to the Treblinka extermination camp for gassing in the summer and autumn of 1942. Of the 1,997 Jews on the two trains, twenty-nine survived the Holocaust, a murder rate of 98.5 per cent.

And thus ends the story of the handiwork of Elkan Ignaz and Karoline Scheuer, and Heinrich and Netty Fischer, four Jews who arrived in Vienna from the Bohemian Crownlands just a few decades before, with a spring in their step and oceans of mistaken optimism.

---

* Otto's father, Heinrich Fischer, died of a heart attack in Vienna in 1924. His eldest sister Irma died soon after birth in 1893. His older brother Alfred died of tuberculosis in 1931.

** One of Max's older sisters, Gisela, died of cancer in 1934.

CHAPTER 7

THE GILDED GOALIE

The Hungarian football authorities introduced a revealing innovation for the national team's forthcoming match against Bohemia, set to take place in early April 1908. For the first time in Budapest, spectators were urged to buy a ticket in advance to avoid disappointment, rather than simply turn up on the day and pay on the door.

A decade previously, the English import of football had been viewed, rather like cricket, as something of an eccentric curiosity. But interest had rapidly become mainstream, and the ticket gambit paid off. More than 8,000 packed out the stands at the Millenáris stadium, forcing the safety-conscious police to shut the gates and setting a new national attendance record for a football match.

The visitors from the Czech lands had been regular and tough opponents in recent years, with games between the two teams closely fought and the results evenly split. This particular clash, however, prefaced a hiatus in this rivalry that lasted for the best part of two decades. As Bohemia did not constitute an independent country, but merely a province of the Austro-Hungarian empire, FIFA subsequently ruled that it could no longer field a national team.

For me, though, the significance of this game does not lie in ticketing arrangements, attendance records or the procedural rulings of sports bodies, but in the presence in the Hungarian goal of a talented scion of an extremely prominent and wealthy Jewish family. Every football team needs a goalkeeper, and this is mine – Paul Goldberger. Or to give him his proper due, Dr Paul Philipp Herbert Goldberger de Buda.

Although only twenty-seven, Goldberger had been making his mark in the nascent football scene in Central Europe for ten years, winning major trophies in Austria and Germany, and also representing teams in Switzerland and Hungary. Indeed, it was his recent performances in goal for the Budapest team 33 FC which had won the nod from the selectors.

Known by fans and journalists throughout the region as 'Gilly', Goldberger did not let himself down on the big stage. 'Gilly, the excellent goalkeeper of 33 FC, who had already attracted the attention of the relevant circles during his short spell in Budapest, had relatively little to do and thus had no opportunity to prove his outstanding class to the full extent,' summarised the reporter from *Pesti Hírlap.* Considered blameless for the two goals conceded in Hungary's 5–2 triumph, the crowd witnessed 'a brilliant save from him in the second half, when he bravely charged out of his goalmouth and saved a shot from close range that looked certain to be a goal'.

Despite this impressive performance, Goldberger's debut appearance for the national team was also to be his last. By the time the national team took to the pitch a month later in Vienna, first-choice goalkeeper László Domonkos had recovered from a brief illness and normal service was resumed.

Goldberger's on-field achievements may not quite put him on a par with some of the greats featured in this book, but his footballing legacy is nonetheless substantial and still resonates today. Three years after the Bohemia game, he played a pivotal role in the founding of Frankfurter Fussballverein (FV), now famous throughout the football world as Eintracht Frankfurt, a club which lists the German league championship and major European competitions among its many achievements.

That same year, 1911, Paul Goldberger also happened to make a fundamental decision in his personal life. Presumably to cement his place in high society, and avoid the slights and barriers that even Jews of his status are wont to suffer, he went down a similar road to all his five living siblings. He walked into a church and converted to Christianity.

Unlike his Frankfurt football venture, it is fair to say, that one did not go quite the way he might have hoped.

* * *

Even though he played his sole international game for Hungary, Paul Goldberger was born and raised in Vienna.* All the same, his surname would have been extremely familiar to the Millenáris crowd. His grandparents had taken an existing small family business in Óbuda, a district of modern-day Budapest, and expanded it into one of the largest textile concerns in Central Europe, supplying the whole of Hungary and the Balkan region with printed fabrics.

The driving force behind the business was by all accounts not Paul's grandfather, the eponymous founder of Sámuel F. Goldberger & Söhne, but his grandmother, Elisabeth. Not content with having brought up seventeen children of her own as well as one adopted son, the redoubtable matriarch officially took the helm after Sámuel's death, running the company throughout her seventies and restoring its fortunes in the wake of a disastrous gamble.

In the year Sámuel died, 1848, the Goldbergers had backed the wrong horse. They threw their weight behind the Hungarian bid for

* Up to 1920, Paul Goldberger's 'country of origin' and later his citizenship were stated on his official documents as Hungarian. At that point, he became an Austrian citizen.

independence from the Austrian empire, providing the rebel army with uniforms. After the uprising was duly crushed, the company had to pay a substantial compensatory tax to the government and hand over much of their stock.

It seems that Elisabeth soon used all her skills of diplomacy to get back into the state's good books, because in 1857 Emperor Franz Joseph even saw fit to visit the company factory in Óbuda. The rapprochement with the highest reaches of Austro-Hungarian society did not end there either. In 1867, after various sizeable donations to patriotic and philanthropic causes, Elisabeth and all her children were elevated to the hereditary Hungarian nobility. As a result, they were all granted a place name to attach to their family name and serve as proof of their aristocratic standing, hence Goldberger de Buda.

Despite forming less than 5 per cent of the overall Hungarian population, Jews were awarded around 20 per cent of such ennoblements in that part of the empire in the decades leading up to the First World War. This disproportionate figure reflected not just the Jewish community's highly impressive contribution, but also a rather naked and extremely expensive bid for social acceptance, born out of deep-seated insecurity.

'The process (towards ennoblements) was long, drawn out, full of pitfalls, and in addition, very costly,' writes the historian Raphael Patai. 'Each rank of nobility and aristocracy had its fixed price, payable to the crown ... Thus a newly acquired title of nobility attested as much to the wealth of the man so "honored" as to his achievements and merits.'

The subsequent rush to assimilation among the newly titled Jews reveals the ultimate intention behind all that investment of time and money. 'About 20 per cent (of the ennobled) ... converted to Christianity, and an unknown but certainly much higher percentage of the others' children followed the same path,' says Patai.

That estimate relates to Hungary. In the city where Paul and his siblings were raised, the trend was even more pronounced. In her book *The Jews of Vienna: Assimilation and Identity*, Marsha Rozenblit writes that 'Viennese Jews converted to Christianity at a rate higher than Jews anywhere else in the Dual Monarchy, Prague and Budapest included.'

For Jews as prosperous as the Goldbergers, a step removed even from the middle-class Jews who were to fill the terraces at Hakoah's rivals Wiener Amateure, and two steps removed from the likes of Max Scheuer and Otto Fischer, conversion was even more likely. By the turn of the twentieth century, Zionist writers in the city were lambasting what they considered to be the sweeping betrayal of the Jewish nation by the moneyed classes. One such article, published in 1902, joked contemptuously that as soon as a Viennese Jew reached his first 100,000 Kronen, conversion was an absolute must. Another remarked that 'there is hardly one (wealthy) family that has not given thought to conversion'.

Viewed within this context, it is perhaps something of a surprise that Paul Goldberger held off for quite as long as he did.

* * *

Goldberger was born in Vienna – on 14 January 1881 – because his father Edmund had recently moved with his wife Charlotte (née Strasser) from their native Budapest to assume a senior executive role in the family's wholesale business in the city. Paul grew up as the eldest of seven children in the family homes in Innere Stadt and Alsergrund, favoured districts of Vienna's wealthiest Jews.

Charlotte would have hardly felt like a kept wife, as her union with Edmund was something of a corporate merger. Her own father, Alois Strasser, had built himself up from modest beginnings in the Hungarian provinces to make a fortune in banking and other commercial activities through his company Strasser & König Corn Trading. If that was not enough, he was also a founder and president of the Hungarian Stock Exchange. Such was the size and opulence of the Strasser family mansion that it now functions as the Croatian embassy in Budapest.

Paul really had everything going for him, and not just because he emerged from a background where money did indeed grow on trees. Athletic, good-looking and bright, he was naturally gifted at whatever he turned his hand to, whether on the sports field or in the classroom, the type of person who attracts admiration and envy in equal measure.

On the academic side, he studied Chemistry at the Technical University in Charlottenburg in Berlin and then an advanced degree at the University of Basel. In 1908, he completed a doctorate in the Swiss city, entitled 'Studies on N-Bromophthalimide'. Few footballers can claim to have made an international appearance in the same year as submitting a doctoral thesis on an obscure scientific topic, but Goldberger moved effortlessly from one great European city to another, leaving notable achievements in his wake.

His sporting talents were diverse. A *Neue Freie Presse* article sees the sixteen-year-old 'Paul von Goldberger' featuring for the Baden water polo team, the 'von' in his surname denoting his noble lineage in the Germanic way, lest anyone might forget it. Almost a decade later, the *Prager Tagblatt* documents a tennis tournament in the Aussee region of Austria that was dominated by Paul and his brother Alfred: 'The lion's share [of the prizes] went to the Goldberger siblings, who play beautifully. Messrs A. and P. von Goldberger are well known from international events.'

It was football, however, that really animated him and occupied much of his time not spent in the chemistry lab. A 1909 profile from *Nemzeti Sport* speaks of Goldberger's 'true love of the beautiful sport'. 'During his university studies,' the article goes on to say, 'he visited several cities in Europe and everywhere he hurried to find the most suitable companions, among whom he could indulge his noble passion.'

From 1898 to 1900, he played for the team in which Otto Fischer later starred, First Vienna. At that point, the most prestigious competition in the Austro-Hungarian empire was the knockout Challenge Cup. Still a teenager, Goldberger managed to lift this cup with First Vienna two years on the run.

Further success soon followed. While studying as an undergraduate at Charlottenburg, he played in goal for Berlin TuFC Britannia, twice winning the local league in the capital city and qualifying for the German championship finals in 1903 and 1904 against the winners of the other regional competitions.

In 1907, he managed to go one better. FC Freiburger, winners of the South German region, were scouring the region for a goalkeeper who could play in the national championship finals to replace Fritz Engelberger, who had recently signed for a Berlin club. Goldberger, then turning out for Old Boys of Basel while writing his thesis, was identified as the ideal stand-in.

FC Freiburger knocked out holders VfB Leipzig in the semi-final before lifting the highly prized national trophy in May after a 3–1 win against Viktoria Berlin in Mannheim. Josef Glaser, Goldberger's teammate on that victorious day and later a German international, recalled that the goalkeeper played out of his skin during the final and emphasised that the only goal he conceded was a penalty.*

* Any Polish Jews in Freiburg were expelled back to Poland in October 1938 to face eventual extermination. On Kristallnacht in November 1938, the synagogue in the city was destroyed and 100 men sent to Dachau concentration camp. There were 474 Jews left in May 1939. The Jews of Freiburg were mostly deported in October 1940 to Gurs internment camp in France, and then to Auschwitz-Birkenau in 1942. Fifteen survivors returned to Freiburg.

These were still the very early days of football – Goldberger is the oldest in my team by a full decade. Press analysis of individual players was then sparse in Germany, making Glaser's subsequent commentary on Goldberger's ability particularly invaluable. 'The basis of his skill was his excellent positioning,' he reflected. 'As a natural goalkeeper, he could almost predict what was going to happen and acted accordingly. He was a very calm goalkeeper whom no one could rattle.'* (His unflappable disposition and wealthy background bring to mind the great French goalkeeper of the modern era, Hugo Lloris.)

Perhaps he could read the game so well because he was not solely a goalkeeper, but had gained significant exposure to various outfield positions during his career. In October 1909, during his three-year stint at Óbuda-based 33 FC, *Nemzeti Sport* featured a profile of Goldberger to commemorate his 300th football game. Saluting 'not only an enthusiastic and first-rate player, but also a professional authority rich in experience and loyal comrades', the article then goes on to present Goldberger's extensive background as a utility player.

> He has played 127 times as a goalkeeper, forty-one times as a right-back and eighteen times as a left-back; he has played fourteen times as a right midfielder, twenty-nine times as centre-half and five times as a left midfielder; he has played four times as a right winger, six times as an inside right, thirty-six times as centre forward, sixteen times as an inside left and five times as a left winger. His versatility is demonstrated by the fact that he was able to perform at a

* On 1 May 1937, Josef Glaser joined the Nazi Party, less than five years before his former teammate and subject of his admiration was murdered for being a Jew. From 1949 to 1964, Glaser was chairman of the South Baden Football Association and the South Baden Sports Association, his Nazi past seemingly little hindrance to career progress.

moderately high level in all of his roles, and as a defender, he proved to be a top-class talent, especially as a goalkeeper.

What exactly couldn't this sporting polymath do? Well, Goldberger's most significant impact on football was actually still to come.

* * *

Those statistics about Goldberger's various positions on the pitch could not have been compiled by the reporter who wrote the article. No journalist would have had access to such granular detail back then, particularly relating to games played in a variety of countries. The only person who could have had such information at his fingertips would have been Goldberger himself.

What does it say about Goldberger that he kept a record of his positions in all the games he played, and then totted them up for an overall tally? I think we can surmise that he had an obsessive and scientifically ordered mind – as might also be gleaned from his academic pursuits – and that this obsession was primarily directed at the structure and interplay of a football team. It is an impression that we see confirmed by his short but highly productive period in Frankfurt, starting in February 1911.

(We saw a similar preoccupation demonstrated elsewhere in the book by the likes of Otto Fischer, József Braun and Árpád Weisz, the latter two even publishing their theories. The difference is that Goldberger was thinking these thoughts two decades earlier, when football was just starting to evolve from fun kick-about to serious pursuit subject to analysis, interpretation and improvement.)

He arrived in Frankfurt for professional reasons. 'Dr Pál Goldberger, known throughout the sporting world as Gilly, is bidding a final farewell to Hungary and settling in Höchst, near Frankfurt am Main, where he will work as a chemist for a large paint factory,' reported *Pesti Hírlap*.* Another newspaper, *Sportvilág*, saw fit to promote him, declaring that his job title would be 'chief chemist'. He almost certainly went to work for Hoechst AG, headquartered in the town that bestowed its name, one of the largest chemical and pharmaceutical companies in Germany throughout the twentieth century.

It looks like a plum post for an aspiring professional scientist. However, in his recollections published in the Eintracht Frankfurt magazine in 1928, Goldberger admits that his attention was not primarily focused on his Bunsen burners. 'When my job took me to Höchst, my first thought was of course football,' he wrote. 'The second was a letter with my application to Frankfurter Kickers.'

Within three months of his arrival at the club, two events occurred that were to shape his legacy as a founding father of Frankfurt football. By April 1911, he had already impressed the club so much with his knowledge and experience that he was appointed as club captain by the general assembly of its members. One month later, he was the driving force behind the merger of Frankfurter Kickers with its rival Frankfurter Victoria to form Frankfurter FV, soon to be known as Eintracht Frankfurt.

At the start of the following season, 1911/12, Goldberger managed to convince his colleagues to introduce the various ideas he had developed during his fourteen years in football, in particular those plucked from the innovative hothouses of Austria and Hungary. By the end of

* The nickname 'Gilly' is almost certainly a play on Goli, the nickname Budapest locals gave to the huge family business. Given Goldberger's favoured position on the pitch, Goli might have been a more apt nickname.

that season, both the hierarchy and the fans had been swept off their feet.

An edition of the club magazine in July 1912 hailed 'Gilly', who had played in outfield positions during the season in question, as 'a master in the finer techniques of football'. The article went on to describe the way Goldberger had fended off initial internal resistance to his revolutionary approach: 'Unperturbed by all the attacks, which of course did not fail to come from our members, our doctor went his own way. Instead of a pronounced individual game, we were treated to a passing game that had never been seen before in Northern district clubs.'

Rather confusingly, the district referred to in the magazine was the northern area of the Southern German Championship. As we saw with Julius Hirsch, the champions of each area in the southern region would then play off against each other to earn the right to compete in the national finals. The team inspired and moulded by Goldberger ran away with the northern district league to reach the Southern German Championship finals for the first time in the club's history, before being thrashed by an identical scoreline – 7–0 – in two matches against an extremely strong Karlsruher FV in the play-offs.

I have checked the team-sheets, and in a moment of intense excitement which not everyone would necessarily understand, discovered that 'Dr Paul von Goldberger' came up against a young and unstoppable Hirsch in both games. The records state that Hirsch, fresh from his four-goal salvo for Germany against the Netherlands just a month before, notched at least another four goals against Goldberger's team. I would give a lot to hear what the experienced old hand said to the young starlet at the end of those encounters.

It was not just marked on-field improvement that Goldberger brought to Frankfurt. In his 1928 reminiscences, he recounts how he sat on the club's board of directors and played a key role in planning the club's new ground on Roseggerstrasse. The new state-of-the-art facility, which comprised stands, a cinder track, reserve pitches and a clubhouse, constituted a major strategic upgrade that showcased the club's new-found ambition.

After an eighteen-month whirlwind, however, the love affair ended as suddenly as it had started. 'It is characteristic of his modest nature that he informed the board of his departure so late that he was able to avoid the honours that would have been showered on him at his farewell party,' reported the *Frankfurter FV* magazine. 'It is very difficult to appreciate fully what he has done for our club.'

With the benefit of hindsight, we can see that Goldberger had in fact done as much as anyone to set the Eintracht ball rolling. When the club lifted the Europa League in 2022 on a hot night in Seville in front of millions watching worldwide, I would like to imagine that the good doctor was smiling down from a better place.

* * *

Work demands had pulled him away from Frankfurt to spend short periods over the next couple of years in various cities throughout Germany, from Hamburg in the north to Munich in the south, making appearances for local teams wherever he found himself.

However, war soon arrived to put paid to any lingering footballing ambitions. Aged thirty-three when fighting broke out, Goldberger was assigned the rank of captain in the Austro-Hungarian army. He served at the front right at the start of the war, before injury or illness consigned him to a Viennese hospital for several months in 1915. He then appears to have been seconded by the wartime authorities to industrial enterprises, no doubt for his expertise as a chemist, first to

Tangermünde in Northern Germany and then to Deutschbrod (now Havlíčkův Brod) in Bohemia.*

Once hostilities ceased, he elected to settle back in Vienna on a permanent basis. He lived first with his mother Charlotte, left widowed after Edmund died in 1908 at the young age of fifty-six. It was not too long, however, before Paul finally got serious in his personal life, entering into a relationship with the divorcée Emanuela Schlesinger – known as Nelly and a mother of two teenage boys. The couple married in January 1923, settling in the prosperous and leafy suburb of Döbling in the northern outskirts of the city.

A couple of aspects of this marriage drew my curiosity and attention, not least because I think they can help us draw a rather more complete picture of who Paul Goldberger was.

I first pondered on his relatively advanced age of forty-two when he got married – significantly older than the average Viennese groom at the time, and also than any of his siblings on their own wedding day. It is true that he lost the war years, and that his itinerant student and working life perhaps pushed thoughts of settling down to the back of his mind, but it still seemed a very late marriage in that era for someone so clearly eligible.

When I first considered this point, I had an image in my mind of a fantastically wealthy, prodigiously gifted bachelor playing the field for as long as he could. However, a couple of comments from people who knew him spoiled this convenient conclusion. These insights persuaded me that Goldberger was actually a studious introvert who

* Tangermünde hosted a slave labour camp during the Holocaust for deported Austrian Jews. In August 1939, Jewish families from Deutschbrod were deported to Prague, from where they were eventually sent to concentration or extermination camps. In June 1942, any Jews still living in Deutschbrod, together with those from the surrounding villages (a total of approximately 130 people), were deported to Theresienstadt concentration camp, where their traces were lost.

was happy to remain in his own company for long periods, no doubt spending his time developing what *Pesti Hírlap* referred to as 'his extensive theoretical knowledge of sport'.

First, we have the *Frankfurter FV* magazine's description of his 'modest nature'. In fact, the relevant German adjective used was *schlicht*, which can also be translated as unpretentious, unostentatious, simple or quiet. Goldberger did not want a farewell party, they implied, because he felt uncomfortable being the centre of attention.

We also have at our disposal an article written in 1935 by Gyula Kiss, the former Hungarian national team player, national team coach, elite referee and by this time a renowned sports journalist. In the relevant article in *Budapesti Hírlap*, Kiss recalls when Goldberger joined his club team, noting his new colleague's shyness on entering the dressing room for the first time. 'After completing his studies, Gilly returned to Budapest, joined 33 FC and served our team for a long time with his goalkeeping talent,' writes Kiss. 'His reserved nature completely changed among us – he became just like the other members of the 33s, and earned a worthy place in the history of the club.'

In their comprehensive compendium of Hungarian footballers published in 1969, Zoltán Antal and József Hoffer combed the available archives to summarise Goldberger as 'the extremely quiet player' who 'was the most versatile Hungarian footballer'.

The other aspect that struck me about his marriage was his choice of a Jewish wife, despite the fact that he had converted to Christianity more than a decade earlier. Indeed, although all his five living siblings left the Jewish religion as well, all but one also ended up marrying someone themselves born a Jew.

It appears that conversion – either to Christianity, or to a third category, *konfessionslos*, indicating a rejection of all religious affiliation – seldom produced the desired goal. As hard as a Viennese Jew like Goldberger might try to fit into the broader society, they rather spectacularly failed to carry it off.

The Austrian researcher Georg Gaugusch spent fifteen years compiling his detailed Who's Who encyclopaedia of the 500 leading families of Viennese Jewry. He told me that these upper middle-class Jews still remained very much in their social milieu even after conversion, mixing almost exclusively with other converted or totally irreligious Jews. It appears that Goldberger was no exception to this rule.

I found him in several *Fremdenlisten*, the published registers of the various affluent guests staying for an extended period in plush resorts. Two such lists from the Altaussee resort from 1912 and 1913 – the two years after Goldberger converted – place him in the company of a plethora of people with giveaway Jewish names such as Goldmann, Rubinstein, Löwy, Levisson and Korngold.

It was a similar story throughout Central Europe. Peter Gay, a historian who fled Berlin as a teenager, argued that assimilation 'took several generations, several intermarriages, possibly a change of name or of residence, before the past of the new Christian faded into invisibility'.

Gay implies here that an antisemitic host community was the obstacle to assimilation, just as it was for the *conversos* of medieval Spain and Portugal, many of whom faced widespread ostracism and discrimination even after pursuing a similar path. And given what ultimately happened to the Jews of Central Europe, it is difficult to argue too much with this logic. However, I think it is also true that thousands of years of shared and often painful history make a common imprint on the soul that shapes distinct personalities and worldviews, binding people together at a very profound level. Try as one might, those bonds are very difficult to shift.

Paul Goldberger and Nelly Schlesinger were married in a civil ceremony. They had actually converted to the status of *konfessionslos* in the weeks leading up to their wedding – he from Roman Catholicism and she from Judaism. In reality, however, all this converting this way and that was just pointless paper pushing that ultimately fooled no one. By the bitter end, they were surely not even fooling themselves.

As it happens, the marriage did not last, and Paul and Nelly divorced in 1930. The woman who had officially renounced Judaism went on to notch a hat-trick of Jewish-born husbands, marrying the publisher Felix Waller in October 1938. The allegedly ex-Jewish Nelly then proceeded to flee with her new partner to France and then to the United States because they were Jews, leaving behind her ex-husband and allegedly fellow ex-Jew Paul Goldberger to face mortal danger because he was a Jew.

The head spins. All that bobbing and weaving, and for nothing.

* * *

Settling back into life in post-war Vienna, Goldberger moved away from the work he had studied for and towards the work he loved. In 1920, he stated his occupation on an official document as 'chemist'. By 1925, however, 'Dr. Paul Goldberger' (after the dissolution of the monarchy in 1918, the 'von' and 'de Buda' disappeared from all references to him) was writing a regular column on Viennese football for *Fussballwoche*, a well-regarded magazine based in Berlin. 'Hakoah has become extremely popular in Poland and the team attracts large crowds of spectators to the games everywhere,' he wrote in July of that year in a detailed description of the Austrian champions' tour games.

It is difficult to pinpoint when or why this column was terminated (there is a period missing in the archives), but it is safe to say that magazine editor Ernst Warner would not have played the role of career-enhancing mentor. Warner was an ardent antisemite who was to enjoy continued popularity under the Nazis. Writing in *Fussballwoche* in 1928, he described the great Jewish coach Hugo Meisl's appearance at the FIFA congress in Amsterdam as typical of 'the smoothness of his race and its destructive spirit'.

A 1929 Eintracht publication commemorating the club's history describes Goldberger as a 'recognised football journalist' in Vienna, part of what was now a booming and high-quality industry in Central Europe heavily dominated by Jews such as Willy Meisl, the so-called 'king of sports journalism' and Hugo's younger brother.*

A search in the Austrian newspaper archives, however, reveals no trace of Goldberger's journalism. We can explain the apparent contradiction in two ways. First, many newspaper articles were not bylined in Austria during that era. Second, his journalistic contribution may soon have moved behind the scenes. Indeed, when he starts to appear in the Viennese telephone directories from 1932 onwards, his occupation is stated as *redakteur* (editor).

The divorced Goldberger was by this stage living alone in an apartment on Josefstädter Strasse in Vienna's upmarket eighth district, as befitting a man of such ample means. Almost directly opposite his apartment still sits one of Vienna's great institutions, Café Eiles, virtually unchanged since his day. One can imagine the unassuming Goldberger sitting by himself in one of the booths with his coffee and notebook, lost in his own thoughts on the development of the game that so fascinated him.

Now in his fifties, his life continued in this quiet way until he was

---

* Willy Meisl fled from Berlin to London in 1934, from where he continued to write sports columns for newspapers all over Europe. In his English-language book *Soccer Revolution*, published in 1956, he criticised what he saw as the backward insularity of English football, urging it to embrace the possession-based game favoured by his brother in the years after the First World War. The Meisl brothers' ideas were arguably not fully understood and implemented in England until the twenty-first century.

forced to witness, with increasing fear, the humiliation and brutality of the Anschluss and Kristallnacht of 1938. However, unlike Max Scheuer and around 120,000 Austrian Jews who managed to escape the country if not necessarily eventual death, Goldberger stayed put.

Nor is there any evidence that he even applied to leave. His three brothers all succeeded in emigrating at various stages – Alfred to the United States in 1920, Stephan to Argentina in 1939 and Felix was listed as an 'enemy alien' in the United Kingdom after the war broke out. Of his three sisters, two had died – Jeanne as a baby and Louise in 1920. I could find nothing in the archives to confirm the wartime whereabouts of his other sister, Elisabeth. However, the official document confirming her immigration to the United States in 1946 stated her 'last place of foreign residence' as Budapest, suggesting that she survived the Holocaust in the Hungarian capital.*

My hunch, therefore, is that the eldest sibling Paul opted to fulfil the role of dutiful child and stay in Vienna to look after their elderly mother, Charlotte. A selfless but ultimately suicidal decision.

At the beginning of September 1939, he was forcibly evicted from his apartment and placed in alternative accommodation with other Jews on nearby Hebragasse. Almost exactly a month later, Charlotte died from a heart condition at the age of eighty-three.

The following day, 2 October, she was buried next to her husband Edmund in the Jewish section of the Vienna Central Cemetery. Paul Goldberger, now totally alone and unemployed, returned from the

* Paul's first cousin Leó Goldberger was also in Budapest during the war. He had been the chief executive of Sámuel F. Goldberger & Söhne since 1920. As one of the wealthiest Jews in the city, he was arrested on the day of the German invasion of Hungary, 19 March 1944. He was murdered the following year in Mauthausen concentration camp in Austria, aged sixty-seven. The post-war Communist government expropriated and nationalised the family's company.

graveside to his apartment of strangers, with only monotony and gloom on the horizon.

* * *

Goldberger may have harboured hopes that his official repudiation of Judaism would somehow come to his rescue. Reality soon intervened to dash them.

The Nuremberg Race Laws of 1935 had classified as Jewish any person with three or more Jewish grandparents. Conversions were deemed irrelevant. The authorities used all available means – such as census information, synagogue membership lists, parish records (for converted Jews), mandatory police registration forms, and interviews with relatives and neighbours – to track down anyone meeting these conditions.

In the mandatory registration of his move to Hebragasse, he stated his religion as '*konfessionslos*'. But his name at the top of the form – 'Dr Paul Philipp Herbert Israel Goldberger' – revealed the Nazis' nonchalant disdain for what they regarded as mere window dressing. As we saw earlier with Julius Hirsch, the German government had by this stage compelled all Jews who bore first names not immediately recognisable as Jewish to adopt an additional name – Israel for men and Sara for women.

In March 1941, the so-called Central Office for Jewish Emigration ordered a further large-scale resettlement of Viennese Jewry. This time round, the purpose was not to rob the Jews of their property and hand over their front door keys to grateful non-Jewish recipients. It was to squeeze them into concentrated areas to facilitate their future deportation to the east.

At the beginning of July, Goldberger was moved to an apartment on Zirkusgasse in the Leopoldstadt district, the area into which most Jews were packed. To avoid any potential confusion, a red letter 'J' was now stamped on the official documentation of his move. The records state that forty-seven Jews were placed in the various apartments in that one building.

In homage to the way Goldberger kept tabs on his games and positions, I decided to take a pen and paper and go through the fates of all forty-seven, one by one. None survived. Gassing on arrival at Sobibór was the most frequent story – this accounted for seventeen. In total, more than 65,000 Jews were deported from Vienna, 15,000 more than the current capacity of the city's Ernst-Happel-Stadion, scene of the UEFA Euro 2008 final. Of those 65,000, it is thought that less than 2,000 survived.

Goldberger was first transferred to an assembly camp in a former school on Kleine Sperlgasse, just ten minutes' walk from Zirkusgasse. 'Sometimes as many as 2,000 people were stranded for days – even weeks – at the site, awaiting deportation,' the relevant page on the Yad Vashem site tells us. 'They would sleep on the floor or on bags filled with straw. The sanitary conditions at the site were terrible, as was the mood of the deportees. Some people suffered nervous breakdowns and some even committed suicide.' Everyone was forced to hand over all cash and valuables to the state.

On 23 October 1941, Goldberger was taken on a cattle cart to the now defunct Aspangbahnhof, the rail station in central Vienna that served as the deportation point for the vast majority of the city's remaining Jews. Nini Ungar, a rare survivor of one of the transports, recalled her own journey from the assembly camp to the station.

'The Viennese were standing and laughing,' she said. 'Finally, they got the Jews out!'

* * *

Goldberger found himself on Transport 9, among 1,000 Jews deported on a train to the city of Łódź in central Poland, known by the Germans as Litzmannstadt. À la Goldberger, I went through this list too. Again, I failed to identify any survivors. According to Yad Vashem, the average age on the transport was fixty-six; 426 were at least sixty-one years old. We do not know whether Goldberger was included in the 143 identified as sick, elderly or invalid.

Łódź had the second largest ghetto in German-occupied Europe after Warsaw. Around 210,000 Jews lived in the ghetto at some point, more than one third of the total population of the city. Almost all were squeezed into an area of less than one square mile, mostly comprising wooden houses without cooking gas, running water or connection to a sewer system. Most Jews subsisted each day on one bowl of watery cabbage or potato soup, a piece of bread and perhaps a snack of radish greens or potato peels. Barbed-wire and wooden fences encircled the ghetto, imprisoning the Jews.

Paul Goldberger was one of 19,554 Jews from more fashionable cities in the western part of Central Europe who entered this worst of nightmares in the autumn of 1941. As we can see from the various written records from the time, the arrival of these upmarket Western Jews caused quite the stir. 'The German Jews keep arriving,' wrote seventeen-year-old Dawid Sierakowiak in his diary entry for 22 October, two days before Goldberger's arrival. 'From Frankfurt am Main, Cologne, and also from Vienna and Prague … Almost all are "big fish". At least so they look.'*

* Sierakowiak's diaries were discovered after the war at what had been his last residence. He was murdered soon after his nineteenth birthday, tuberculosis being the formal cause of death.

'We were struck by their elegant sports clothes, their exquisite footwear, their furs, the many various coloured capes the women wore,' documented the Chronicle of the Łódź Ghetto, a daily record of life written for posterity by a team of authors between 1941 and 1944, then buried and later recovered. 'They often gave the impression of being people on some sort of vacation … You couldn't tell there was a war on from the way these people looked.'

Wind the clock forward six months, and reality had plundered the same deportees' former personalities. 'Events outpaced time, people changed visibly, at first outwardly, then physically, and finally, if they had not vanished altogether, they moved through the ghetto like ghosts,' the same chronicler wrote. 'The turnips and beets they had at first disdained, they now bought at high prices, and the soups they had scorned became the height of their dreams. Once it had been others, but then it was they who prowled the "city" with a cup or a canteen on a chain to beg a little soup.'

By that stage, however, Paul Goldberger had indeed 'vanished altogether'. The ghetto records first inform us that Goldberger listed himself as a 'chemist', perhaps thinking that his old profession would make him useful to the German authorities just as it had in the First World War, and thus improve his chances of survival. He started out on Richter Strasse (now Tokarska) but was soon moved round the corner to Kreuz Strasse (now Krzyżowa). One record states that he 'died' (*gestorben*) on 25 March 1942, while another prefers the following day. He was sixty-one.

The formal cause of death is not stated. Suicide, whether by hanging, poison, slashing wrists or jumping from bridges, is one possibility. In the previous month or so, the Chronicle had reported that more than twenty ghetto inmates ended their lives in one of these ways, no doubt unable to cope with the loss of relatives, the desperate hunger, debilitating illness or anxiety about the ongoing mass deportations to Chełmno extermination camp, situated around eighty kilometres to the north-west of Łódź.*

Statistically speaking, the more likely explanation is that he simply expired from illness and malnutrition. Despite comprising only around 10 per cent of the ghetto population, the generally more elderly and less hardened Western Jews constituted around 50 per cent of the recorded deaths from October 1941 to May 1942.

We might also note that the weather took a sharp turn for the worse around the time of Goldberger's death. 'Winter has returned today,' Sierakowiak wrote on 19 March. 'Thick snow fell, and it's really freezing cold. We have no way to get out of this cold. To say nothing of the hunger.' The Chronicle states that five people actually froze to death on the train station platform towards the end of the month while waiting to be transported to Chełmno.

In one way or another, the life of Paul Goldberger – the riches-to-rags story par excellence – thus reached its conclusion amid extreme squalor and misery. We are left only with the Chronicle's haunting portrayal of the Western Jews in their final moments, so many of whom had spent years persuading themselves, just like Goldberger, that they had unburdened themselves of their heritage and gained acceptance.

'They had been stripped of all their European finery, and all that remained was the Eternal Jew.'

---

* Estimates of the number of people murdered at Chełmno vary greatly, from 172,000 to 320,000. The overwhelming majority were Jews. Execution was carried out by pumping carbon monoxide into vans, each containing between fifty and seventy people. Only four Jews who had been in Chełmno survived the war – Mordechai Podchlebnik, Mordechai Zurawski, Shimon Srebnik and Abram Roj. A survival rate of between 0.00125 per cent and 0.0023 per cent.

CHAPTER 8

THE MASTER AND THE APPRENTICE

After being comprehensively beaten in the Champions League finals of both 2009 and 2011, Alex Ferguson admitted that his flummoxed Manchester United team had been powerless on both occasions to halt Barcelona's intricate system of perpetual motion and interchange. 'They get you on that carousel and they make you dizzy with their passing,' he said.

As we have already seen throughout this book, Barcelona were not the first exponents of the passing carousel. And once upon a time, they were the victims of it, made to feel as dazed and second-rate as United.

Over the Christmas and New Year holiday of 1922/23, the Spanish public enjoyed a special treat, hungrily gorging on a footballing delicacy. MTK Budapest had arrived in the country for a much-anticipated seven-game tour against the top domestic clubs – Barcelona first, and then Real Madrid, Athletic Bilbao and Real Sociedad. Following the festive period, MTK returned home undefeated from these now world-renowned footballing citadels, leaving in their wake a mixture of awe and wonder.

The first two games, against Barcelona, ended in goalless draws. But even the local journalists, spellbound by a style of football that they had never previously encountered, admitted that only rank bad luck had saved the hosts from successive defeats.

El Mundo Deportivo eulogised

> the high class and absolute mastery of the technique of the precise pass, together with the most suitable positioning to lose a marker and receive the ball … As a scientific demonstration in ball control, in movement off the ball, in absolute harmony between the lines and between the elements of each line, we believe that MTK's performance is the greatest we have seen in our stadiums, and that even includes the English professional teams.

The carousel glided on to the capital to take on Real Madrid, a team which included Santiago Bernabéu, whose name now adorns the club's iconic stadium. When Real were defeated 4–3, the local media was again reluctant to be deceived by a mere scoreline. 'Let's have no illusions,' counselled *La Accion*.

> In yesterday's match between MTK Budapest and Real Madrid, our visitors played only half-heartedly. It would be useless for us to try to convince you that the difference between the two teams was only one goal. MTK is one of the best, if not the best team we have seen in Spain. If we analyse each player in isolation, we find eleven aces, each in his own specialist position. Then, in unison, there is nothing so well-matched, so perfect, so harmonious.

As few football fans outside Hungary now have even heard of MTK, and as Real Madrid is now recognised as by some distance the most consistently successful club in the history of European football, and as Barcelona recently boasted arguably the greatest club side in the past few decades, we can perhaps pause to reflect that much has changed in Europe since this tour took place.

And undoubtedly one of the most seismic changes in the intervening period – in terms of the way the continent looks and feels, and its general productive output – has been the obliteration of its Jews.

In this brilliant, mould-breaking MTK team that humbled Real Madrid on their own turf, five were Jews – Gyula Mándi, Vilmos Kertész, György Molnár, Antal Vágó and Henrik Nádler. Two more Jews, József Braun and Alexander Fábián, later to star as the one-armed hero of Hakoah Vienna's finest hour, were included in the touring squad of sixteen.

This final chapter hones in on two of those players – Antal Vágó and Henrik Nádler – who graced the left side of the MTK and Hungary midfield, pretty much one after the other, for two decades. The Real Madrid match took place in the brief period when their careers intersected, before Vágó retired and Nádler fully assumed his mantle. By the time the latter bowed out, their combined haul had reached fifteen domestic league titles.

These two wonderfully gifted footballers were eventually to fall victim to an obsessive and frenzied panic. In the very final stages of the war, with the Red Army striding swiftly through Eastern Europe and with Allied forces making similar progress from the west, the German regime and their many local devotees still clung to a burning ambition. To eradicate the Jews of Hungary – the one large-scale Jewish community in the European mainland to have thus far remained mostly intact – before such a golden opportunity could be stolen from their clutches. And even if that meant diverting vital resources from the last lines of their now defensive war.

* * *

Antal Vágó was born on 8 August 1891, but not with that name. He reached young adulthood with his original name of Weisz, before the entire family opted to swap its conspicuous Jewishness for the Hungarian Vágó.*

His father József married Antonia (née Binét) in her home town of Pápa in western Hungary, but the couple moved to Budapest in time for the birth of their eldest child and only daughter, Olga.

Antal, always known by his family as Toni, was born during the family's brief interlude in Pásztó in the north of the country, most probably because József had been relocated there to perform his work as a postal clerk and railway telegrapher.** Three more sons, including the future MTK coach Zoltán, followed. The family eventually settled in Terézváros, a central Budapest district to which young tourists now flock for its buzzing nightlife, largely unaware and perhaps uninterested that 40 per cent of its population were Jews a matter of decades ago.

Already by his early teenage years, young Toni's footballing ability was starting to make tongues wag within his local community. His

* Antal Vágó is thus one of three Weiszes to qualify for inclusion in my team. As well as Árpád, there was Ferenc Weisz, a prolific forward who represented Hungary on seventeen occasions, before being transported with his wife Gizella to be gassed at Auschwitz-Birkenau in July 1944. Incidentally, Ferenc was also inspired to change his surname later in life, from the Yiddish word for white (Weisz), to the Hungarian equivalent, Fehér. It would thus be remiss not to make explicit a rather obvious observation – one famous footballing Weisz converted his children to Christianity; two famous footballing Weiszes stripped their surname (an intrinsic component of an individual's identity) of any semblance of Jewishness; but all three were murdered for being Jews.

** In 1942, the young Jewish men of Pápa were forced to perform labour service, often on the Eastern Front, resulting in almost inevitable death. On 4 and 5 July 1944, the remaining 2,565 Jews of Pápa, forming 10 per cent of the local population, were deported to Auschwitz-Birkenau. Less than 10 per cent of that number returned. There are no Jews in Pápa today. The 362 Jews of Pásztó had already been deported to the same destination seven weeks earlier, on 16 May 1944. Fewer than forty returned. There are no Jews in Pásztó today.

subsequent rise was lightning fast and stratospheric, the stuff of boyhood dreams.

In 1907, he won the national youth championship with the local team Fővárosi, soon to change its name to the more appropriate Terézvárosi. By the following year, he was turning out for the first team in the country's top division. And before he had time to breathe, he earned his first cap in November 1908 against Austria, at the age of just seventeen years and two months.*

In June 1911, still not yet twenty, Vágó was transferred to MTK, already the aristocrats of Budapest football and soon to reign supreme once coach Jimmy Hogan had got his feet under the table. He went on to become the virtually ever-present mainstay of the club's midfield until his retirement twelve years later, by which time he could point to a tidy collection of eight league titles and four cup medals.

What type of player was he? Just as we can draw a direct line between the MTK of that era and the Barcelona team of almost a century later, so we can compare Vágó, in terms of style, position and impact, to the great Andrés Iniesta. Except that Iniesta was a supreme practitioner of a type of football that was already well established. His Jewish predecessor, on the other hand, had no such copybook to draw on.

Vágó's principal role in the unit was to keep everything moving, to receive the ball in a deep position and recycle it without any fuss to a

* Hungary's captain on the day of Vágó's debut was another Jew, Sándor Bródy. Born in 1884 in Székelyfalva (now known as Sekule in Western Slovakia), Bródy won the Hungarian league eight times as a midfielder for Ferencváros and represented the national team on seventeen occasions. He also later coached Ferencváros, as well as the Swedish team, IFK Göteborg. Although he died in April 1944 after the Nazi invasion of Hungary, I believe it unlikely that he was murdered, at least directly. According to the historian of IFK Göteborg, Jens Hallberg, Bródy suffered from a grave heart condition. Moreover, the ghettoisation, starvation and deportation of the Hungarian Jews had not by this stage entered its most brutal phase.

teammate in space. His passing range was extensive, with both short and long in his armoury. He was in essence the purring engine of the MTK Rolls-Royce – as it happens a very fitting metaphor, as we shall see.

However, he was by no means just a luxury player who neglected the less glamorous aspects of the game. He was also expert in dispossessing opponents, persistently and aggressively breaking up attacks before they could threaten the MTK goal.

'If he had a weakness, no one seems to remember it,' writes Andrew Handler in his book *From the Ghetto to the Games*, released in 1985. 'Flawless ball control, accurate passing, unerring instinct for being at the right place at the right time, and an astonishing range of defensive skills were the most often cited characteristics of this complete player.'

In their own compendium, published in 1969, the Hungarian football historians Zoltán Antal and József Hoffer summarise Vágó's career in a similar way. 'His play was characterised by sure ball handling, good vision, accurate passing and reliability,' they write. 'His strengths were clever positioning and excellent timing in the tackle. His heading ability cannot be criticised either. He fought tirelessly and tenaciously.'

Antal and Hoffer also highlight the effectiveness of Vágó's symbiotic partnership with another Jew, Gyula Bíró, for both MTK and the national team. They believe the duo established a blueprint in Hungarian football that was later imitated by their heirs in the Golden Team of the 1950s, when the ripples of past Jewish influence remained powerful despite the recent destruction of the Jews themselves:

> The approach of the two players and the differentiation between their responsibilities show some similarities with the division of labour between their later successors, [József] Bozsik and [József] Zakariás. Bíró, like Bozsik, was primarily active in organising

attacks. At the same time, Vágó – like Zakariás four decades later – was mainly involved in defence.*

Given their respective duties, Bíró appeared on the scoresheet more often than Vágó. However, a careful examination of the newspaper reports from the time suggest that when Vágó did get a goal, it was more likely to be a spectacular strike, courtesy of his trusted left foot, than a prosaic tap-in.

Take, for example, this effort against visiting Rapid Vienna in April 1919, as reported by *Sporthirlap*: 'MTK's series of attacks only paid dividends in the 31st minute of the second half when Vágó scored the third goal with a beautiful long-range shot from 20 metres.'

Or this one, as described in the same newspaper, in the hothouse atmosphere of the derby match against Ferencváros in November 1922: 'In the 30th minute, Vágó passes the ball to Opata, who passes it back to Vágó, who scores MTK's second goal with a powerful, low, curling shot from the edge of the penalty area. [Ferencváros goalkeeper] Amsel was expecting a shot in the opposite corner.'** We can deduce that Vágó 'gave the keeper the eyes' a long while before modern-day commentators even knew such a thing existed.

In all, Vágó represented Hungary on seventeen occasions, a figure that would have been considerably higher had it not been for the

* We saw Bíró earlier in the book as coach of the Poland national team at the 1924 Olympics.

** Nicknamed *Pók*, meaning 'spider', the Jewish goalkeeper Ignác Amsel represented Hungary nine times, vying for the national green jersey with another Jew, Lajos Fischer, who represented the Zionist teams VAC, Maccabi Brno and Hakoah Vienna. Amsel fled to Brazil in 1939, where he became coach of São Paolo and then Atlético Mineiro. He died in Rio de Janeiro in 1974. Fischer somehow survived the Holocaust in Budapest, and died in New York in 1978.

footballing disruption caused by the outbreak of the First World War and his resulting military service for the same country.

A couple of highlights stand out in his international career. In the 1912 Stockholm Olympics, having been thrashed in the first round by a then still dominant Great Britain side that went on to win the gold medal with ease, Hungary were placed in a consolation tournament with the other teams knocked out before the semi-final stage. With the twenty-year-old Vágo as captain, Hungary first saw off a Germany team that included Julius Hirsch and Gottfried Fuchs, before defeating Austria 3–0 in the final.

The consensus was that his best game came against the same familiar opponents in July 1917, inspiring his team to a 4–1 victory. 'The unanimous opinion of those in the know was that it was the superb play of our midfield, on a par with first-class English players, that gave the Hungarian team a well-deserved, supreme victory,' reported *Budapesti Hírlap*. 'If you can manage to differentiate between the three of them, the highest mark must go to Vágó. This uncomplicated, unpretentious and honest player produced the most valuable sporting performance of his life on Sunday.'

Proudly wearing the Hungary shirt alongside Vágó in Vienna that day was Imre Taussig, the right-winger whom the great József Braun soon dislodged in both the MTK and national teams, and a fellow Jew eligible for my team. For a long time, it had been thought that Taussig returned to Austria in 1944 for the privilege of being murdered. Rather more conveniently, it transpires that neither he nor Antal Vágó had to venture very far from their front door to achieve the same outcome.

* * *

Watching and taking careful notes throughout Vágó's glory days was the young Henrik Nádler. Born in Budapest ten years after Vágó, on 19 March 1901, Nádler was raised in an altogether more affluent environment.

After arriving in the capital from his native Navariya in the Lviv region of Galicia, his father Izsák met and married his next-door neighbour Róza (née Ruchel Acht), who hailed from similar origins, in her case Lviv itself.* In the big city, Izsák proceeded to make so good as a highly skilled maker and trader of leather goods that the couple moved into an apartment in the newly built and highly prestigious Anker-palota (Anker Palace) building in Terézváros, a popular choice of residence for wealthy Jews.

Henrik was the fourth of six children, with three sisters and two brothers. The large family looked out from their plush home onto Ferenc Deák square, Budapest's version of Piccadilly Circus, where Izsák's large, bustling and well-known store was located. By joining the dots, we can build a picture of a close-knit, secure and comfortable home environment that laid the foundation for Henrik's perennially sunny disposition and appetite for tomfoolery, as frequently cited by the footballing media.

'(Nádler) has the most beautiful, greatest, best human quality: cheerfulness,' remarked *Sporthirlap* in one profile during his playing career. A short celebrity question-and-answer feature in the *Színházi Élet* magazine confirms the picture of a well-off young man gallivanting about town, with few cares in the world. 'His favourite drink: French champagne. His passion: motorcycles.'

We only need to think of Lionel Messi, a quiet introvert off the field and an attention-grabbing showman on it, to know that not all

* In November 1942, the 450 Jews of Navariya, forming around one third of the total population of the village, were deported to Bełżec death camp, where they were exterminated on arrival.

football players necessarily reveal their intrinsic personalities when they ply their trade. But as we shall see, the fun-loving Nádler was nothing if not consistent, ever the entertainer.

By the age of fourteen, Nádler was snapped up by the voracious MTK youth academy, where the club's distinct playing style was inculcated in a golden generation of talent. 'It was here that he played and grew up to become an outstanding player in the youth team, virtually every single member of which went on to have a great career in Hungarian football,' wrote the sports journalist Gyula Vadas in his book on the top sporting personalities in the country, published in 1927. Indeed, Nádler and his legendary teammates József Braun and György Orth were all born within a few weeks of each other.

He broke through to the first team as an eighteen-year-old in the 1919/20 season, winning the first of six successive championship medals, a period in which few opponents, home or abroad, managed to lay a glove on the all-conquering side. Apart from a handful of games for Hakoah Vienna in 1930 right at the end of his career, Nádler was, like Vágó, a one-club man.

Although he eventually took on his predecessor's position in the team and was also very left-footed, Nádler was a very different type of character and player. Vágó was an unfussy footballer, an exquisite passer and a calming influence, the type of player whom the former Arsenal manager Arsène Wenger liked to describe as 'efficient'. In contrast, Nádler would take more risks, relying more on dribbling runs, a technically brilliant crowd-pleaser but inclined at times to frustrate his teammates and coaches by losing possession of the ball. He was, in this sense, a very un-MTK-like player, an eccentric anomaly in a carefully choreographed team system.

Referring to Nádler by his widely used nickname, Zoltán Antal and József Hoffer write that 'the blue-and-whites' "Pubi" was a technical, ingenious player, full of guile … He was also fond of employing "funny" tricks. He used them to wind up his opponents. But his on-field decision-making could also be reckless and selfish."*

Writing in the 1960s, Antal and Hoffer would have been exploring the same press archives that I have been, although they also enjoyed the enviable bonus of being able to speak to people who remembered watching players like Nádler in the flesh. I can confirm that the archives totally support their concise summary.

Nádler's total technical mastery of the football is a recurrent theme. One journalist for *Le Sport Alsacien* was particularly taken with the midfielder after MTK's victory over AS Strasbourg on a tour game in December 1923: 'Nádler is a ball acrobat of the highest order … the ball seemed to be an extension of his body; it literally stuck to his feet.' The article was even accompanied by a cartoon showing Nádler bamboozling a clueless opponent, with the ball apparently affixed to his boot.

A *Sporthirlap* article from 1924 described Nádler as

> a God-blessed talent, with all the virtues and faults of such a born talent. There is little deliberation and much intuition … his actions are more instinct than consciousness. He is sometimes entranced by his own dazzling technique, just as orators are sometimes captivated by the beautiful sound of their composition. In such cases he is no longer in control of himself; it is not technique that is at his service. He is subordinated to the pleasure of playing.

Nádler competed with the joy and abandon of a schoolboy in the playground. When announcing his semi-retirement to focus on business

* Pubi, Nádler's nickname, is an old Hungarian expression for a cute little boy with an angelic face.

interests in 1927, he reassured the same newspaper that 'I can't stop playing football for good, just like you can't get rid of someone you love. And football is a childhood love for me.'

However, as Antal and Hoffer infer, his uninhibitedness did come at a cost. 'His flaws?' asks *Sporthirlap*. 'There are quite a number. He can be careless, a tad selfish. He can be late to pass the ball, which he likes to hold on to, rather than passing it on straight away.' The consistency of his performances inevitably suffered as a result. 'He is a totally individual player, completely capricious,' remarked *Nemzeti Sport* in 1925.

There is no doubt that this negative flipside to his carefree style had an impact on the number of international caps he won. In the first years of his career, the selectors often opted for another Jew occupying the same position, Zoltán Blum of Ferencváros, a less gifted but more dependable presence. When Nádler did break through in 1924 for the first of his seven international appearances, the media were often predictably ambivalent in their judgement. 'He did some useful things and played some good passes, but the effect was immediately spoiled by his ill-judged dribbling,' reported *Sporthirlap* after a home victory against Poland.

The downsides of his game certainly did not undermine his enduring popularity with MTK's predominantly Jewish fanbase. The team were usually so superior to the opposition at club level that the supporters could enjoy his mercurial talent without worrying too much whether his peccadilloes would cost points and titles.

'Whether it's accompanied by praise or, if he makes a mistake, by a scolding outburst, you can sense the warm affection with which the fans of the champion team cherish this likeable young player,' observed *Sporthirlap*. And those little showboating tricks of his completely brought the house down. '[The goalkeeper] clears the ball brilliantly and Nádler picks up the ball,' recounted the *Az Est* correspondent after a home draw against the touring Bolton Wanderers. '...Nádler turns and swivels at lightning speed and the crowd is now roaring: Bravo Pubi!'

What helped to boost Nádler's popularity further was the incongruity between his physique and his on-field demeanour. He was very small and slender, yet unafraid to mix it with the big boys, a pocket assassin. Along with all his other attributes and shortcomings, this description conjures for me a close comparison with Bernardo Silva in Pep Guardiola's well-oiled Manchester City unit.

'He is also a tough kid who cannot be overpowered, and can often be seen scything down his opponents two heads taller than himself with the utmost calmness,' continued *Sporthirlap*. 'I haven't put together the statistics, but I think I'm right in saying that most free kicks awarded against MTK are because of his fouls.'

Az Újság referred pithily to Nádler as 'MTK's small but big player'. His never-say-die combativeness certainly helped to allay the national selectors' initial fears about his size. 'Until now, he was not chosen for the Hungarian team only because they feared that his small size and weak physique would make him easy to overpower,' remarked the *Magyarország* newspaper after he eventually won recognition. 'Nádler has proven in MTK matches that he can outplay even the most experienced midfield players who tower over him.'

Nádler's refusal to buckle in the face of powerful adversaries contributed to typically rumbustious scenes in the away encounter at Ferencváros in April 1926. Around twenty minutes from full-time, and with the match goalless and tense, József Braun reportedly punched Zoltán Blum in the stomach and was sent off. The feisty Nádler, who had been receiving treatment on the touchline, promptly raced on to the pitch to join a growing throng of brawling players and pitch-invading spectators.

According to the press, Nádler then confronted a police captain by the name of Árkád Kiss who was entering the playing area to restore some semblance of order. The *Az Est* newspaper recounted in full what happened next.

> [Nádler said] 'Please, Captain, don't come onto the field!' 'How dare you talk to me like that?' the police captain replied angrily. 'I am the police officer on duty and I have the right to enter the field.' Nádler was about to answer, but at that moment another police officer ran onto the field after seeing the argument between his superior and the football player. 'Take him away,' said Kiss, pointing at Nádler. The police officer grabbed Nádler's arm, who tried to protest against the police officer's action. Another police officer rushed forward, then the two of them grabbed the football player by both arms and dragged him out.

Were the police captain's actions a little excessive? Some further delving into the archives can offer some valuable perspective.

Fifteen years after this incident, in 1941, the same Árkád Kiss had become a senior figure at the National Central Authority for the Control of Foreigners (KEOKH), an organisation which was now primarily focused on handling the thousands of Jews – mostly from Austria, Germany, Poland and Slovakia – who had over the years escaped the Nazis and ended up in Hungary.

What to do with all these Jews? Two functionaries in the independent Hungarian administration had a brainwave. Randolph Braham, a leading authority on the Hungarian Holocaust, sets out his version of the relevant events in his book *The Politics of Genocide*:

> Following Hungary's entry into the war against the Soviet Union

> on June 29, 1941, and the subsequent acquisition of military-administrative jurisdiction over a considerable portion of Ukrainian territory northeast of Hungary, two rabidly antisemitic KEOKH officers – Ödön Martinides and Árkád Kiss – devised a plan for the resettlement of the 'alien' Jews in the newly 'liberated' areas.

In the ensuing operation, almost 20,000 Jews were duly awarded the Kiss of death, transported over the border from Hungary to the town of Kamenets-Podolsk. Travelling alongside the recent immigrants were a considerable number of Hungarian Jews, thrown out of their native country because they could not immediately produce their citizenship papers upon request.

On the 27 and 28 August 1941, the Einsatzgruppen readily carried out the extermination of the expelled masses. '[The Jews] were compelled to march about ten miles to a series of craters caused by bombings,' writes Braham. 'There they were ordered to undress, after which they were machine-gunned. Many of them were buried while gravely wounded but still alive.'

Seen in this light, the rather overzealous and heavy-handed approach of police captain Árkád Kiss towards the Jew Henrik Nádler becomes rather more straightforward to comprehend.

* * *

In contrast to the metronomic consistency of his performances on the pitch, Antal Vágó's life outside football was beset by extreme vicissitudes. After suffering traumatic personal loss, he hauled himself up to the brink of considerable wealth, only for his dreams to be ultimately turned to dust.

The source of Vágó's tragically temporary good fortune was a fellow

Jew, Alfréd Brüll, whom we came across briefly in the earlier chapter on József Braun. Brüll was one of the richest men in Hungary, an heir to a vast portfolio of companies and property interests. But in contrast to his tycoon father, he was uninterested in business, instead devoting himself to philanthropic causes and to his twin passions – motor cars and MTK Budapest.

During the first years of the twentieth century, Brüll owned and drove one of the first automobiles to be seen in Budapest, and financed and participated in pioneering motor races in the city. In 1905, he became president of MTK, a position he maintained for the next thirty-five years. He was the strategic brains and investment powerhouse behind the club's glory days, employing a succession of innovative British coaches and funding the construction of a brand-new stadium.

It so happened that one of the top MTK players in the early years of his presidency shared his fascination not only with football, but with cars. That player was Antal 'Toni' Vágó. Fifteen years older than his midfield general, Brüll immediately took a shine to his kindred spirit, taking him under his wing for the rest of their lives, a benevolent uncle with pockets deeper than the ocean.

Vágó was hired as Brüll's personal driver pretty much immediately upon his arrival at the club. A profile of all MTK players in *Sportvilág* in October 1912 already spoke of 'Antal Vágó, 21, a car chauffeur'.

It turned out to be a fortuitous line of work. During the First World War, more than a million Hungarian soldiers were killed, wounded or captured, almost certainly including Antal's own younger brother Sándor, who died in Austria in 1915, aged twenty-one. Brüll saw to it, however, that Vágó had a rather easier time of it. As well as donating large sums of money to injured soldiers and civilians and himself volunteering for the Red Cross, Brüll gifted his beloved Mercedes to the army on the condition that his protégé was designated as its driver.

Vágó was duly dispatched with the precious vehicle to the safety of the Austro-Hungarian capital of Vienna, where he would spend his days ferrying assorted military dignitaries around the city. Such was the relative serenity of the assignment that he even managed to fit in a game playing in the Austrian top flight for Wiener AF in April 1916.

Just before the outbreak of hostilities, Vágó had married Irén Kirchknopf, a woman born into another family of recent Jewish migrants to Budapest. The couple settled close to relatives in Terézváros, and two children soon followed, a son György in 1915 and a daughter Katalin (known as Kató) four years later.

In September 1922, however, tragedy ripped through the picture of domestic bliss. 'Vágó's family grief' ran the headline in *Sporthirlap*. 'A heavy blow has befallen Antal Vágó, the MTK national team player. His wife has died, leaving behind two young children and her loving husband. The entire sporting community shares the grief of this outstanding player!' Tuberculosis had claimed Irén's life at the age of just twenty-five.

A single parent of a seven-year-old and three-year-old, and with his glittering football career entering its very final phase, the 31-year-old Vágó suddenly found himself in extremely challenging circumstances. It was primarily Brüll who prevented him from sinking into despond, offering him the necessary friendship, paid work and practical help to navigate to calmer waters.

Vágó soon did far more for Brüll than just serve as a chauffeur. He also ended up being his bodyguard, his business agent and his long-standing companion and confidant. The enduring closeness of their personal and working relationship, ultimately lasting three decades, can be gleaned from various references to them in the Hungarian press. In 1928, for example, the newspaper *Fővárosi Közlöny*, the official journal of the Budapest municipality, reported that Brüll met with representatives of the local administration to discuss his purchase of land on the shore of the River Danube with the aim of building a boathouse. He was accompanied, the article says, by 'his representative Antal Vágó'.

Brüll enjoyed what might now be termed a trust fund lifestyle. He never married, and would travel to exclusive hotels, sometimes with a small group of friends, spending extended periods relaxing in Nice or hobnobbing in the fashionable Paris of the inter-war era. Vágó was his most frequent travelling companion, as well as his trusted driver, spending many long hours in his sole company and thus cementing the bond between the two men.

'This is the third time in two years I've made the [1,500 kilometre] trip from Paris to Budapest and not once have I had the smallest puncture,' Brüll told *Sporthirlap* in August 1930.

> So I'll go against the grain and say that the Cadillac engine offers the smoothest possible ride, although it is true that Antal Vágó's excellent driving plays a part. Although Rolls-Royce cars cost three times as much, can we really imagine that they are worth three times as much? That is completely out of the question.

We get a further illustration of both Brüll's taste for luxury and his attachment to Vágó in March 1936, when the magazine *Kerékpár és Motorsport* ('Cycling and Motorsports') caught up with him in the Hotel Negresco in Nice, still today a favourite haunt of celebrities, royalty and other fully paid-up members of the international jet set:

> 'What do you do all day in Nice?' (we ask). 'Not much. I wake up earlier than in Budapest, have breakfast, then Toni Vágó arrives in the Negresco, and we go for a walk, usually in the morning. I

> normally have lunch elsewhere, then go to bed, read the paper in the afternoon, sometimes play a little rummy, always have dinner at the Negresco in the evening, and then either go to the cinema or play cards until midnight.

The resourceful Vágó also pursued various other lines of work outside his employment with Brüll, establishing something of a portfolio career. He became assistant coach for a while at his first club Terézvárosi and dabbled in refereeing. Clearly talented with his hands, he set himself up in 1923 as 'a paper merchant and a cabinetmaker'. A year later, *Sporthirlap* announced that Vágó had 'opened an electrical installation workshop in the courtyard of the house at 9 Andrássy Street'.

Even here, however, we see Brüll's unmistakable imprint. At 9 Andrássy Street in Terézváros stood Brüll's magnificent three-storey mansion, built in 1882 by his father Ármin under the auspices of the eminent Hungarian architect, Mór Kallina. By the time the then 43-year-old Vágó remarried in 1935, to Szeréna Weisz, his address was stated as 9 Andrássy Street, suggesting that the couple made their home in the palatial residence.*

As they looked out on to the opulent boulevard, Budapest's nearest equivalent to the Champs Élysées, the newlyweds no doubt dreamt up all manner of plans for their future together. Alfréd Brüll's will, originally written in 1931 and later confirmed in 1938, bequeathed the sum of 200,000 Hungarian pengö to his friend Antal Vágó, equivalent in purchasing power today to around 2 million US dollars.

---

* Szeréna Weisz was born in 1900 into a small Jewish community in the town of Pilisvörösvár on the outskirts of Budapest. There were seventy-eight Jews in Pilisvörösvár in 1941. Several were sent to labour camps, leaving the sixty-six who remained in July 1944 to be sent to Auschwitz-Birkenau. Seven survived.

But not so fast. As the Yiddish proverb has it, *Mann Tracht, un Gott Lacht*.

Man plans, and God laughs.

* * *

Henrik Nádler started to wind down his playing career at the premature age of twenty-six. Although he continued to dabble in the sport he loved, playing sporadically for MTK and then Hakoah Vienna, his focus had switched to the family business.

'It's time for me to get more involved in the suitcase business that is my future,' he told *Sporthirlap* in July 1927.

> We also plan to open a new business in the near future and have other important business matters to deal with. All these things take all my time and I am not able to spend four afternoons a week training, let alone go on a tour … The money I made from football is not what I need to make a living.

The happy-go-lucky Nádler had clearly decided to get serious, the more so because he had recently met and become engaged to a local Jewish woman, Lili Friedmann, a similarly talented athlete who went on to win multiple national table tennis championships representing MTK.

Finding himself in a much more fortunate position upon footballing retirement than many of his former teammates, his future certainly appeared promising. Back in 1924, *Nemzeti Sport* had run a piece describing the ruinous impact of the country's raging financial crisis on the MTK players and supporters. The exception, the article stated, was Nádler, who lived 'in very good financial circumstances'.

His new life appeared to start well enough, too. Together with his older sister Rozália, he registered a 'suitcase and leather goods business' with the authorities in April 1928, no doubt seeking to exploit their father Izsák's expertise and network of contacts from many years in the trade.* That same year, he got married to Lili, and the couple's only child was born in Vienna during Henrik's brief spell at Hakoah in 1930.

But reading between the lines of the available evidence, it was not all sunshine and roses for very long. In 1932, the bankruptcy announcements section of *Budapesti Közlöny* reported that the courts had ordered his company to enter into a debt repayment plan with its insistent creditors, or else face the inevitable consequences. Another severe recession at the time did not create a conducive environment for budding entrepreneurs.

Three years later, the family lost its patriarch and the brains behind its prosperity. A notice in the *Újság* newspaper in September 1935, on behalf of Róza Nádler and her six children, communicated the family grief: 'The whole family report with a broken heart that their father Izsák Nádler has passed away after a short period of suffering.'

To achieve a clearer understanding of Henrik Nádler's life in the 1930s, I tried, as I did with all the players in my team, to locate family members. I knew from the genealogical site Geni that he had a child, but was initially none the wiser about his or her identity. The relevant entry on the site was designated as 'private', and I was told by an expert genealogist in Hungary that 'due to current privacy laws, there is no publicly available database connecting someone born after 1925 to their parents'.

---

* Rozália's grand-daughter Judit Varnai-Shorer believes that the main focus of the family's leather goods business was high-end fashion handbags for women, rather than suitcases. She says that Henrik and Rozália also ran their own store on Váci Street in central Budapest.

After several vain enquiries to the administrators of the various Nádler family pages on Geni, I struck gold. I found Richard Panchyk, a New York writer descended from Henrik Nádler's maternal grandparents, who told me that he had been in touch with Nádler's daughter in 2005. From the depths of his email archive, Richard rescued for me photographs of Henrik that she had shared with him, as well as two email messages with scant but nevertheless invaluable biographical details.

Having herself lived in New York for close to fifty years, the then 75-year-old had anglicised the spelling of her name from her birth name Veronika to Veronica, which she also shortened to Vera. 'We all came home [from Vienna] when I was three months old,' she recalled. 'After that he helped out in their store, Nádler luggage at the Anker-palota.'*

Working in the store alongside various other siblings and family members equally eager to put food on the table would have been unlikely to maintain the quality of life that Henrik had enjoyed in his youth, nor would it have satisfied the ambitions of this ever-optimistic, energetic character. With his own business continuing to struggle against the tide of the prevailing economy, he eventually returned to what he knew best – football.

In June 1937, he was appointed to his first coaching role, taking the reins at Gloria Arad in the Transylvanian region of Romania, the same club József Braun was briefly rumoured to be joining in 1940. The club had pushed for the national title several years before, but had since fallen off the pace somewhat.

'Local sporting circles hope that Nádler will manage to lift Gloria back to the leading position it used to occupy in the Romanian football hierarchy,' commented the national sports newspaper, *Gazeta Sporturilor*. Although he had been out of top-level football for close

* Three of Izsák's children continued to run both family stores into the 1950s.

to a decade, the combination of Nádler's own outstanding reputation as a player and the general esteem for Hungarian football had landed him a plum job.

He made a swift and powerful impression when the 1937/38 campaign got underway. 'Gloria has had a great start to the championship season,' reported *Aradi Ujság*, the newspaper that served the city's large Hungarian-speaking population. 'Nádler, the club's excellent coach, has prepared the players in a carefully planned way so that they can now put in better performances match by match.'

The pinnacle came in October, when Gloria travelled to the capital to take on champions Venus Bucharest and secured a 1–1 draw. 'The Arad players showed sensational form, and on this evidence, they are one of the best teams in the country,' argued *Gazeta Sporturilor*. 'They are very physical, the players are fighting with all their might, they can maintain the pace through the game and they again gifted the capital's fans with a great display. All eleven players excelled and the team is a homogeneous unit.'

Beaming with local pride, *Aradi Ujság* chimed in with its own message of acclaim: 'The highest praise must go to Henrik Nádler for his professional work as Gloria's coach, having got his team into such great shape that they have now stood up to the national champions.'

The upturn in Nádler's fortunes was short-lived. In December, after six months at the helm, he returned to Budapest for the mid-season break. What happened next was disputed. Nádler subsequently claimed to the football association that he reported back for duty in Arad in January 1938, but the club president told him that his services were no longer required, an ostensibly surprising decision on footballing grounds alone.

He sued the club for the 67,000 Romanian lei he believed he was owed for the rest of his one-year contract. However, the resulting tribunal ultimately ruled against him 'on the grounds that Nádler had not been dismissed by anyone, but had left without notice'. By way of background, *Aradi Ujság* also reported that 'a disagreement had arisen between Nádler and the management, leading to his departure'. The judgement evidently accepted the club's assertion that the coach had jumped before he was pushed.

As with the Árkád Kiss episode, however, we should not necessarily take the story at face value and assume that the tribunal was carrying out justice in an entirely impartial way. In the very same month that Nádler had returned to resume his duties at Gloria Arad – January 1938 – Romania's openly antisemitic prime minister Octavian Goga announced his intention to expel thousands of foreign-born Jews from Romania, before making the following comment to an interviewer from the *New York Times*: 'I shall be most grateful if you can obtain full publicity for the declaration I want to give you now. The Jewish problem is an old one here, and it is a Rumanian tragedy. Briefly, we have far too many Jews.'*

Indeed, one might argue that Nádler's legal case was forlorn from the outset, and hopelessly naive. The erstwhile cheeky chappie about town was now having the rug pulled swiftly from under his feet. He arrived back in Budapest in good time to learn the details of the First Jewish Law in May 1938, severely restricting Jewish participation in all manner of professions and trades and throwing thousands into

* There were 9,402 Jews in Arad in 1942, more than 10 per cent of the population. The previous year, all adult Jewish males below the age of fifty-five had been drafted into forced labour service by the Romanian authorities. A joint Romanian-German plan to deport the Jews of Arad to the Bełżec death camp was rescinded in October 1942. This volte face saved them from the fate suffered by more than 300,000 other Romanian Jews, including around 48,000 (the capacity of Sunderland's Stadium of Light) murdered by their 'compatriots' in the last ten days of 1941. After the war, most Arad Jews emigrated to Israel. Fewer Jews reside in the whole of Romania today (less than 9,000) than in Arad alone in 1942.

poverty and destitution. It was a move applauded enthusiastically by the country's highly influential Christian church.

The pusillanimous leadership of the Jewish community reacted to the legislation with what the historian Raphael Patai describes as 'a pathetic and cringing emulation of the government position in support of the anti-Jewish law'. 'Some,' he continues, '...actually *advocated* the introduction of "mildly restrictive" measures as a kind of vaccine to prevent the outbreak of a virulent anti-Semitic epidemic.'

As Nádler, Vágó and more than half a million Hungarian Jews would soon discover, the cowering calculation was as pointless as it had always been.

* * *

The Second Jewish Law, adopted by the independent Hungarian government in May 1939, went further than its predecessor and forbade Jews from working in public bodies, such as the MLSZ (the Hungarian Football Association). The interior minister appointed the antisemitic Pál Gidófalvy, whom we saw earlier refusing to save József Braun, to oversee a more widespread purge of Jews within the game.

The accompanying government statement lamented 'the antagonism that has recently developed between Hungarian football and the Christian middle class', pointing out that 'among the leaders of Hungarian football, who are supposed to play an effective role in national education, a large number of people who are not suitable for leading Hungarian youth in the national spirit have been included'.

The far from 'suitable' Alfréd Brüll, the employer, friend and promised benefactor of Antal Vágó, had a big target marked on his forehead. According to various witnesses, he and his fellow Jewish directors Lajos Preiszman and Henrik Fodor offered to stand down from their positions at an MTK general meeting in June 1940, thinking that this gesture may protect the club. However, the membership voted not to continue without their beloved president and colleagues and opted instead to disband the team. MTK, which had changed the name of its football team in 1926 to Hungária to demonstrate its loyalty to the country, had learned that such patriotic gestures tend only to be noticed by Jews.

Soon after the team's disbandment, Brüll managed to flee to neutral Switzerland. Ensconced in this safe haven, however, he soon realised that the psychological switch from respected local celebrity to dislocated and friendless refugee is far from easy. By 1943, the 66-year-old had started to hanker for the good old days. His capability for rational thought overwhelmed by homesickness, he made what in hindsight seems the insane decision to return to Hungary. He was soon to have it confirmed, in the most brutal way imaginable, that the place he was sick for had never really been his home.

Suspecting that Hungary might change sides to join the rampant Allies, Germany invaded the country in March 1944 and appointed an even more amenable government. The Nazi henchman Adolf Eichmann and his experienced team of extermination experts were awarded the prestigious task of completing the final large piece of the genocidal jigsaw – Hungarian Jewry.

No doubt sensing that the tide of the war was turning and that time was therefore running out, they proceeded to act with maniacal speed to set their plans in motion. Between 15 May and 8 July 1944 – a period of 54 days – the German SS, the Hungarian gendarmerie, the Hungarian civil service apparatus and much of the Hungarian population joined forces to round up and deport 437,402 Jews (Old Trafford x 6) on 147 trains, almost all to Auschwitz-Birkenau, where approximately 80 per cent were gassed on arrival.

These deportations doomed Jews from the Hungarian provinces only. Just before the Jews of Budapest were to meet the same fate, the Hungarian government under Miklós Horthy opted to halt the transports, allegedly because it had started to fear Allied punishment in the wake of the country's inevitable and imminent defeat. It was a decision that saved around one half of the city's 200,000-strong community.

However, certain prominent Budapest Jews, such as Alfréd Brüll, were so despised that they ended up being deported with the provincials anyway. In May, Brüll was seized at his mansion on Andrássy Street and eventually sent to the city of Kecskemét, around 100 kilometres south of Budapest, where more than 5,000 Jews from various communities were crammed into a disused brick factory for at least two weeks. The overcrowded conditions were so unbearable that seventy people managed to kill themselves with poison during this time.

Two transports of cattle cars left Kecskemét at the end of June bound for Auschwitz, one of which contained Brüll. Post-war testimonies conflict on the actual timing of his murder – either gassing on arrival at the death camp, or in December 1944. Given his advancing age, and the fact that the gas chambers were destroyed at the end of November 1944 in order to eliminate evidence of mass murder, a more instantaneous liquidation seems much more likely. Brüll's lightning descent from the luxury of Hotel Negresco to the depravity of Auschwitz serves as yet one further symbol of the fragility of Jewish life in the Diaspora through the ages.

Antal Vágó himself was spared deportation, but not his life. We can piece together what happened to him from various sources – including the general history of Budapest in 1944, Holocaust archives and the research of György Rudas, who still lives in the city. Rudas is the grandson of Zoltán Vágó, Antal's younger brother who was himself a former footballer and MTK coach.

On 16 June 1944, the mayor of Budapest ordered the Jews of Budapest to leave their homes within five days and move in to almost 2,000 specially designated apartment buildings in the city. As all these buildings were marked with the same insignia that Jews were forced to wear on their clothing, they became known as the 'yellow star houses'. The purpose of these houses, a unique phenomenon in the European Holocaust, was to make it easier to identify and arrest the city's Jews when the time came for deportation.

In the entry on the Yad Vashem database that records Antal Vágó's murder, his permanent address is stated as 9 Andrássy Street, Alfréd Brüll's mansion. We can therefore assume that Antal and his second wife Szeréna were still living at this address in May 1944 to say a last farewell to Brüll when he was dragged from his beloved family home. Moreover, as we know from the records that 9 Andrássy Street became a designated yellow-star house, we can deduce that the couple stayed there after the mayor's June decree, albeit now joined by dozens, if not hundreds, of disorientated and frightened fellow Jews.

On 15 October 1944, after Horthy had attempted to break with Nazi Germany, the fanatically antisemitic Arrow Cross party seized power. Although it barely seemed possible, things rapidly went further downhill for the Jews. Tens of thousands more Jews were recruited for slave labour, and as we shall see with Henrik Nádler, many were even handed over to the Germans and taken out of the country for the same purpose.

At the end of November, the regime ordered the remaining Jews in the yellow-star houses to move into two ghettos. One was a fenced-in ghetto of a type replicated throughout Europe, located in the Jewish area of Erzsébetváros, into which 70,000 Jews were packed. The other was the 'international' ghetto, so called because the Jews there had managed to secure real or forged protective passes from benevolent foreign diplomats representing countries that were neutral during the war.

Throughout the summer and autumn of that year, the Swede Raoul Wallenberg and the Swiss Carl Lutz coordinated the distribution of these pieces of paper, which indicated that the person or family was under the protection of the relevant foreign government. At least 15,600 Jews possessing such passes moved into a cluster of apartment buildings in Újlipótváros, an area close to the River Danube and around thirty minutes' walk north-west of the main ghetto. Many thousands more without genuine passes either sought safety in these protected buildings too, or went into hiding elsewhere in the city.

Whether or not he had a legitimate pass, we know that Antal Vágó was in a house protected by Wallenberg and his staff, marked by a Swedish flag fluttering from a window, and supplied with food deliveries and any urgent medical treatment. We know this because a close family friend was with him at 21 József Katona Street right until he was taken away to be murdered.

After the war, Erzsébet Frank told the surviving Vágó family that Arrow Cross soldiers had force-marched the residents of the house towards the Danube. Along the way, they had been split into two – men in front, women at the back. The men were shot into the river, but the women were saved.

Her version of events is corroborated by stories told about the fate of Gedeon Richter, who had found himself in the same house as Vágó on József Katona Street. The 72-year-old Richter was a pioneer of the Hungarian pharmaceutical industry and founder of the organisation that still bears his name, now a multinational public company with an annual revenue of more than $2 billion. As he was a Jew, however, his end did not exactly reflect a brimming gratitude for this remarkable contribution.

In 2009, an elderly female survivor of the massacre, named only as Zsóka, was interviewed about her experience in the newspaper *Népszabadság*. 'On December 30, at around 11am, eight Arrow Cross soldiers stormed the house,' recalled Zsóka. 'All the residents, about 170 people, were herded into the courtyard, including the elderly and infants.'

The Jews were taken to 60 Andrássy Street, the Arrow Cross headquarters situated down the road from the Brüll mansion. 'The people of (József) Katona Street were looted, stripped to their underwear and even had their shoes taken,' she continued. After being alerted to what was happening, 'Wallenberg appeared in the house and made a huge fuss, but the Arrow Cross soldiers reassured him that it was just a routine check, and that those under Swedish protection would be escorted back to Katona Street as soon as the raging air-raid had ended. Unfortunately, Wallenberg made an error, gave in to the Arrow Cross and left.'*

'At dawn the next day, the barefoot group – men in front, women behind – was lined up in the courtyard,' said Zsóka.** 'Several women …were subjected to the roughest physical beating possible. The group was herded along Vilmos Császár Street [now known as Bajcsy-Zsilinszky Street] and Kálmán Street towards the Danube, and was split into two at Zrínyi Street.'

Zsóka says that Richter hugged his wife at this point, before he,

* Wallenberg later intervened again, this time successfully, to save the women from the same fate as the men. The Swedish hero was arrested the following month by the invading Soviet forces. It is thought that he was murdered in captivity in Moscow in 1947, aged thirty-four.

** Vágó's date of death is stated in the Holocaust archives as Saturday 30 December 1944. However, given Zsóka's recollection that the József Katona Street residents were taken first to spend a night at 60 Andrássy Street, we have to consider the possibility that he was actually murdered on the Sunday morning, 31 December.

Vágó and the other men were marched to the river.* Her recollection of what happened next can just as easily be applied to the great footballer as to the great pharmacist: 'Ten minutes later, with a bullet already in his head, he was swimming in the Danube with his companions.'

And this, we must picture in our heads, is how the Jewish Iniesta – Antal 'Toni' Vágó – departed this world.

* * *

Ten years younger than Vágó, who was fifty-three at the time of his murder, Henrik Nádler was more vulnerable to a summons to forced labour service. In her email correspondence with Richard Panchyk in 2005, Nádler's daughter Veronica confirmed that he did indeed suffer this indignity. She attached a photograph of her father standing on a railway track with two colleagues, and wearing the compulsory armband that distinguished him as a lowlife Jewish slave labourer. In her submission to the Yad Vashem archives in 1986, Nádler's niece Eva Varnai, herself a survivor, lists her uncle's place of residence during the war as *munkaszolgálat* (labour service).

It is left to us to determine the date of his conscription. The Hungarian government's recruitment of Jews to the labour service came in

* We do not know for sure that Szeréna was with her husband Antal Vágó in József Katona Street, and therefore with him on the march to say good-bye at this point, but it seems highly likely. I could find no official documentation about her Holocaust experience, and György Rudas says that his side of the family, for whatever reason, did not stay in touch after the war with Szeréna or with Vágó's two children from his first marriage. However, György's research revealed that Szeréna, György and Kató all survived. Szeréna died in 1978. 'I found Szeréna's grave in the Kozma Street Jewish cemetery, inscribed with the name of Antal Vágóné Weisz Szeréna, leading me to believe that she never remarried,' Rudas said to me. Remarkably, Vágó's three surviving siblings and his two elderly parents József and Antonia also emerged alive from the ruins of Budapest in 1945.

several waves. As we saw with the story of József Braun, for example, more than 40,000 Jews were sent as slave labourers in 1942 to support Hungarian troops on the Eastern Front, an ordeal which very few survived. After the start of the German occupation in 1944, the Hungarian and German authorities agreed to round up 150,000 able-bodied Jews as labourers to alleviate the country's acute manpower shortage, and thereby ensure the continued production of the industrial and agricultural goods that the military required.

This recruitment drive, which ironically delayed or even prevented the deportation and extermination of thousands of Jews, was at its most intense in May 1944. A perfunctory obituary notice in the official Hungarian government journal *Magyar Közlöny*, published almost four years after his eventual murder, confirms that Nádler was picked up in this wave:

> No. 583.048/1948. Henrik Nádler, born on March 19, 1901 in Budapest, son of Izsák Leib and Rachel Acht, former resident of Budapest (District VII., Éva Street 15), enlisted for labour service in May 1944, disappeared. Budapest Central District Court. 21158.*

The resulting official death certificate, completed on 9 March 1949, stated Nádler's date of death as 15 June 1944. In most cases, the Hungarian authorities ruled that those who disappeared in the war, concentration camps, or while on labour service were declared dead on the fifteenth of the month in which the applicants for the death certificate, normally the bereaved family, last had irrefutable evidence that the said individual was alive. It could be that Veronica's photograph of her father

* Éva Street is now known as Asboth Street. Nádler's apartment was two minutes' walk from the Anker-palota where he was brought up and where his mother still lived.

was sent in June 1944, during the first stage of his labour service when he still looked relatively healthy and well nourished.

In actual fact, Henrik Nádler was murdered several months after his official date of death. Moreover, even when that erroneous date was confirmed by the court, the family knew full well that it was hogwash.

In April 1946, as the sparse and discombobulated remnants of Jewish Europe were coming to terms with the terrible reality that had befallen them, Henrik's sister and business partner Rozália placed the following heart-rending advert in half a dozen Hungarian newspapers:

> Does anyone know anything about my brother, Pubi (Henrik) Nádler, the MTK national team football player, who was taken from Benczúr Street, and from the Józsefváros railway station in November 1944? And does anyone know about my brother, Illés Nádler, who was taken from the village of Bucsu in Vas county at the end of March 1945? They were the owners of the Anker-palota luggage store in Ferenc Deák square, Budapest. Wanted by his sister: Imréné Székely Nádler Gizi, leather decorator, Budapest IV, 17 Váci Street, mezzanine floor.*

Benczúr Street and Józsefváros station (which no longer exists) were both in central Budapest. We are therefore left to assume that Benczúr Street was the location of Nádler's forced labour camp, and Józsefváros station was the site of his deportation. But where was he taken to, and why?

At the end of October 1944, shortly after its ascent to power, the Hungarian Arrow Cross government transferred around 50,000 labour servicemen over to the Germans, mostly for the purpose of building

* Confusingly, Henrik Nádler's sister Rozália was also known by the name Gizella, shortened to Gizi. Her husband's name was Imre Székely, hence the formulation of her name in the advert.

fortifications on the border between Hungary and the Austrian part of the Reich. Most of these Jews were marched on foot in brutal fashion from the Hungarian provinces to this border. However, the historian Randolph Braham notes that several labour companies stationed in Budapest 'were entrained at the Józsefváros Railway Station under conditions reminiscent of the deportations from the provinces.'

The first trace of Nádler after his deportation is a document which proves that he was in the Ohrdruf camp in the German state of Thuringia on 24 December 1944. Ohrdruf was administered by its more famous parent camp, Buchenwald, around sixty kilometres away. Established only in November 1944, Ohrdruf's principal purpose was to use slave labour to construct an underground bunker that could serve as an alternative headquarters for the embattled government of the German Reich. Although 10,000 labourers had been brought in by the end of 1944, the project was in fact never completed.

Michael Löffelsender, a historian of the Buchenwald camp, has looked at the testimonies of survivors who were also transported from Budapest to Ohrdruf around this time. Weighing up the evidence, he believes 'it is very likely that he [Nádler] was transported from Budapest via Sachsenhausen concentration camp directly to Ohrdruf subcamp at the beginning of December'. Löffelsender sent three such survivor testimonies to me, all recounted in July 1945 to interviewers from the Jewish Agency for Palestine. These accounts offer us an invaluable insight into Henrik Nádler's descent from footballing celebrity and family man to prisoner number 105,177.

Sachsenhausen, an otherwise infamous camp that itself claimed tens of thousands of victims, was not far from Berlin and therefore nowhere near Ohrdruf. In this instance, it served as a redistribution hub for labourers. 'On December 1, I was put in a wagon at the Józsefváros railway station...and taken to Sachsenhausen,' said György Beretvás.

> It took ten days and we were given food twice during the journey. Hungarians escorted us to Hegyeshalom [on the Western Hungarian border], and the SS took us to Zurndorf [across the border in Austria]. In Oranienburg, they stripped us, shaved our hair and took us to the Sachsenhausen distribution camp. Two days later, they put us in a wagon and took us to Ohrdruf in Thuringia.

'We travelled for ten days,' recalled another survivor, Jenö Kahan. 'At the Austrian border, in Zurndorf, we were given one kilogram of bread per person for the entire journey. The train car was not opened the entire time.'

If you want to know what hell is like, Ohrdruf in December 1944 must bear at least a passing resemblance. 'This was a new camp, one of the most horrible,' reported György Kunstädter. '...They put us in blocks, and we slept on the floor. There was no running water, you couldn't wash or undress. We got lice ... Twice in one day I received ten blows with a broken pickaxe handle. They simply called people from their workplaces and beat them, for no reason.'

'We had very hard work, very poor nutrition, and beatings,' György Beretvás told the interviewers. 'There was no medical care, you had to work when you were sick. We had a lot of dead people ... some of the people starved, and some were beaten to death by the SS. I worked in a 200-person commando, and here they beat four to five people to death every day.'

In early April 1945, Ohrdruf became the first camp to be liberated by American forces. The stupefied soldiers were confronted by piles upon piles of dead bodies. The remains of Henrik Nádler, however, were not among them.

In the intervening period, the SS had transferred some sick and emaciated prisoners to other camps, most notably to Bergen-Belsen, more than 300 kilometres to the north of Ohrdruf. We have at our disposal two documents proving that Nádler was in Bergen-Belsen.

One is a Buchenwald prisoner identity card which indicates that he was transferred to Bergen-Belsen on 1 February 1945. (It is worth just taking a moment to speculate just how bad the treatment of a still relatively young – 43-year-old – former athlete must have been to cause such physical deterioration in just two months in Ohrdruf, or to reflect how the gravely ill Nádler must have felt on the long, cold journey to Bergen-Belsen after being dumped in a wagon). A second identity card is stamped with the date of 26 February 1945 and with the name of Bergen-Belsen. It is highly probable therefore that the final day of Henrik Nádler's protracted murder occurred on this latter date, his remains very probably left to rot among the thousands of unburied bodies discovered by the liberating British forces a few weeks later.*

* * *

For each of the players in my team, I have worked hard to identify,

* As Rozália's desperate newspaper advert implies, Henrik's younger brother Illés was also murdered as a slave labourer. Their mother Róza survived the onslaught but died from complications of diabetes and with a broken heart in March 1945, aged seventy-three. From the available Holocaust archives, it appears that Henrik's wife Lili survived by hiding several kilometres outside the ghetto, on Egressy Street in the Zugló district of Budapest. We are left to assume that their daughter Veronica, then aged fourteen, was also there with her. Lili remarried in 1946. An article about her sporting achievements appeared in the table tennis magazine *Asztalitenisz* in July 1986, at which point she was seventy-nine years old. Recalling the golden age of Hungarian table tennis, the article states that 'Lili Friedmann is one of the few who is alive, living among us'. Veronica emigrated to the United States in 1957, pursuing a successful thirty-year career in advertising in New York. She was married and divorced twice, with no children. 'As you requested, I went to look for all the pictures of my father,' she wrote to Richard Panchyk in 2005, sixty years after Henrik Nádler's death. 'It is always a bitter-sweet experience. After all this time I still get emotional about losing him.'

where at all possible, their date of death. Not primarily for the purposes of finding out the date in the Gregorian calendar. This means little to me, simply yet another date when Europe murdered a Jew. What matters to me is finding the equivalent date in the Hebrew calendar – or to use the Hebrew or Yiddish words, the *azkarah* or *yahrzeit* – when Jews contemplate and honour the life and soul of the late individual.

I like the date 26 February 1945 because the ancient annual Jewish festival of Purim, which commemorates the saving of the Jewish people from annihilation in Persia in the fifth century BCE, began that year on that very day. In the story of Esther that has been recited on Purim for more than 2,000 years, the instigators of the planned extermination ended up suffering the exact same fate they had reserved for the Jews. The enemies of the Jews were thus cast aside by history, while the Jews themselves emerged to a bright, new dawn.

What is the relevance of Purim to Henrik 'Pubi' Nádler, the onetime diminutive midfield dynamo and arch crowd-pleaser of Budapest football?

After the war, Nádler's 20-year-old niece Eva Varnai decided, not unfathomably, to abandon Hungary and Europe, and to immigrate to the newly born State of Israel, then and now an inspiring symbol of hope and renewal for Jews throughout the world.*

'Vowing not to be a victim anymore, she and her husband, Gyuri, tried three times to be smuggled across the border to Austria and were incarcerated for that [by the newly installed Communist regime in Hungary],' read Eva's obituary in the *Atlanta Jewish Times* after her death in 2017.

During her stay in prison, Eva had a miscarriage. Still, they were not

* Eva was the daughter of Henrik's sister Rozália, who eventually followed her to Israel.

daunted by their failure, and in 1950 they succeeded in boarding a moving train late at night that crossed into Austria. They boarded the train from two sides and were not certain, clinging to the train's sides, that both made it across the border until they got well into Austria. They then were taken by a ship from Italy to Israel.

Like many Holocaust survivors, Eva vowed never to return to the scene of her people's degradation and torment. That was until a half a century after her escape, when her daughter Judit was appointed as Israel's ambassador to Hungary. Eva broke her vow, and looked on with indescribable joy at the swearing-in ceremony in Budapest as Hungarian soldiers stood to attention and presented arms for her daughter, the great niece of a great Jewish footballer, the official emissary of the reborn nation-state of the Jewish people.

I spent years investigating the desperate fates of my eleven players, my brother Jews whose lives and careers I had researched in depth, and with whom I now felt a strong connection. To discover the circumstances of their murder, I was forced to wade through the putrid sewers of history. If I told you that none of this took its toll, I would be lying.

Which is why Eva's visceral emotion at the Budapest ceremony resonated with me so deeply.

Because just like after the Purim story, and despite everything, we are still here.

Am Yisrael chai. The Jewish nation lives.

CONCLUSION

EUROPE, MEMORY, FOOTBALL AND THE JEWS

Before the Second World War, Richard Coudenhove-Kalergi became a leading authority on the phenomenon of antisemitism. In 1935, he neatly summarised his findings, declaring that 'the overwhelming majority of non-Jewish Europeans today are more or less antisemitically disposed'.

Within a few years, 'non-Jewish Europeans' had acted on their disposition and more or less disposed of European Jewry. 'You can't understand the Holocaust without understanding the degree of complicity,' said the historian Simon Schama. 'It was as though the Germans were simply doing what millions of other people wanted to happen, that Jews should disappear for ever from Europe.'

The fate of several of my players – whose stories will be similar to those of countless others who never achieved their level of fame – illustrates Schama's point more eloquently than words.

Hungarians worked and beat József Braun to death and shot Antal Vágó into the Danube; Italians expelled Árpád Weisz and the Dutch deported him to his death; Ukrainians almost certainly participated in the murder of Zygmunt Steuermann; Latvians probably fired the bullet that ended Otto Fischer's life; the French imprisoned Max Scheuer and facilitated his deportation to an extermination camp.

Eighty years on, with the last Jewish witnesses to this pan-European endeavour rapidly diminishing, now seems a natural time to ponder an important question.

Has Europe come to terms with what it did?

* * *

Several decades after the gas chambers ceased operating, the continent embarked on something of a remembrance frenzy. It began to mark an annual Holocaust Memorial Day. It started erecting monuments and plaques left, right and centre, some of which contain cursory details of the murdered Jews that may even engage the fleeting interest of passers-by.

Since Matteo Marani's comprehensive biography belatedly brought his remarkable story to light, the maestro coach Árpád Weisz has had many such tributes paid to him. There is a plaque at the Stadio Renato Dall'Ara, the scene of Weisz's double championship triumph at Bologna. There is a plaque at the San Siro, now home to Inter Milan, the club at which Weisz established his still unbroken record as the youngest coach to win Serie A. At a match between his two former clubs in January 2013, the two teams emerged from the San Siro tunnel wearing T-shirts bearing the slogan 'No to Racism' and a picture of Weisz. The mayors of the respective cities exchanged *Rossoblù* and *Nerazzurri* shirts with Weisz's name printed on the back.

A statue of Weisz stands in a cultural centre in Budapest, not far from his adolescent home. The local authorities in nearby Solt, Weisz's birthplace, granted him posthumous honorary citizenship at a ceremony in 2013. In Dordrecht in the Netherlands, where Weisz coached the city's team after fleeing Italy, a pathway in one of the city's parks bears his name, with several signs honouring the 'Hungarian [!] …

victim of the Nazis.' (In 2020, Chelsea even joined the craze, displaying a mural at Stamford Bridge depicting Weisz, Julius Hirsch and, rather oddly, Ron Jones, a British soldier who suffered terrible hardship in the prisoner-of-war camp next to the Auschwitz concentration camp complex, though was not a Jew, was therefore not targeted for murder and died in Wales at the age of 102.)

'Of all the things that commemorate Weisz today, and there are many, there is one thing that touches me more than anything else,' writes Marani at the very end of his biography.

> It is a small plaque located at the Bombicci school in Bologna, where [Weisz's son] Roberto attended first and second grade, unable to continue in third grade due to the racial laws. If Árpád is the prominent figure that everyone has come to know, almost a symbol given that his martyrdom symbolises the fight against discrimination in football, that stone is necessary to remember a boy who died in Auschwitz at the age of just twelve. In Castel Maggiore, just outside Bologna, there is also a soccer pitch named after his little sister Clara, who also died in Auschwitz at the age of eight. These are reasons that make me feel proud to have been born and raised in this city.

I find it interesting that Marani chooses not to focus on the numerous expulsions and humiliations, the cruelty and ghettoisation that litter the long and shameful history of antisemitism in Bologna. Neither does he dwell on the Italian racial laws that threw the Weisz family out of the city and the country, and which led to their eventual murder. Rather, it is a plaque and pitch in memory of the two Weisz children who 'died' that stir his local pride.

Despite Europe's often rather self-satisfied view of its ability to grapple with the past, I think that the deluge of Holocaust memorialisation camouflages multiple layers of denial. Indeed, I think that Europe is still a very long way from coming to terms with what it did to the Jews. If truth be told, I think it has barely scratched the surface.

* * *

When people refer to Holocaust denial, they normally have in mind the belief held on the extreme fringes (in Europe, at any rate) that the Holocaust did not happen or that the number of victims has been greatly exaggerated.* Much more widespread, however, is a softer form of denial – a disingenuous interpretation of the Holocaust that hides as much as it reveals, a narrative subtly distorted to suit the aims of its originators.

This denial has multiple forms but let us touch on just a few. I have already alluded to the first – the practice of drastically reducing the categories of perpetrator. In a 2018 survey by the University College London Centre for Holocaust Education, more than half of younger students in the UK (aged eleven to fourteen) judged that the systematised murder of 6 million Jews was solely attributable to one man – Adolf Hitler. This viewpoint did not enter young minds by magic. It is a product of a collective reaction over decades against the challenging reality – namely, that much of Europe wanted the Jews dead or gone.

'Holocaust deflection entails admitting that the Holocaust happened while denying the complicity or various types of participation of countries, specific groups, or individuals despite ample evidence to the contrary,' writes the Holocaust historian Manfred Gerstenfeld.

* In an Anti-Defamation League survey from 2024, 43 per cent of respondents from the Middle East and North Africa believed either that the Holocaust is a myth, or that the number of victims has been greatly exaggerated.

'Major examples of deflection occur in those countries where, during the war, Germans were helped massively in the killing, deportation, and despoliation of the Jews.' In a similar attempt to define the widespread distortion, the historian and Nazi hunter Efraim Zuroff adds a further element into the mix, namely 'the exaggeration of the number of, and scope of the assistance provided by, local Righteous Gentiles'.

Indeed, it seems to me that the ubiquitous term 'the Nazi Holocaust' has denial lodged deep inside it, representing an unconscious linguistic device to preserve Europe's self-image and reputation. Throughout this book, I have therefore used the more appropriate term – the European Holocaust.

Just as the range of culprits is narrowed, the victims are routinely expanded and generalised to include just about anyone who suffers from intolerance and bigotry. Marani talks about Weisz as 'a symbol' in 'the fight against discrimination'. Bologna and Inter walked on to the pitch with T-shirts with the words 'No to Racism'. This propensity to take the Jew out of the Holocaust, to avert eyes from the very specific hatred that caused it, is very much the norm.

On the website for the Anne Frank House in Amsterdam, which attracts 1.2 million visitors a year, a video on 'discrimination' highlights the sin of 'treating people unequally, for instance because of their age, skin colour, or sexual preference'. But were Anne Frank and up to 1.5 million other Jewish children really gassed, shot or starved, as the museum seems to imply, because of regrettable but commonplace discrimination? Or was it because they had been ruthlessly hunted down and marked for extinction, from Trondheim to Rhodes, because they were Jews?

Another fundamental aspect of the denial is the depiction of the Holocaust as a horrendous blip, an appalling but isolated event which must never be repeated. However, as many episodes recounted in this book illustrate, the advent of the Holocaust can only really be understood in its proper historical context. It was innovative for its highly methodical, industrial method of mass slaughter, its geographical scale and its obsessive, even self-defeating zeal, making the genocide unique in human history. But the actual intention to murder, torture, expel and humiliate Jews is as much a part of Europe's cultural heritage as its most spoken languages and the Roman empire.

Holocaust memorialisation, writes the commentator Haviv Rettig Gur, 'downplays a long history of persecution, ignores the Holocaust's deeper roots in favor of the emotional salve of simplistic moral lessons, and detaches the specific gas chambers and killing fields from a broader history of which they are an apotheosis, not an aberration'.

For a period often said to be among the most propitious for Jews in their history, the years since 1945 also seem to have contained an awful lot of antisemitism. 'Never again,' world leaders like to say to project their gravitas. But amid all the empty rhetoric, the 'agains' just kept on coming, and to the Jews themselves – to stress again, the actual victims of the Holocaust.

We can point to the widespread murders of surviving Jews returning to their former homes in Europe immediately after the Holocaust, to decades of Soviet repression, to the breathtakingly efficient ethnic cleansing of 850,000 Jews from the Arab world. And now, with the Arab Jews totally gone and the last remnants of European Jewry (around 0.15 per cent of the total population) entering into demographic irrelevance, the obsessive focus has inevitably shifted to the place where it just so happens that millions of Jews now live proudly in the ancestral homeland of the Jewish nation.

From 2015 to 2024, the United Nations General Assembly adopted 171 resolutions against Israel and seventy-seven against all other countries combined. 'Having rehabilitated themselves against considerable odds in a minute corner of the earth,' writes the journalist Matti

Friedman, 'the descendants of powerless people who were pushed out of Europe and the Islamic Middle East have become what their grandparents were – the pool into which the world spits.'

A coincidence, they claim.

Do they think we were born yesterday?

* * *

Rabbi Jonathan Sacks described antisemitism as 'a virus that has survived over time by mutating'. He set out the three stages: 'In the Middle Ages, Jews were hated for their religion. In the nineteenth and early twentieth century, they were hated for their race. Today, they are hated for their nation-state, Israel.' Although it is not a wholly comprehensive framework – some aspects of antisemitism are omitted, while those mentioned can overlap in time and substance – Sacks nevertheless provides us with a useful summary of the dominant strains of the virus in the relevant eras.

As football is the most popular sport in the world and a central part of global culture, it inevitably reflects the prevailing mutation at any given time. There was no football in the Middle Ages. In the era of racial antisemitism, we saw how Hungarian football sought to purge itself of Jewish influence, how Jewish players and spectators and Jewish-dominated clubs in various countries were habitually subjected to violence and abuse, how Hasmonea Lwów's stadium was reduced to ashes, how Hakoah Vienna was closed down and its results annulled from the history books, its league championship win deemed too much of a vile perversion of the moral order to be allowed to stand.

Now, as the latest mutation assumes an ever-tighter grip, it's the turn of Israeli teams to be threatened with the same banishment as their Zionist predecessors in Europe. As their compatriots busy themselves with erecting monuments to Árpád Weisz and bemoaning 'discrimination', the Italian Coaches' Association decided in 2025 to join a growing campaign within football to ban Israel from international competition, a country founded not least to prevent Jews like Weisz from being terrorised in places like Italy.

The coaches' accompanying statement, accusing Israel of 'vicious genocidal' actions, managed to be antisemitic in three ways – invoking an objectively false slander against the Jews to rival the blood libels of the Middle Ages; corrupting the intended meaning of the word genocide – a word coined by a Jew to describe the destruction of European Jewry – and thus belittling the scale and bloodlust of the Holocaust; and charging an innocent people of the very same crime that has caused them such indescribable pain and trauma.

Gary Lineker, the poster boy of English television football broadcasting and long-time presenter of the BBC's flagship *Match of the Day* programme, took to social media to repost a similar call for the Jewish state to be expelled from international football. He deleted the post, alleging that he had misunderstood its meaning.

The behaviour established something of a pattern. A year later, in 2025, Lineker reposted a video entitled 'Zionism explained in less than 2 mins', later claiming not to have noticed a large image of a rat on the post, or to be aware that Jews were habitually equated with rats by the Nazis. His comment that the British government's asylum policy was 'not dissimilar to that used by Germany in the 30s' displayed a similar historical cluelessness and insouciance about the reality of anti-Jewish persecution.

Lineker complained that 'there is a lot of heavy lobbying on people to be quiet', a not-so-subtle allusion to the shady Jewish influence of antisemitic fantasy, but in reality probably just referencing the continual distress voiced by the tiny, declining and beleaguered UK Jewish population, whose number is dwarfed by Lineker's followers on the social media platform X by a factor of thirty-two (that figure will have increased by the time you read this).

The presenter's social media timeline was unusually silent in the aftermath of the unprovoked Gazan invasion of Israel in October 2023, a savage onslaught branded by the historian Jeffrey Herf as an 'arrested genocide'. The selective silence was contagious. Accepting an honorary degree at the University of Manchester in 2025, the world-famous coach Pep Guardiola pointedly chose to focus his speech on civilian suffering in Gaza, declaring that he longs to see people 'showing up … refusing to be silent or still when it matters most'.

Much of the media gushed in admiration of Guardiola's moral leadership, with Paul Hayward in *The Observer* praising his 'deft and heartfelt intervention'. Not quite deft and heartfelt enough, alas, to pay even passing reference to the massacre, hostage-taking and planned, systematic mass rape that precipitated the defensive war in Gaza to begin with – the largest single-day mass murder of Jews outside of the Holocaust since the Proskurov pogrom in Ukraine in 1919. A massacre, one may add, to rank in the annals of Jewish history alongside the eradication of the large and formerly thriving community (15 per cent of the population) in Guardiola's beloved Barcelona in 1391 – the last time a Jewish community of any significance existed in that city – achieved through a frenzied campaign of mass murder, forced conversion and subsequent prohibition.

'The prevalence and persistence of the anti-Israel agenda in Europe is a stain on its integrity,' wrote Robin Shepherd in his book *A State Beyond the Pale: Europe's Problem with Israel*. 'Cocooned in their own self-righteousness, large numbers of influential Europeans have no idea of the damage that is being done to Europe's reputation. Contempt in Europe for Israel will be repaid by contempt among the civilized for Europe.'

Whatever its cost – and pervasive antisemitism is always a sign of deep moral and cultural decay – the modern-day variant of the virus has only intensified and spread since Shepherd wrote those words back in 2009. Moreover, as the proportion of the world's Jews living in Israel (already around 50 per cent) continues to increase steadily, and as any residual guilt about the Holocaust is overpowered by the desire to turn the tables on the Jews for inspiring the guilt in the first place, I would wager that it will get a whole lot worse still.

* * *

How will Jews respond, in particular those outside Israel?

Fortunately, we have many examples in history to help us answer this question. Indeed, the stories of the players in this book offer some valuable case studies of how different types of Jews responded to the surrounding, increasingly hostile society in the years before and after the First World War.

The period immediately preceding and during the Holocaust itself is less instructive. By that stage, anyone who could do so was trying to get out of harm's way as soon as possible, whatever their previous relationship with their host societies. By then, there was little choice. The Zionist Max Scheuer fled to Marseille from Vienna; the Orthodox Jew Leon Sperling escaped to Lviv from Kraków; the German patriot Julius Hirsch tried desperately to find work in Paris; Árpád Weisz, who baptised his children, thought the Netherlands to be the safest available bet after being expelled from Italy.

You could say too that the millions of Jews approaching the doors of the gas chambers or standing by their self-dug graves had converged ideologically, and forgotten their long-held disputes. The liberal dreams of inter-faith harmony held by Josef Steuermann, Zygmunt's father, had been shattered; the Hirsch family's love of country had been exposed as hopelessly deluded; the ideology of Jutrzenka, Józef Klotz's team in Kraków, advocating Jewish cultural autonomy outside of Israel within a socialist framework, was dead in the water; Soviet Communism had ruthlessly crushed Jewish life. If rolling elections had been held on the train platforms at Birkenau, I think it is safe to say that the victory for the Zionists would have been overwhelming. All the others had got it so fatally wrong.

We are not at that desperate juncture yet. The impact on Jews of the third mutation of the virus, the obsessive animus towards Israel, currently has more in common with the pressure they experienced during the first stage, religious antisemitism. The demands in the Diaspora to conform to the received wisdom – then Christianity, now anti-Israel beliefs – are intense. The costs of any reluctance to do so – social exclusion, career damage, even threats to physical safety – will mount. And unlike the Holocaust period, but very much like the period of religious antisemitism, the Jewish responses to this predicament will be diverse.

The historian Bernard Lewis took the same framework as Sacks and explained how Jewish reactions have fluctuated according to the various mutations. 'In anti-Semitism's first stage, when the hostility was based in religion and expressed in religious terms, the Jew always had the option of changing sides,' he wrote in 2005.

> During the medieval and early modern periods, Jews persecuted by Christians could convert. Not only could they escape the persecution; they could join the persecutors if they so wished, and some

> indeed rose to high rank in the church and in the Inquisition. Racial anti-Semitism removed that option. The present-day ideological anti-Semitism has restored it, and now as in the Middle Ages, there seem to be some who are willing to avail themselves of this option.

In other words, some Jews will join in the general Israel bashing and hope that does the trick. Among them will be some particularly fervent converts to the cause. They will be used as battering rams in the propaganda war – see, I told you so, even Jews are saying it! They will figure that their route to career success will be cleared, that they will be welcomed into the community of decent, right-thinking people.

They would perhaps do well to remember that the motives of many Jewish *conversos* in the Middle Ages were ultimately mistrusted and they were persecuted all the same. They must hope too that the virus does not transform into a much more violent and even lethal mutation and catch them unawares, as it did with Paul Goldberger and Árpád Weisz. Indeed, we should recall that, in all probability, the parents of Roberto and Clara Weisz listed their children as Catholic when the family boarded the train to Auschwitz in October 1942, praying in vain that their outdated understanding of antisemitism was still valid.

Many other Jews will resolve to keep their head down, completely abstaining from any discussion of all things Israel, the great transgressor of all the nations. We can interpret this quest for anonymity as the contemporary equivalent of Jews changing their names and assuming native mannerisms and habits when they migrated to the major cities of Central and Western Europe. They may feel the same discomfort about Israel as the established Jews of Berlin and Vienna did in the early decades of the twentieth century in relation to the *ostjuden*, the recent religious arrivals from further east whom they accused of stirring up the hornet's nest of antisemitism with their foreign ways.

Some will assertively state their agnosticism, openly declaring that they have no interest in Israel whatsoever. 'I kind of think "Fuck Israel". … For those who might be wondering, my position on Israel is: I don't care about it more than any other country,' writes David Baddiel in his book on antisemitism, *Jews Don't Count*. One could say that Paul Goldberger adopted a similarly public neutrality when he opted for official *konfessionslos* status just before his wedding in 1923.

Others will believe that things will turn around, that the antisemitism will subside once whichever war is over, or when an Israeli Prime Minister is more agreeable to the cultured sophisticates of Europe and the West. We can imagine that Zygmunt Steuermann and Leon Sperling were similarly hopeful about their domestic environment when they declined the opportunity to move to the Land of Israel in the 1920s and 1930s.

In a bid to gain acceptance, still others will make proactive, unsolicited concessions, even when irrelevant to the discussion at hand. In the words of Dave Rich, in his own book on antisemitism, 'they will declare their own unhappiness at Israel's political direction or the policies of the current government. It is a kind of tax you have to pay to get a hearing on this subject, an entry ticket to the debate'. A twist, perhaps, on the special Jew tax regularly levied throughout European history, or the *jizya* tax imposed on non-Muslims in the Islamic world. Rather than a financial payment to the host, it is an offering of ideological orthodoxy.

But the good news, for me at least, is that the direction of travel will not be one-way. If the inter-war period is anything to go by, we are also set to witness the continued flourishing of a counter-movement of Jews who grasp, ever more clearly, that all we are seeing now is just one further expression of the longest hatred.

'There has been a great change since the [First World] war,' the leading German Zionist activist Sammy Gronemann told the *Jewish Chronicle* in 1925.

> Almost all the Jews in Berlin who formerly proudly emphasised their Germanic and Berliner purity were only within three generations of Lodz or Pinsk, but they made it appear as if their forefathers had fought as Visigoths against the Romans … All this is now being changed … For the children are returning to Judaism. They suffered so much from anti-Semitism in the schools, both from their teachers and their fellow pupils…(that) they no longer conceal their Judaism, nor do they want to do so. On the contrary, they openly join Jewish organisations, and under the blue and white flag they march on excursions into the country singing Jewish songs.

At exactly the same time, we saw the pandemonium throughout Europe, not to mention in Tel Aviv and New York, when the Zionists of Hakoah Vienna came to town – a club that symbolised, more than any other in football history, a spirit of steadfast national defiance in the face of naked hatred. Although so many of those young Berlin Jews and Hakoah supporters were soon to be engulfed in the flames of the Holocaust, that never-say-die spirit – so perfectly embodied by the dogged little fighter, Max Scheuer – will forever burn brightly in the Jewish soul.

* * *

'Europe without the Jews is no longer Europe,' said Frans Timmermans, first vice-president of the European Commission, in 2015. 'There is no Europe without European Jews,' agreed Ursula von der Leyen, president of the European Commission, in 2022. These statements, unsurprisingly both made to audiences of Jews, sound peculiar to my ears for one simple reason. They came one hundred years too late. European Jewry was virtually obliterated in the Holocaust, and is now entering its very final phase before petering out altogether.

Timmermans and von der Leyen are nevertheless right to say that Europe is not the same without the energy and enterprise of the Jews. It is certainly not controversial or original to say that the continent's artistic, literary and scientific output has suffered immeasurably through their absence. 'Europe is Simone Veil and Hannah Arendt,' said von der Leyen in the same speech. 'Europe is Mahler and Kafka, and Freud.' But what will be surprising to many – and what I myself did not know until I embarked on this odyssey of discovery – was that European Jews had played a similarly pivotal role in the development of football.

'History is written by the victors,' is a common aphorism. The obliterated, on the other hand, don't get much of a look-in. You can read Kafka, study Freud and listen to Mahler, but who's going to tell you that European Jews were so prominent and influential in football when those most likely to brag about that fact were wiped off the face of the earth?

Most football historians attribute the decline of Hungarian football, for example, to the defection of many stars from its Golden Team that reached the World Cup final in 1954. 'It survived the ravages of fascism, just, to have its golden period in the early 1950s, but already by then Communism had struck at its roots,' writes Jonathan Wilson about Hungarian football culture. 'But it could not survive the [1956] Uprising and that final, decisive emigration.'

But what about Austria? There was no Communism there, nor any mass emigration from there. They were a top footballing nation before the Holocaust and also went into decline after themselves reaching the World Cup semi-final in 1954.

So maybe we can put forward another theory.

Perhaps the main reason why Hungary and Austria failed to perpetuate their footballing success is precisely because of the Holocaust, in which so many Hungarians and Austrians willingly participated? Perhaps either Hungary or Austria might have won the World Cup in 1954 if a generation of their young Jewish talent had not been decimated a decade before? Perhaps when their pre-war, largely Jewish-built footballing culture evaporated, they lost the ability to renew themselves, like a plant without water? Perhaps the reason why the decline of Hungarian and Austrian football is not attributed to the disappearance of the Jews is because there are so few Jews left to raise the point?

The Jews of Europe were not on the periphery of football, a contribution deserving only of a pleasant museum exhibition or obscure academic paper. They were right at its very heart. One of the main reasons I wrote this book was to bring this remarkable narrative to the fore.

My most powerful motivation, however, was simply to tell the stories of my eleven players, to raise their profiles within the pages of football history. And through the years of researching and writing, I felt that I got to know each one of them like friends.

Csibi, Dusko, Józek, Munio, Juller, Csili, Maxl, Schloime, Gilly, Toni and Pubi – I will miss you all. I just wish I could have seen you play.

Yehi zichram baruch. May their memory be blessed.

ACKNOWLEDGEMENTS

Many people have helped me in all sorts of different ways to write this book.

I would first like to thank the trustees of the Toni Schiff Memorial Fund, whose grant enabled me to go the extra mile in my research.

A special thank you must also go to some of the relatives of my players who provided me with so much invaluable information on their families' stories: Veronika Mermelstein, the niece of József Braun, and her daughter Eva Kulcsar; Danny Dekel, the nephew of Józef Klotz; and György Rudas, the great-nephew of Antal Vágó. It has been a great pleasure to get to know all of you.

Andreas Hirsch helped me to source photographs of his grandfather, Julius. Robert Beig sent me a marvellous photograph of his great-uncle, Otto Fischer. Judit Varnai-Shorer, the great-niece of Henrik Nádler, provided some details about the family's business in Budapest. My thanks too to Tamás Bodrogi, an expert on the history of MTK, for introducing me to the families of József Braun and Antal Vágó.

Hajnalka Deák was a fantastic support throughout, translating from Hungarian and sourcing relevant information and photographs in Hungary.

Robert Rozett from Yad Vashem and Péter Szabó provided details about József Braun's slave labour company on the Eastern Front and the date and whereabouts of his 'disappearance', allowing me to speculate further on the circumstances of his murder. Matej Hanula from the Institute of History at the Slovak Academy of Sciences and Tomáš Černak from Cornelius University in Bratislava supplied information on Braun's coaching career in Slovakia. Zoltán Tibori Szabó at the Institute for Holocaust and Genocide Studies at Babeş-Bolyai University in Cluj suggested why Braun never took up the coaching post at Gloria Arad. I am grateful to Frank Lowy for his vivid childhood recollections of watching FTC Fiľakovo. Vladimír Cirbus provided photographs of Braun in his Fiľakovo days.

Pawel Rogala translated several items from Polish and sourced information on the Polish players. Thomas Urban forwarded to me the replies received by the late Andrzej Gowarzewski when he interviewed contacts and former teammates of Zygmunt Steuermann in the 1970s and 1980s, in order to determine how the player was murdered. With this and other information to hand, I could try to construct a feasible scenario surrounding Steuermann's eventual fate. Thomas also sent to me various relevant links to articles on all the players from Poland and introduced me to other experts.

I am similarly grateful to Katharina Prager, a biographer of Salka Viertel, who unearthed some excerpts from the scriptwriter's correspondence with or about her brother Zygmunt Steuermann held at the *Deutsches Literaturarchiv* (German Literature Archive) in Marbach in Germany. The Lviv historian Khrystyna Kharchuk advised me on the exact location of Hasmonea's stadium in relation to Janowska camp. Maciej Lisicki provided information on the fate of various Jewish footballers from Poland, as well as precious photographs.

Piotr Figiela, curator at the Kraków Museum, supplied useful links and articles about football in the city, and the very considerable Jewish influence on it. Adam Musial, an expert on the history of Kraków Jewry, frequently gave me the benefit of his knowledge.

Anna Przybyszewska-Drozd at the Emanuel Ringelblum Jewish Historical Institute in Warsaw contacted the family of the late Jarosław

Rokicki on my behalf. Rokicki died while compiling an encyclopaedia of pre-war Polish footballers, which therefore remained unpublished. The family very kindly passed on to me his draft entries for Klotz, Steuermann and Leon Sperling, which contained invaluable information on their careers and military records and for which I am extremely grateful.

Paweł Gaszyński, an archivist at Jagiellonian University, provided me with information on Józef Klotz's university career. Matan Shefi and the POLIN Museum of the History of Polish Jews discovered material about Klotz's court case in 1930. The historian Alexander Watson helped me to understand army conscription rules in the Austro-Hungarian empire in the First World War.

Marek Węgrzyn, an archivist at the Institute of National Remembrance in Kraków, was kind enough to send to me the text of a talk he gave on Leon Sperling, which contained important descriptions of his football career. Mike Taylor and Michael Tobias both provided useful genealogical information on Sperling's family.

Werner Skrentny, whose comprehensive research into the life of Julius Hirsch was a huge help to me when writing the relevant chapter, also went out of his way to answer any further queries I had. The Karlsruhe City Archives provided photographs of Hirsch.

Matteo Marani's book on Árpád Weisz was similarly invaluable for me. Karesz Vandor of the company Hungarian Roots supplied some facts about the family histories of Weisz and his wife Ilona Rechnitzer. Karesz also explained to me the complexities of the Jewish histories of Weisz's birthplace Solt and nearby Kalocsa. Gábor Andreides forwarded the Budapest directories from the early twentieth century which listed the veterinarian practices belonging to Lázár Weisz in Kőbánya. Thamar Barnett sent to me the official property inventory for the Weisz home, recorded by the Dutch authorities after the family had been deported. Bologna FC provided a photograph of Weisz in his later years as a coach.

It took me a long time to find out who Max Scheuer's parents and siblings were. Alexander Juraske helped me to crack the code after finding a reference to a Lina Scheuer at the same address as Max in 1932. I was then able to source her records, which revealed details about other members of the family. The Vienna-based genealogist Wolf-Erich Eckstein then filled in any remaining gaps. Laurence Ritter at the Fondation du Camp des Milles explained to me the function of the Miramas camp. Marcus Patka and Daniela Schmid from the Jewish Museum in Vienna located photographs of Scheuer in their archives.

Gunnar Persson, an expert on all things Hakoah Vienna, was always on hand to answer any questions about the club and its players.

Alexander Juraske's extensive research on Otto Fischer helped me to build a detailed picture of his life. Vince Hunt knew a great deal about Fischer's period as coach of Olimpija Liepāja. He introduced me to Ilana Ivanovna at the Liepāja Jewish Heritage Foundation, who provided further invaluable information about Fischer and his wife Anna Lemkin. The local sports historian Raimonds Kaže supplied various photographs of Fischer from a game between Hakoah Vienna and RFK Riga in 1926.

Ulrich Matheja shared his important findings on Paul Goldberger for Eintracht Museum's research project on its key pre-war Jewish players, officials and supporters. Georg Gaugusch provided missing pieces of information and incisive observations on Goldberger's marriage, divorce and conversions as well as key details about his parents and siblings. Marsha Rozenblit explained to me the rules on interfaith marriage in Austria in the 1920s. Alexander Juraske helped me to interpret Goldberger's First World War record. The Hungarian football historian Attila Kapási sent through a photo of the Hungary team in Goldberger's sole international game and explained the background to other photos of Hungarian footballers in my possession.

György Rudas introduced me to the writings of Barnabás Koltai (who also goes by the pen name of Alfréd Joó), an expert on the history of MTK and Hungarian football in general. Koltai has conducted research into the lives, careers and deaths of Henrik Nádler and Imre Taussig, among others. The IFK Göteborg historian Jens Hallberg provided me with important facts about the life of Sándor Bródy.

Eszter Hörcher from the Holocaust Memorial Center in Budapest supplied me with information on the policeman and later antisemitic bureaucrat, Árkád Kiss. Richard Panchyk shared a priceless and extremely moving email exchange from 2005 with Henrik Nádler's daughter Veronica, as well as photographs of her father that she had sent to him. Michael Löffelsender, a historian at the Documentation Centre and Archive at Buchenwald, helped me to understand the circumstances leading up to Nádler's murder.

Others who introduced me to key contacts or helped in other important ways include Clémence Atlas, Ana Barbulescu, Sofia Dyak, Mark Freiman, Robert Friedman, Tom Gross, Lili Haber, Horst Hötsch, Tomasz Jankowski, Sue Klauber, Adél Nagy, Catherine Nicault, Robert Knight, Judy Petersen, Nicolas Robert, Barbara Rubinstein, Georg Spitaler and Gerd Valchars. If I have missed anyone out – so many helped me – I apologise and thank you.

Many archives, databases and online resources – both historical and football-related – were indispensable to me throughout. Examples include Yad Vashem, the United States Holocaust Memorial Museum, the Arolsen Archives, Budapest City Archives, Vienna City Archives, Austrian State Archives, the Vienna Jewish Community Archive, Centropa, The National Committee for Attending Deportees (DEGOB), Memento Wien, The YIVO Encyclopedia of Jews in Eastern Europe, Encyclopaedia Judaica, Jewish Telegraphic Agency, Jewish Virtual Library, Wirtualny Sztetl, Kriegsarchiv, Arcanum Newspapers, Austrian

Newspapers Online (ANNO), Jagiellonian Digital Library, Deutsches Zeitungsportal, Worldfootball.net, Österreichische Fussballdatenbank, Magyarfutball.hu, EUFootball.Info, MTK Család, the Rec.Sport. Soccer Statistics Foundation (RSSSF) archive, Transfermarkt, Voetbal Archieven, Ancestry, FamilySearch, Geni, JewishGen and MyHeritage.

Thank you also to the Hungarian Sport Museum, MTK Budapest and the National Digital Archives of Poland for providing various additional photographs.

Paul Lewis, Robin Shepherd, my brother Richard and my wife Janie read through several sections and offered suggestions for improvement.

I would like to thank James Stephens and Olivia Beattie at Biteback for believing in this book. Thanks also to my editor Alex Pathe and the rest of the Biteback team. I also want to pay tribute again to Jeremy Robson, my original publisher at Biteback, who set the whole ball rolling when he embraced the idea of my Béla Guttmann biography. He immediately grasped what I was trying to achieve when no other publisher or agent gave the idea the time of day.

It is a source of continuing sadness and disappointment for me that I could not find out everything I wanted about the players' families. If anyone knows further details – in particular what became of Józef Klotz's wife Regina and their (painfully unnamed) daughter, or of Zygmunt Steuermann's wife/partner Hania and son Adam – I implore you to get in touch with me.

So many people – too many to mention – have taken a genuine interest in my research and encouraged me in writing this book. First and foremost on this list are my wife Janie and our children Yael, Joe and Tali, who have lived and breathed the entire experience with me throughout the many ups and downs, all the discoveries and all the frustrations. I dedicate this book to them with huge love and gratitude. When I say I couldn't have done it without them, I mean what I say.

BIBLIOGRAPHY

Gábor Andreides & Tamás Dénes (2018), *Weisz és a Többiek - Magyarok az Olasz Fociban, 1920-1960.* Jaffa Kiadó.

Zoltán Antal & József Hoffer (1969), *Alberttől Zsákig. Válogatott labdarugók könyve.* Sport Kiadó.

Jo Araf (2021), *Generazione Wunderteam. The Rise and Fall of Austria's Wonder Team.* Pitch Publishing.

Jo Araf (2023), *The Forgotten Cup: History of the Mitropa Cup, Mother of the Champions League.* Pitch Publishing.

Moshe Arens (2011), *Flags over the Warsaw Ghetto: The Untold Story of the Warsaw Ghetto Uprising.* Gefen Publishing.

Arolsen Archives (2021), *Football Players in Focus: Educational Materials on Sports, Persecution, and Remembrance.*

Susanne Asche, Ernst Otto Bräunche, Manfred Koch, Heinz Schmitt & Christina Wagner (1998), *Karlsruhe - die Stadtgeschichte.* Badenia Verlag.

Arthur Baar (1959), *50 Jahre Hakoah, 1909-1959.* Verlagskomitee Hakoah.

Arthur Baar (1961), *50 Jahre Hakoah, 1909-1959. Supplement.* Verlagskomitee Hakoah.

David Baddiel (2021), *Jews Don't Count.* TLS Books.

Susanne Barth (2021), 'Revisiting the "Cosel Period": A Fresh Perspective on the Stopping of Western Deportation Trains En Route to Auschwitz, 1942–1943' in *Shofar: An Interdisciplinary Journal of Jewish Studies.*

Maciej Władysław Belda, Piotr Figiela, Anna Hałambiec, Michał

Luberda & Krzysztof Śmiechowski (2012), *The Maccabees of Sport. Jewish Sport in Kraków*. Muzeum Historyczne Miasta Krakowa.

Steven Beller (1989), *Vienna and the Jews 1867-1938: A Cultural History*. Cambridge University Press.

Szymon Beniuk (2023), 'Na Pograniczu Sportu i Polityki Tournée Hakoahu Wiedeń po Polsce w 1924 r. w Swietle Relacji Prasy' in *The Journal of Polish and World History*.

Waitman Wade Beorn (2024), *Between the Wires: The Janowska Camp and the Holocaust in Lviv*. University of Nebraska Press.

Waitman Wade Beorn (2018), 'Last Stop in Lwów: Janowska as a Hybrid Camp' in *Holocaust and Genocide Studies*.

Susanne Helene Betz, Monika Löscher & Pia Schölnberger eds. (2009), *Mehr als ein Sportverein: 100 Jahre Hakoah Wien 1909-2009*. Studienverlag.

Dominic Bliss (2014), *Erbstein: The Triumph and Tragedy of Football's Forgotten Pioneer*. Blizzard Media.

Ulrich Alexander Boschwitz (2021), *The Passenger*. Pushkin Press.

William Bowman (2011), *Hakoah Vienna and the International Nature of Interwar Austrian Sports* in Central European History.

Randolph Braham (1981), *The Politics of Genocide: The Holocaust in Hungary*. Colombia University Press.

Randolph Braham (1977), 'The Hungarian Labor Service System', 1939–1945 in *The East European Quarterly*.

Andreas Brandtner & Drahomír Havlíček (2001), *Šafov/Schaffa*. Euro-Sola.

Michael Brenner & Gideon Reuveni eds. (2006), *Emancipation through Muscles: Jews and Sports in Europe*. University of Nebraska Press.

Eva Brown (2007), *If You Save One Life*. Upper Story Press.

John Bunzl ed. (1987), *Hoppauf Hakoah: Jüdischer Sport in Österreich Von den Anfängen bis in die Gegenwart*. Junius Verlag.

Vicki Caron (1985), 'Prelude to Vichy: France and the Jewish Refugees in the Era of Appeasement' in *Journal of Contemporary History*.

Giovanni Cerutti (2020), *L'allenatore ad Auschwitz - Árpád Weisz: dai campi di calcio italiani al lager.* Interlinea.

Norman Davies (2003), *White Eagle, Red Star.* Pimlico.

Lucy Dawidowicz (1990), *The War Against the Jews: 1933–1945.* Penguin.

Tamás Dénes, Mihály Sándor & Éva B. Bába (2016), *A Magyar Labdarúgás Történet*, Volumes 1–3. Alexandra Kiadó.

Patrick Desbois (2009), *The Holocaust by Bullets.* Palgrave Macmillan.

DFB-Kulturstiftung (2021), *Auf den Spuren von Julius Hirsch. Die Deportation nach Auschwitz im März 1943.*

Lucjan Dobroszycki, ed. (1984), *Chronicle of the Lodz Ghetto 1941–44.* Yale University Press.

Michael Elkins (1982), *Forged in Fury.* Corgi.

Amos Elon (2002), *The Pity of it All: A History of Jews in Germany, 1743-1933.* Metropolitan Books.

Andrew Ezergailis (1996), *The Holocaust in Latvia, 1941-1944: The Missing Center.* The Historical Institute of Latvia.

Daniel Finkelstein (2023), *Hitler, Stalin, Mum and Dad.* William Collins.

Norman Fox (2003), *Prophet or Traitor? The Jimmy Hogan Story.* Parrs Wood Press.

Georg Gaugusch (2023), *Wer einmal war: Das Jüdische Großbürgertum Wiens 1800–1938.* Amalthea Signum.

Robert Gawkowski & Jarosław Rokicki (2010), 'Stosunki polsko-żydowskie w sporcie II Rzeczpospolitej' in *Parlamentaryzm, konserwatyzm, nacjonalizm.*

Martin Gilbert (1989), *The Holocaust: The Jewish Tragedy.* HarperCollins.

Daniel Goldhagen (1996), *Hitler's Willing Executioners: Ordinary Germans and the Holocaust.* Alfred A. Knopf.

Kazimierz Górski (1995), *Pół Wieku z Piłką.* Sport i Turystyka.

Andrzej Gowarzewski (1991), *Biało-czerwoni. Dzieje Reprezentacji.* Katowice.

Andrzej Gowarzweski (1997), *Lwów i Wilno w ekstraklasie:dzieje polskiego futbolu kresowego.* GiA.

Andrzej Gowarzewski (2017), *Mistrzostwa Polski. Ludzie Fakty 1918-1939 (encyklopedia piłkarska).* GiA.

Jan Grabowski & Barbara Engelking eds. (2022), *Night Without End: The Fate of Jews in German-Occupied Poland.* Indiana University Press.

Bernhard Hachleitner, Matthias Marschik & Georg Spitaler eds. (2019), *Sportfunktionäre und Jüdische Differenz: Zwischen Anerkennung und Antisemitismus Wien 1918 bis 1938.* De Gruyter.

Miklós Hadas (2000), 'Football and Social Identity: The Case of Hungary in the Twentieth Century' in *The Sports Historian Journal.*

Andrew Handler (1985), *From the Ghetto to the Games: Jewish Athletes in Hungary.* East European Monographs.

Suzette Hazzan (2017), 'Des républicains espagnols aux juifs, de l'internement à la déportation, les Groupes de travailleurs étrangers de Miramas' in Robert Mencherini ed. *Provence-Auschwitz: De l'internement des étrangers à la déportation des juifs 1939-1944.* Presses Universitaires de Provence.

Uli Hesse (2022), *Tor! The story of German football.* Polaris Publishing.

Raul Hilberg (1961), *The Destruction of the European Jews.* WH Allen.

László Hoppe (1970), *Labdarúgó-bajnokságaink: 1901–1969.* Sport Lap- és Könyvkiadó.

Dara Horn (2021), *People Love Dead Jews: Reports from a Haunted Present.* WW Norton.

Ryan Hubbard (2019), *From Partition to Solidarity: The first 100 years of Polish football.* RAH.

Hungarian Football Association (1981), *Válogatott labdarúgóink arcképcsarnoka.* MLSZ.

Vincent Hunt (2017), *Blood in the Forest: The End of the Second World War in the Courland Pocket.* Helion and Company.

Ashley Hyne (2019), *Jimmy Hogan: The Greatest Football Coach Ever?* Electric Blue Publishing.

Colin Jose (1998), *The American Soccer League: The Golden Years of American Soccer 1921–1931.* Scarecrow Press.

Alexander Juraske (2024), *Otto 'Schloime Fischer': Ein Jüdischer Fußballstar aus Wien.* Heintrich and Heintrich Verlag.

Attila Kapási (2023), *Válogatottak - Az előidőktől az első világháborúig.* Self-published.

David Kertzer (1997), *The Kidnapping of Edgardo Mortara.* Knopf Publishing.

Serge Klarsfeld (1978), *Le Mémorial de la Déportation des Juifs de France.* Klarsfeld.

Ignaz Hermann Körner (2008), *Lexikon jüdischer Sportler in Wien 1900–1938.* Mandelbaum Verlag.

Alexander Manor, ed. (1980), *Sefer Sambor-Stary Sambor; pirkei edut ve-zikaron le-kehilot.* Irgun yots'e Sambor.

Matteo Marani (2007), *Dallo Scudetto ad Auschwitz. Vita e morte di Arpad Weisz, allenatore ebreo.* Aliberti.

Geoffrey P. Megargee ed. (2009–2022), *Encyclopedia of Camps and Ghettos, 1933–1945,* Volumes I–IV. Indiana University Press.

Anda Meisels Rosen (2005), *Middle Andzia: A Memoir.* BookSurge Publishing.

Adam Musial (2024), 'Three Jewish Football Stars from Kraków' in *The Galitzianer.*

Catherine Nicault, François Virag & Ronald Virag (2008), 'Edmond Virag, dit Eddy Weiskopf, International de Football' in *Archives Juives.*

Darren O'Byrne & Christopher Young (2025), *Willy Meisl, 'King of the*

Sports Journalists': A Jewish Career in Times of Change. De Gruyter Oldenbourg.

Raphael Patai (1995), *The Jews of Hungary: History, Culture, Psychology.* Wayne State University Press.

Bruce Pauley (1992), *From Prejudice to Persecution: A History of Austrian Antisemitism.* University of North Carolina Press.

Lorenz Peiffer & Henry Wahlig (2014), *Verlorene Helden: von Gottfried Fuchs bis Walther Bensemann - die Vertreibung der Juden aus dem deutschen Fussball nach 1933.* 11Freunde Verlag.

Gunnar Persson (2004), *Stjärnor på Flykt : Historien om Hakoah Wien.* Norstedts.

Hannah Pick-Goslar (2023), *My Friend Anne Frank.* Ebury Publishing.

Istvan Pluhár & Stefan Pluhar (1977), *Játszottam, oktattam, tudósítottam: A magyar labdarúgás őszinte története. 1901-től.* Corvin.

Katharina Prager (2007), 'Ich bin nicht gone Hollywood!: Salka Viertel - Ein Leben' in *Theater und Film.* Braumüller.

Bernhard Press (2000), *The Murder of the Jews in Latvia 1941-1945.* Northwestern University Press.

Jacob Presser (1968), *Ashes in the Wind: The Destruction of Dutch Jewry.* Souvenir Press.

Waldemar Rezmer (2015), 'Inter-religious Relations in the Polish Armed Forces 1918–1939' in *Procedia – Social and Behavioral Sciences.*

Dave Rich (2023), *Everyday Hate: How antisemitism is built into our world – and how you can change it.* Biteback Publishing.

Donna Rifkind (2020), *The Sun And Her Stars: Salka Viertel and Hitler's Exiles in the Golden Age of Hollywood.* Other Press.

Marsha Rozenblit (1983), *The Jews of Vienna 1867-1914: Assimilation and Identity.* State University of New York Press.

Robert Rozett (2014), *Conscripted Slaves: Hungarian Jewish Forced Laborers on the Eastern Front.* Yad Vashem.

Donna Ryan (1996), *The Holocaust and the Jews of Marseille: The Enforcement of Anti-Semitic Policies in Vichy France.* University of Illinois Press.

Elemér Saly (1945), *Mozgó vesztőhely*. Idegennyelvű Irodalmi Kiadó.

Lewinter Schalom et al. (1961), *Hasmonea Lwów 1908–1961.* Tel Aviv.

Dietrich Schulze-Marmeling, ed. (2003), *Davidstern und Lederball.* Die Werkstatt.

Karl Heinz Schwind (1994), *Geschichten aus einem Fussball-Jahrhundert.* Carl Ueberreuter Verlag.

Gusztáv Sebes (1981), *Örömök és csalódások. Egy sportvezető emlékei.* Gondolat Kiadó.

Ilan Shchori (2012), *Hakoah Vienna's Journey to the Holy Land* in Eretz Magazine.

Robin Shepherd (2009), *A State Beyond the Pale: Europe's Problem with Israel.* Weidenfeld & Nicolson.

Dawid Sierakowiak (1996), *The Diary of Dawid Sierakowiak: Five Notebooks from the Łódź Ghetto*. Bloomsbury.

Kevin Simpson (2020), *Soccer under the Swastika: Defiance and Survival in the Nazi Camps and Ghettos.* Rowman & Littlefield.

Werner Skrentny (2012), *Julius Hirsch. Nationalspieler. Ermordet: Biografie eines jüdischen Fußballers.* Die Werkstatt.

Werner Skrentny (2012), *"Gott" and "Juller": International soccer players, friends and Jews.* Die Werkstatt.

Mark S. Smith (2012), *Treblinka Survivor: The Life and Death of Hershl Sperling*. Spellmount.

Simon Levis Sullam (2018), *The Italian Executioners: The Genocide of the Jews of Italy.* Princeton University Press.

Péter Szabó (2020), *Magyarok a Don-kanyarban*. Kossuth Kiadó.

Krisztián Ungváry (2006), *The Siege of Budapest: One Hundred Days in World War II.* Yale University Press.

Thomas Urban (2011), *Schwarze Adler, Weiße Adler: Deutsche und Polnische Fußballer im Räderwerk der Politik.* Die Werkstatt.

Gyula Vadas, ed. (1927), *100-ak könyve. Száz magyar versenyző írásban és képben.* Nemzeti Sportkönyvtár.

Jeffrey Veidlinger (2021), *In the Midst of Civilised Europe: The Pogroms of 1918–1921 and the Onset of the Holocaust.* Picador.

Salka Viertel, (1969), *The Kindness of Strangers.* NYRB Classics.

Henryk Vogler (1994), *Wyznanie Mojżeszowe: Wspomnienia z Utraconego Czasu.* Państwowy Instytut Wydawniczy.

Bernard Wasserstein (2012), *On the Eve: The Jews of Europe before the Second World War.* Profile Books.

Árpád Weisz and Aldo Molinari (2018), *Il Giuoco del Calcio.* Minerva Edizioni.

Leon Weliczker Wells (1963), *The Janowska Road: Survival in a Nazi Death Camp.* Macmillan.

Josef Werner (1988), *Hakenkreuz und Judenstern: Das Schicksal der Karlsruher Juden im Dritten Reich.* Badenia Verlag.

Bogna Wilczyńska (2017), *Makkabi, Jutrzenka, Wisla and Cracovia. Polish-Jewish Kraków from the Perspective of Football.* De Gruyter.

Jonathan Wilson (2019), *The Names Heard Long Ago.* Blink Publishing.

Robert Wistrich (1989), *The Jews of Vienna in the Age of Franz Joseph.* Oxford University Press.

Marcin Wodziński (2002), 'Languages of the Jewish communities in Polish Silesia (1922–1939)', in *Jewish History.*

Michal Zichlarz (2021), *Stefan Żywotko. Ze Lwowa po Mistrzostwo Afryki.* Instytut Pamięci Narodowej.

Susan Zuccotti (1993), *The Holocaust, The French, and the Jews.* Basic Books.

INDEX

INDEX